K

Sex Therapy

Sex Therapy
A Behavioral Approach

William Caird, Ph.D.

Associate Professor, Department of Psychiatry, University of British Columbia; Chief Psychologist, Department of Psychiatry, St. Paul's Hospital, Vancouver, British Columbia, Canada

John P. Wincze, Ph.D.

Associate Professor, Section of Psychiatry and Human Behavior, Brown University, Medical School; Chief Psychologist, Veterans Administration Hospital, Providence, Rhode Island

Medical Department
Harper & Row, Publishers
Hagerstown, Maryland
New York, San Francisco, London

Cover and text designed by Alice J. Sellers

77–78–79–80–81–82—10–9–8–7–6–5–4–3–2–1

Library of Congress Cataloging in Publication Data

Caird, William, 1926–
   Sex therapy.

   Includes index.
   1. Sex therapy. I. Wincze, John P., 1943– joint author. II. Title.
[DNLM: 1. Behavior therapy. 2. Sex disorders—Therapy. WM610
C136s]
RC556.C34   616.6   76–54208
ISBN 0–06–140595–7

To our wives, Margaret and Linnea;

our children, Leslie, Paula, Susan,
Jeffrey, Larissa and Brent;

and our parents, William and Martha
Joseph and Blanche

Contents

Preface

The title of this book *SEX THERAPY: A Behavioral Approach* fairly well describes what the book is about and admits of a particular point of view, a specific orientation. We view sexual problems as learned problems and once learned, frequently maintained by anxiety or other inappropriate behavior patterns. The major treatment approach is directed towards the alleviation of this anxiety, thus allowing more adaptive behaviors to emerge or to be developed. Systematic desensitizing is the procedure advocated. This has proven to be both rapid and effective.

Although sexual problems are commonly presented to psychiatrists, clinical psychologists, marital counselors and sex therapists, they often first come to the attention of non-sex therapists—general and family practitioners, obstetricians and gynecologists, and social workers. This book is addressed to all these groups. Causes of the most commonly encountered male and female sexual dysfunctions are outlined, and rational treatment procedures for dealing with these are detailed. The focus is on the description, assessment and treatment of sexual problems using a straightforward behavioral approach derived from empirically established principles. Simple but efficient and efficacious therapeutic strategies are clearly spelled out.

We try to dispel some of the myths currently surrounding sexual expression and sexual problems and to indicate that in many cases these can be dealt with in a relatively short time period.

However, this is not to suggest that all sexual problems can be readily solved by some simple advice and judicious instruction. This would be a gross oversimplification and to believe this would create its own problems. Sexual problems are real problems and, by and large, a "common sense" approach is not likely to prove therapeutic for many of them. If it were, life would be so much simpler for those with problems and for those attempting to help remedy such problems. Nevertheless, it is our belief that a comprehensive assessment procedure will enable a therapist to distinguish between those people who require some psychologically sophisticated therapeutic procedures and those who require something less intense. This, along with the procedures outlined, provides the raison d'être for the book.

Acknowledgments

The authors express their gratitude to Carrie Carton for her exhaustive work in transcribing patient interviews and in performing other secretarial duties and to Goldie Bjerke and Patricia Baligian for their tireless typing of the manuscript.

We are also deeply indebted to the Dalhousie audio visual staff for their invaluable contributions to the development of audio visual material for our research.

Finally, we express our sincere appreciation to the Medical Research Council of Canada for their financial support and to President Henry Hicks, Dalhousie University, for his administrative support of our research.

Sex Therapy

Introduction

THE BEHAVIORAL APPROACH COMES OF AGE

It has become abundantly clear over the past few years that the treatment of sexual dysfunctions is undergoing radical changes. No longer are therapists, be they psychiatrists or psychologists, content to follow rigidly the traditional, dynamically oriented approach to these problems. The view that sexual problems as well as other behavioral problems are rooted in unresolved infantile conflicts, or that they are the outward manifestation of repression (the observed behavior being simply a symptom of a deep and underlying problem), is becoming increasingly unacceptable to a good many therapists. The corollary of this change in thinking is, of course, that new ways of dealing with these problems must be devised. One of the objects of this book is to describe some of the procedures currently in use. The focus is on the immediate and observable behavior of the individual. That is, how did he or she acquire this behavior, how is it being maintained, and how can this behavior be altered or modified? The answers to these questions are sought in theories of learning.

The fact that the behavioral treatment of sexual dysfunctions is gaining prominence is reflected in both books and journal articles dealing with maladaptive behavior. Perhaps the best known and most widely publicized book dealing with sexual problems is *Human Sexual Inadequacy,* by Masters and Johnson (1970). There is no question that the therapeutic procedures they use are behavioristic, albeit somewhat more eclectic than those used by behavior therapists such as Joseph Wolpe and Arnold Lazarus (1966). Nevertheless, it is obvious that Masters and Johnson have moved away from a purely medical model interpretation of maladaptive sexual behaviors, both in thought and deed.

The same is true, but to a lesser extent, in a more recent book, *The New Sex Therapy* (Kaplan, 1974). While Dr. Kaplan acknowledges herself as a psychoanalytically oriented therapist, her book contains numerous references to the effectiveness of behavioral approaches in the treatment of sexual disorders. That is, behavior modification is shown to be a brief and effective method of treating sexual dysfunctions in some men and women.

This will come as no surprise to practicing behavior therapists. It has been known for a long time that some sexual disorders are readily ammenable to a behavioristic approach (Lazarus, 1963). However, only in fairly recent years have systematic attempts been made to determine the efficacy of behavior therapy for sexual dysfunctions. This area of research is still in its infancy, but some progress has been made. It is the object of this book to indicate and analyze one specific line of behavioral research which holds a good deal of promise for alleviating the misery which accompanies sexual inadequacies or dysfunctions in men and women.

PURPOSE AND AIMS

Although our primary intention is to detail a specific type of behavior modification for sexual disorders, we also hope to provide an evaluation of other types of therapy currently in use, noting their effectiveness and their limitations. So far as our own work is concerned, we will also be emphasizing the assessment of sexual dysfunctions, since this is an area long neglected in both professional and nonprofessional writing. That is, what are the constituents of sexual dysfunction? What are the characteristics of men and women who complain of sexual problems?

When we considered writing this book there came to mind the question, "For whom are we writing it? Students of psychology? Medical students? Nursing students? Psychiatrists? Gynecologists? General practitioners? People suffering from sexual problems? Sex therapists? We never resolved this question to our own satisfaction. So, to avoid having to make the decision, we decided to write for the widest possible audience. This imposed its own problems and limitations. For the book to be comprehensible to students in a wide variety of disciplines as well as to nonprofessionals, it would be necessary to avoid an excessive use of technical terms, psychological jargon, and elaborate and convoluted theoretical notions. But then we would be forced to sacrifice some of the precision expected by knowledgeable professional readers. In our view, the magnitude of the problems justified this approach.

We hope that this book will prove informative and useful, and thus lead to a better understanding of sexual dysfunctions and how they may be dealt with. At the same time we believe that it will dispel some of the myths and erroneous notions surrounding the topic of human sexual conduct. This is important because despite the widespread dissemination of literature on the topic, sex continues to be a profound mystery to a great many people, including those who should know better. Misconceptions, misunderstanding, and downright absurdities characterize this area of knowledge—frequently engendered and fostered by well-meaning but misleading articles in popular publications.

We make no pretense to know all there is to know about sexual dysfunctions. On the contrary, although both authors have been engaged continuously for the past five years in the experimental investigation of male and female sexual problems, we, as well or better than anyone, appreciate how much we do not know and how much we have to learn. Despite this bald admission, we have gained some knowledge, some insight, over this time period and believe that we can add to the growing body of knowledge in the field. We have attempted to provide a source of information on some limited aspects of sexual dysfunctions, and to show how these might be dealt with by means of fairly simplistic procedures. For the nonprofessional reader, this book may furnish some basic information and dispel some common fallacies. For the professionals, it will (it is hoped) make them cognizant of, and acquaint them with, additional or alternative modes of treating a most serious and distressing problem.

ALTERNATIVES AND ATTITUDES

Quite clearly there is no single or best way of treating sexual problems. Therapeutic strategems that are highly effective with some clients are completely ineffectual with others. As we will indicate, these phenomena arise from client, procedural, and therapist variables and the complex interaction among these three. Recognizing this complexity, perhaps the therapist will be in a better position to consider alternative procedures for recalcitrant clients. For example, one might consider the relationship between social class and therapeutic outcome.

In reviewing two recent books, Masters and Johnson's *Human Sexual Inadequacy* and Helen Kaplan's *The New Sex Therapy,* one is struck by the kind of people treated. That is, the vast majority of both Masters and Johnson's and Kaplan's clients appear to be from middle or upper middle class backgrounds. In the Masters and Johnson book these data are not explicitly presented. However, common sense dictates that this must be so. Since their therapeutic procedures involve the couple's attending their clinic in St. Louis,

Missouri, for a two-week period (90% of their referrals are from outside the St. Louis area) this means that their clients must be able to afford two weeks away from home. In addition there is a substantial fee ($2500). Under these conditions it seems unlikely that very many of their clients are in the lower income brackets.

Similarly with Dr. Kaplan's clients. Of the 33 case studies she documented in her book, it is possible to conclude that at least 26 of these were from middle or upper middle class backgrounds, e.g., successful businessmen, attorneys, stock or real estate brokers, physicians. There was not sufficient information to determine the status of the remaining 7 cases, but it might be reasonable to conclude that they were from the same population. Of those cases where occupation or socioeconomic status was stated or could be reasonably inferred, not one was a plumber, a carpenter, an unskilled worker, or unemployed. What this means is that in both examples, the clients represent a very biased sample of the population suffering from sexual dysfunctions. One obvious conclusion to be drawn from these facts is that the therapeutic procedures advocated in both books may be effective only for clients who are reasonably well educated and who come from the higher strata of society. This may be something of an exaggeration, but our experience with low income and poorly educated clients makes it clear that the therapies of Masters and Johnson and Kaplan would simply not be efficient and perhaps not even effective in the forms described.

Kinsey and his colleagues (1948, 1953) made it explicit more than 20 years ago that real differences exist between social and educational classes *viz a viz* sexual behavior and attitudes; while no direct reference was made to the affect of these variables on therapy, it seems safe to conclude that they are bound to be important. Behaviors which one class considers normal may be viewed by a different class as being abnormal or perverted. A good example of this is provided by Kinsey (1948) where he notes that while 90% of upper social level males (highly educated) regularly have intercourse while nude, only 43% of those who reach only grade school do so. The same trend is true for females. While 91% of women with graduate school educations reported premarital intercourse in the nude, only 67% of women who did not go beyond high school reported the same experience. Clearly there are differences, and it seems unlikely that these differences are not transferable to the therapeutic situation.

The specific procedure which we advocate in this book is systematic desensitization (SD) and its variations, as first formally enunciated by Wolpe (1958). We appreciate that there are serious shortcomings to this approach, both theoretical and procedural (Locke, 1971; Wilkins, 1971). Nevertheless, in the treatment of *primary* frigidity and in the majority of male sexual problems, we know of no other procedure which comes close to approaching its efficiency and efficacy. At the same time, we do not recommend a slavish adherence to a particular form of SD. We believe that SD can be viewed as a general descriptive term which encompasses a variety of procedures and strategies. It is not a type of therapy, well formulated with rigid guidelines, which one can routinely apply in a standard fashion with each and every case. Furthermore, SD is not a mechanistic procedure, and more goes on in therapy than many behavior therapists are willing to acknowledge. That is, many nonspecific aspects of therapy contribute to it.

If there is any consistency in this volume, it is our belief that individual differences and the recognition of these differences are paramount in therapeutic intervention. What this means in practical terms is that therapists are frequently thrown back on their own devices when attempting to solve sexual problems. While one has general principles to dictate the direction of therapy, the uniqueness of men and women ensures that one will frequently have to be imaginative and creative in one's therapeutic endeavors. We believe that within the general parameters of SD the therapist should adopt a flexible approach and, if necessary, tailor or adjust the *modus operandi* to suit the case. The majority of problems fit well into a more or less standard SD framework and in these instances therapy is fairly straightforward. However, there are exceptions, and the degree to which the therapist can effectively cope with these provides a measure of one's skill and, in the final analysis, one's usefulness.

SEX AND STATUS

There are anomalies in treating male and female sexual dysfunctions. These arise, in large part, from the psychological and psychosexual differences between men and women. As suggested earlier, the major concern of the book is with the treatment of primary frigidity in women, and impotence and premature ejaculation in men. (Primary frigidity usually has no discernible immediate antecedents but for one reason or another is being maintained by anxiety.) We are less concerned with the problem of secondary frigidity, an absence of sexual response or an aversion to sex with a particular partner. Not that these are unimportant, because they clearly matter. However, in secondary frigidity (as the term suggests) the major problem is not so much a sexual one as it is a relationship problem or a communication problem, or the like. That is, the dysfunction has obvious immediate antecedents. For example, a woman who has lost her desire for sex because she has a husband who demands it whenever he is drunk, is unlikely to benefit from any kind of therapy in the absence of altering her husband's behavior. Or as in one of the cases cited later, a woman who no longer desires sex with her husband because she had discovered his extramarital affair, is not going to derive a great deal of benefit from therapy directed exclusively at the sexual problem. Cases like these, of which we admit there are many, require a different approach. Once the primary problem has been solved it may then be necessary to attempt to deal with the sexual one. On the other hand, it may well be that once the immediate, nonsexual difficulties have been ameliorated, the sexual problems will have disappeared.

Men, as contrasted to women, seem to be less vulnerable although not impervious to the development of primary sexual disorders. More often than not when a man presents himself with the sexual problem of impotence, this is of a secondary nature. That is, he has been performing at par for him, but for one reason or another suddenly discovers that he can no longer get an erection—or if he can, he is unable to maintain it. As one man explained it: "I can get it up a little, but not enough to do any damage." There are a variety of reasons for erectile failure (e.g., drugs, depression, pressure of work, or fatigue) but whatever the cause, once this happens it can have long-range repercussions. Failure breeds failure. One unsuccessful attempt at coitus leads to anxiety, which in turn reduces the probability of success on a future occasion. If this too is a fiasco, a vicious circle is being established where every failure increases the anxiety which drastically reduces the probability of future success, and so on.

Premature ejaculation may be quite different, and comes close to approximating primary frigidity, although the etiology is not the same. Various explanations have been offered to account for this disorder. For example, it has been viewed as a conditioned response to early stressful sexual experiences such as masturbating as quickly as possible to reduce the risk of being caught, or by experiences with prostitutes where speed of ejaculation is viewed as a virtue—at least from the prostitute's point of view. The validity of these hypotheses are open to question, but whatever the cause, they are frequently a part of the male "dowry," and are not responses to his wife. The same is probably true of inability to ejaculate. The problem may be of long standing, with the cause being a conditioned fear of impregnating a girl.

Surprisingly, and this is what we mean in making the distinction between male and female psychosexual responses, few men (in our experience) accuse their wives of being responsible for their problems. They may complain about specific aspects of their wives' sexual behavior or nonbehavior, but rarely do they say that she is the cause of their impotence or premature ejaculation. (Although occasionally they may accuse her of failing to understand or help him alleviate the problem.)

Men are much less emotionally involved in sex and are much less influenced by the immediate situation than are women. The fact that his wife is drunk does not prevent a man from having intercourse with her. A man is quite capable of intercourse following hours of bitter argument with his wife, often to her dismay and chagrin. It is no accident that the vast majority of houses of prostitution cater to men, and it is also understandable that women find a man's use of a prostitute incomprehensible.

The fact that men are psychosexually different than women has implications for treatment. Since men seldom see their partners as being the source of their problems, and because they view the male–female interaction in a quite different light, it appears to make little difference, so far as therapeutic design is concerned, whether the problem is of recent onset and a response to a specific set of circumstances, or whether it is one of long standing with the cause obscure or unfathomable. It has been our experience that the same general treatment procedures are as effective with one as the other.

"IF HE IS IGNORANT, TEACH HIM."

Intuitively one might expect in this sexually enlightened age that everyone over the age of twelve would posses a vast store of factual information about sex: anatomy, physiology and procedures for satisfying inherent sexual needs and desires. This is obviously not the case (so much for intuition). While the therapeutic procedures described in this book are designed for problems of some magnitude, it is not necessary that the therapist view every problem as being of such enormous proportions that one must trot out the most sophisticated therapeutic equipment to deal with it. One does not typically use an elephant gun to kill flies.

One of the virtues of a comprehensive interview and assessment technique is that it allows one to distinguish between the flies and the elephants. Frequently, a client, a man or a woman, may seek therapy for what is considered a serious and debilitating problem, and often it is. However, it may well be that the problem is one which can be solved with some straightforward talk and information. Models of the male and female sexual anatomy are a good investment for any sex therapist. A good demonstration and explanation of these is often worth fifty therapeutic hours. The therapist should, when using these, make it clear that these are only models to demonstrate how *most* people look. Just as there are differences in people's mental apparatus, there are differences in their sexual trappings as well. A simple explanation of the mechanics and physiology of the sexual act and response may frequently alleviate a worrisome problem.

Related to the foregoing is the possibility that a client, particularly a woman, may have physical problems which interfere with or prevent normal sexual relations, e.g. an intact hymen (maidenhead), polyps, or infection. While these account for relatively few clients, it should be standard practice for the women to have a thorough gynecologic examination prior to any psychological intervention.

There has been a burgeoning of "sex clinics" in recent years. It has been estimated that in the United States there are (at this writing) between five and six thousand of these, with perhaps less than fifty being legitimate. That is, of this vast number, only a handfull are properly equipped in terms of trained personnel to offer therapy which will prove beneficial to their clients. This is a serious and distressing problem, not simply because the client receives nothing for money spent (although this is a consideration), but because of the possible risks and dangers that people may encounter as a result of falling into the hands of charlatans, quacks and swindlers. Unfortunately, people in trouble seek solace wherever they find it, and few are in a position to discriminate between the knaves and fools on the one hand and the qualified people on the other. Usually a phone call to the local psychological association or medical society will suffice. Or, if there is a university nearby, a call to the department of psychology or psychiatry may solve the problem. Many of the reliable and authentic sex therapy clinics are operated within universities, or if not, have university affiliations. As a rule of thumb, one should avoid as the plague anyone who guarantees rapid and reliable cures for sexual dysfunctions.

Inherent in this proliferation of sex clinics is the question of why? Why, in the course of relatively few years, have so many men and women decided that their sex lives are less than adequate, to the degree that they need professional help? It is unlikely that there is an epidemic of sexual dysfunction, so that's not the answer. A more likely explanation is that it reflects a combination of a new awareness of the role of sexuality in contemporary society and the changing role of women in society. There is an increasing tendency for women to view themselves no longer as merely suppliers of sexual service to men. Equal rights has invaded the sexual sphere as it has so many other areas. Superimposed on this change, and contributing to it, is the widespread circulation of books and articles in popular magazines directly concerned with sexuality, e.g., *The Female Eunuch, The Sensuous Woman, The Joy of Sex*. It is being brought home to women that sex should be fun, shared fun, and that if they are to enjoy the fruits of their labors they had better do something about it. And doing something about it ranges all the way from learning to engage in and enjoy sex, to simply enhancing an already minimally satisfying experience. That could mean broadening their sexual repertoires, perhaps bringing them into line with their husbands' desires and expectations, or in some cases, using their new-found knowledge to teach their husbands a thing or two.

Another explanation for the dramatic increase in people seeking help for sexual problems is the availability of therapists. That is, therapists create their own demands, and as the number of therapists increases so does the number of people seeking help. This is a phenomenon which has not gone unnoticed in psychiatry.

CLIENT–THERAPIST RELATIONSHIP

Before concluding this introduction we would like to comment briefly on client–therapist interaction, particularly the nonspecific ways in which the therapist modifies the client's behavior. The relationship between client and therapist is an intensely personal one and this is most clearly and obviously manifested in the way a client will freely discuss the most intimate details of his or her sex life with an opposite-sex stranger. Clients will tell their therapists things they would never tell their spouse, their best friends or their priests. They do this on the expectation that what they say is confidential, and this is as it should be. But this is not the only reason for baring their sexual souls. The nature of the relationship is such that the client can use the therapist-stranger as a sounding board in ways not possible with any other individual. Because the therapist is considered to be an expert and a professional, the sounds that come back are received in a very special way; they are words of authority.

This makes the client vulnerable, and puts the therapist in a position whereby he or she can exert great influence on the client. The question then becomes, to what extent should a therapist use this power to influence the client's behavior, and to what degree should the therapist attempt to impose his or her value system on the client? To the first part of this question it might be argued that therapists should use whatever power the client gives them in order to alter the client's behavior for the better. However, the trouble with this argument is that it tends to contradict the second part of the question, for how, in the absence of some values, can the therapist chart a course? Whose values and what values should be stressed or advocated when attempting to modify behavior? Clearly, the most obvious (the ones one has had most experience with) are the therapist's own. But do these gibe with the client's, and if not, how may one justify imposing these on a client?

These questions are brought sharply into focus when therapeutic procedures are in direct conflict with long and strongly held attitudes and beliefs. Can a therapist, in good conscience, advocate or perhaps insist, that a woman or a man practice masturbation when she or he strongly believes, in a theological sense, that masturbation is sin? Should a therapist recommend a surrogate partner for a client when the client views this as little more than prostitution? How forceful should a therapist present a case for using a variety of coital positions when the male client strongly believes that the man should always be on top and anything else is a serious reflection on his maleness?

There are no clear answers to these questions. Nevertheless, the therapist should be aware that these are of serious concern and, recognizing that one is not omnipotent, strive to maintain a sense of objectivity and of responsibility consistent with the client's welfare. This is a problem which medicine has had to face but which has not been adequately solved. The obvious example is the question of abortion *viz a viz* the dedicated, Catholic physician.

One thing which has become abundantly clear in our work is the validity of the old adage that "an ounce of prevention is worth a pound of cure." Many of the problems we have encountered in dealing with sexual dysfunctions need never have arisen. Despite the lip service paid to sexual education, this in fact barely exists. What passes for sex education turns out on closer inspection to be "reproductive" education. The assumption seems to be that sex and reproduction are synonymous, and this is patently absurd. What is really required if the frequency of sexual dysfunctions is to be seriously reduced, is education in sexuality—not just in reproduction, not only in coital techniques, but in the broad range of behaviors encompassed by human sexuality. Only in this way, we believe, will sexual problems assume their proper perspective in the human scheme of things.

1

Female Sexual Dysfunction: Description

Sexual dysfunctions come in many guises and have varied causes. Psychologically they are an enigma. Situations and experiences which result in a sexual problem with one woman may leave another unscathed. Experiences which, at least superficially, should herald no long-term effect can result in lifelong sexual entanglements, while severe sexual traumas which might be expected to have profound effects on future behavior, may have no long-lasting effect whatsoever. These phenomena are not peculiar to sexual disorders; they are seen in all psychological problems. There are a variety of explanations offered to account for individual differences in response to specific stimuli, but these are hypotheses which encompass only fragments of the totality of human behavior. Describing behavior is much easier than predicting or explaining it.

In this chapter we will consider, in general, some types of sexual dysfunctions and, where possible, their antecedents and/or causes. The object is to provide a flavor of the kinds of men and women and problems which we will be discussing throughout the remainder of the book.

These brief descriptions are only a sample of the variety of sexual problems that clients present, the kind that virtually every medical practitioner or psychotherapist has heard repeated time and time again. The women described here share a common problem: they derive no pleasure from sex, or they find it distasteful, or they consider it downright objectionable. They also share the experience of having sought help for what they recognize as being an impediment to a satisfying and fulfilling marriage. And without exception, the help they so desperately need has not been forthcoming. Too often have they been told not to worry, that they will get over it. Much too frequently have they spent months (and in some cases years) on weekly visits to a psychiatrist or a nonmedical psychotherapist, only to discover that these soul-baring experiences were having no effect. Increasing frustration and depression were the only consequences of a seemingly endless dialogue.

DYSFUNCTION ASSOCIATED WITH TRAUMA

Some, but obviously not all, sexual problems in women are the aftermath of bad sexual experiences, e.g., rape or attempted rape, severe pain during an initial sexual encounter, or anxiety from observing and perhaps misinterpreting the sex act of their parents. The experience of being raped is certainly not conducive to convincing a woman that sex is love and love is sex. More likely she will believe that men are in fact animals—and dangerous animals at that—and the way to avoid future distressing sexual experiences is to avoid such beasts. If one can invoke conditioning as an explanation for sexual avoidance, a case of rape would appear to provide a good example. Similarly, if a woman's first sexual experience is painful and by definition unsatisfying, the probability of her seeking or acquiescing in future sexual activities is seriously reduced. Typically people do not voluntarily repeat actions which are painful or uncomfortable.

Traumatic experiences like these can have deep and long-lasting effects on a woman, and effectively prevent her from engaging in sex in a meaningful and satisfying way.

Generally speaking, sex is an intimate activity carried out in the absence of an audience. However, this is not always true, and we have frequently treated women whose introduction to intercourse was the observation of their parents in the act. As everyone knows, coitus is not something which can be carried out with decorum. There are sounds and physical activities, even when both participants are enjoying it, which can be readily misinterpreted by children. They may think that father is hurting mother, and consequently become extremely upset. This feeling is magnified when the father *is* actually hurting his wife, when he is forcing himself on her and she is responding with tears. Clearly, learning about sex from this kind of observation is not satisfactory, and from what is known of the effects of learning through modeling, one might expect a girl to develop distorted notions about marriage and sex.

Two examples from our files may help clarify some of these points.

Case Report 1

Janice can have intercourse with her husband only after she has had three or four drinks. She has been this way during her six years of married life. Even though she can engage in sex while under the influence of alcohol, she never enjoys it and never experiences an orgasm—although she can achieve this through masturbation or through digital stimulation by her husband. She is a very unhappy woman on this account and becomes increasingly depressed when discussing her sexual and attendant problems. Her husband, too, is unhappy and feels that he is in some way deficient or inadequate, particularly when his advances are repulsed, which they frequently are. The clear knowledge that his wife has to be on the verge of drunkenness before she can tolerate him is not designed to bolster his ego nor lend credence to his manhood.

Janice's early experience with sex was not designed to convince her that what she had read in women's magazines of the fulfilling properties of love, marriage and sex were entirely accurate. One of five children, she was raised in a tiny, poverty-stricken fishing village. Her home was a four-room shack, and she shared a bedroom with her two brothers and two sisters. The girls slept in the same bed. Her father, a sometimes fisherman, was drunk whenever he could afford it and sex between her parents was anything but private or loving. For the most part it consisted of her father physically and brutally forcing himself on her mother whenever he arrived home under the influence. No attempt was made to shield the children from his drunken overtures towards his wife.

When she was 13 Janice was raped by an older cousin in the presence of her sisters. Her parents became aware of this but treated it as a joke. The effect on Janice was devastating, and eventually through the intervention of a social worker she was seen by a psychiatrist on a number of occasions over the ensuing two years. This apparently had little effect and she continued to have nightmares and hysterical attacks when approached by a man. When she was 15 it was suggested that she visit the minister of the local church, in the hope that by discussing her problems with him she could somehow resolve them. This well-intentioned advice proved to be her undoing. After forcing her to divulge the intimate details of the rape, the minister attacked her and attempted to rape her. She managed to escape and ran screaming from the house. No one would believe her story and attributed it to her imagination or misinterpretation of the minister's behavior and intentions.

She received no further treatment and her attitude toward men only slightly altered over the next seven years when, by good fortune, she met and married a gentle and understanding man. Nevertheless, she remained extremely anxious about sex, finding it tolerable only under the conditions mentioned earlier.

Case Report 2

Norma, 19, and *Josephine,* 17, are sisters. Both have identical sexual problems; they find sex in all its manifestations unpleasant, repugnant, and unsatisfying. That they should feel this way is not surprising in light of their history (which graphically points up the role of learning in the etiology of sexual dysfunctions).

These two young women come from a family of four children. In addition to themselves, there is a sister, 15, and a brother, 21. Their homelife, from as far back as they can remember, has been one of constant and bitter strife. The father, a semiskilled laborer, is an alcoholic who, after he has a few drinks, becomes violent and physically aggressive, particularly with his family. This takes the form of assaulting the mother and female children, particularly Norma and Josephine. These assaults are serious and he has, on occasion, choked them to the point of unconsciousness. The family live in deadly fear of him, with justification, and they are in a bind because he has threatened to kill them if they ever report him to the police or attempt to have him committed to a mental hospital.

These physical assaults are only part of his behavior. His major topic of conversation after drinking is sex. Long before the girls reached their teens he preached to them the evils of sex; sex is "filthy" and "dirty" and if they "play with themselves" or engage in sex, something terrible (although unspecified) will happen to them. This preaching is a frequent occurrence, done graphically and with no attempt at subtlety. He recounts to the girls how his sister masturbated with a cucumber, and threatens that if he ever catches them doing this, he will kill them. This is the general tenor of his attempts at sex education.

However, his chronic decrees on the evils of sex do not prevent this father from behaving in the most loathsome manner toward Norma and Josephine. From the time both girls were 13 he has made a practice of grabbing them and fondling their breasts and genitals. He does this in front of the mother, who is too frightened of him to object. He has also done this in front of the girls' boyfriends and girlfriends, and in fact has done the same thing to girls who visit his daughters, to the point that none will enter the house while he is there. He has threatened both Norma and Josephine that if they walk around the house in their nighties, despite the fact they are wearing housecoats, he will take them into bed and "do it to them." His meaning is abundantly clear, and they dread the sight of him.

In addition, constantly and in front of the children, he refers to his wife as a whore and claims that neither Josephine nor her brother are his children. (There is no evidence whatsoever to justify such a statement.) The fact is that although this man constantly chases other women, he either ignores or denies it when this is mentioned. He is also a sadist with animals, and has spitefully killed cats and other pets in front of the children.

This, then, is a very abbreviated summary of their background.

Norma married and left home when she was 17, and Josephine followed when

16. Despite the constant discussion of sex in their childhood home, both young women are abysmally ignorant of the most elementary and basic facts about most things concerned with sex. For example, despite the constant harangues about masturbation, neither girl is really aware of what masturbation actually is. They think that only by having a climax can a girl get pregnant. Even so, they are not really aware of what a climax or an orgasm is, although they suspect it's similar to a man's ejaculating. They do not know what or where the clitoris is, and believe that if a man has not been circumcised this will prevent a woman from getting pregnant. They continue to believe, to some extent, what their father has told them about sex, because as Josephine explained: "He should know. He always wants it."

Given a background like this, it is small wonder that these young women are now experiencing sexual problems. One might reasonably expect the youngest sister to develop similar problems.

DYSFUNCTION AND EARLY LEARNING

No one will dispute the fact that what children learn has long-lasting effects, that adult behavior is in large part determined by childhood experiences. This is as true of sexual behavior as it is of other behaviors. Attitudes, values, modes of thinking and acting are all acquired from significant others. If a child observes her mother acting in particular ways, then in all likelihood she will act in the same way. If she notes that her parents are affectionate and loving towards each other, this provides a model for her future behavior. On the other hand, if constant and bitter strife characterize her parent's relationship, this too will affect her adult behavior.

The point is that children can learn maladaptive responses in the absence of severe emotional and/or physical hurt, as easily as they can learn adaptive ones. As children they are not capable of discriminating between what is good or bad, useful or useless, adaptive or maladaptive. In general they learn and retain, in some cases to an astonishing degree, those behaviors which are in one way or another reinforced through some mode.

Very often a woman will experience intercourse prior to marriage and, depending on the woman, her background, and perhaps the situation in which this is done, feel guilty about it. The degree to which she experiences guilt feelings, and the extent to which she is unable to rationalize these feelings, may well interfere with or prevent future sexual relationships. Girls are forever being warned of the perils of premarital sex and being threatened with dire consequences if they transgress. A constant diet of this kind of ill-advised conversation cannot fail to have an effect on the ways in which they view men in general and sex in particular. Unfortunately, many parents consider it their duty to provide sex education of this type and too often it makes little difference in the long run whether this is done brutally or with some effort at tact. The end result is the same.

The effects of early "normal" and more or less "conventional" learning on future sexual behavior are illustrated in the following examples.

Case Report 3

Ellen is a 32-year-old attractive woman who dresses provocatively—too-tight sweaters and miniskirts—and for the most part presents a picture of cheerful good-naturedness. Her smile vanishes, however, when the subject of her husband comes up; his major interest in life is sex, and sex to Ellen is anathema and has been all ten of her married years—and before. She has never enjoyed sex, she has never had an orgasm through intercourse, and she finds the whole process repulsive and disgusting. To avoid her husband's advances (which are becoming more and more infrequent) she has adopted a variety of stratagems—she will go to bed early and feign sleep when her spouse arrives, she will stay up late in the fond hope that he will be asleep before she arrives, she will "develop" a headache or will start an argument—anything to avoid sexual intercourse.

In her ten years of marriage, Ellen's husband, a carpenter, has never seen her completely naked and only once, inadvertently, has he seen her bare breasts. It has been no easy task for her to maintain this modesty. She achieves it by never getting completely undressed when her husband is around. When preparing for bed she undresses to her panties and bra (with her back to her husband) and dons a nightgown which stretches from neck to ankles. She may then, if in a particularly daring mood, remove her bra, which requires some gymnastic manipulation. Most times, though, she sleeps with it on. Not being completely undressed provides her with a measure of safety and security. And it's proven effective in that it keeps her husband at arm's length.

Her single concession to her husband's sexual desires is to subtly convey to him, perhaps once a month, that he may have intercourse provided he does it quickly and does not fondle her breasts. On these rare occasions she removes her panties before retiring, but not her bra or nightgown. Intercourse is carried out in the dark with both participants completely covered by the bedclothes. She makes this concession only from a sense of guilt and what she considers to be her marital duty.

To an observer, Ellen's behavior is not what one might expect from a married woman. Faced with behavior like this, the question that immediately comes to mind is, why? How can it be explained? Unfortunately there is no ready answer, although a knowledge of Ellen's background does cast some light on the problem.

This woman was raised in a moderately strict Catholic household where it was believed the "good" girl walked nearer to God than the "bad" girl. All of Ellen's education was received in a convent school where proscriptions against sin, where this was equated with sexual adventures, was the order of the day. The girls were constantly warned of the perils, both physical and spiritual, attendant on moral and theological lapses. Sex was sin and sin was sex and traffic with boys should be avoided because everyone knows what boys are always thinking about.

A surprising and unwanted pregnancy or two, in girls whom Ellen knew, only provided additional grist for this antisexual mill. Twelve years on this kind of an intellectual diet, particularly for an impressionable young girl, was not something to be readily discarded just because the proscriptions were no longer appropriate. This was a problem with Ellen. So impressed was she with her early training that she was unable to distinguish between married and unmarried sex. If sex was sinful before marriage, how could a priest, by saying a few words, suddenly and arbitrarily remove the sinfulness of sexual intercourse? Her answer to this question was simply that it could not be done; sex was a sin, and marriage vows could not and did not alter this basic fact. Her married life then consisted of a series of sinful acts for which she felt guilty and disgusted. It was as if God was ever-present, looking over her shoulder. It should be added that her convent training was buttressed and reinforced at home; her mother was not a strong believer in sexual freedom, and seized upon any reports of an illegitimate birth as evidence that the way of the transgressor was indeed hard, albeit justified. This she constantly pointed out to Ellen.

The rigid sex education Ellen received would not pose serious problems for the majority of girls, who are able to make the necessary adjustment once they marry. However, in Ellen's case the constant injunctions at school against sex, combined with her mother's ever-present suspicion that more goes on in automobiles than is ever publicly acknowledged, proved too much for her to cope with and she remains unable to make a realistic distinction between married and unmarried sex. Unfortunately for her, her husband does not share her views on sexual matters and this results in a good deal of nonsexual friction between them.

Such phenomena are not restricted to children raised in religious or superstrict households. Kinsey (1953) has quite rightly pointed out that from an early age children are taught that physical contact with children of the opposite sex is to be avoided; they learn to inhibit their emotional responses towards members of the opposite sex. Many continue this restraint with marriage, and often a great deal of stress and turmoil results. Following marriage, all these learned inhibitions are supposed to vanish, and the fond expectation is that partners will automatically and immediately be able to make the physical and emotional adjustments consistent with a good and satisfying marital relationship. Kinsey notes that: "Unfortunately, there is no magic in a marriage ceremony which can accomplish this. The record indicates that a very high proportion of the females, in particular, and a considerable number of the males find it difficult after marriage to redevelop the sort of freedom with which they made contact as children, and to learn again how to respond without inhibition to physical and emotional contacts with other persons."

What is surprising, in this context, is not that some men and women are unable satisfactorily to make this readjustment, but that so many in fact can. It says something about the malleability of the human species.

Case Report 4

When she got married, *Brenda* found sexual intercourse, and everything connected with sexual intercourse, aversive. That she occasionally reached a climax during intercourse made no difference. Twenty-two years and three children later, she still finds sex aversive and, moreover, finds her husband aversive too, even in the absence of his demands for what he considers his connubial rights.

Despite Brenda's strong and ever-present negative feelings about sex, her husband appreciates neither the extent nor depth of her repugnance. He is aware that she is something less than thrilled at the prospect of sexual intimacy, but two factors, his insensitivity and her skill as an actress, have been sufficient to shield him from the stark reality of the situation.

Brenda, it should be added, is ambivalent toward her husband; she would like to love him because she recognizes that in many ways he is a kind and gentle man. On the other hand, she resents his sexual advances and feels that in this area he is insensitive, selfish and inconsiderate, despite the fact that she has never discussed her feelings about sex with him, and indeed has contributed to the problem by feigning pleasure during intercourse—or at least masking her distaste.

This failure to discuss her problem with her husband is not restricted to the sexual sphere; a general reticence to mention or talk about unpleasant things is one of her central characteristics. She rationalizes this attitude by saying that she does not wish to hurt his feelings, despite the fact that this lack of communication creates far more problems than it solves. For example, every birthday, even before her marriage, her husband has given her a bouquet of roses in the belief that she loves these flowers. The truth of the matter is that Brenda hates roses and would be quite happy if she never saw one again. She would much rather receive a bottle of sherry. Nevertheless she has perpetuated, through acquiesence, the myth that she is fond of roses, and in the absence of expressing views to the contrary, will probably continue to receive a bouquet on her birthday until the day she dies. It is improbable that she will express her true feelings about this because she is afraid that if she does, her husband will be offended. Her entire married life has been governed by the avoidance of such a possibility.

It is difficult to pinpoint the source of Brenda's sexual difficulties; however, one possible source lies in her early education. Brenda's parents were divorced when she was a young girl and she went to live with her maternal grandparents. Her grandmother, a Victorian when the age of Victoria had passed, was a stickler for personal modesty and viewed nakedness and semi-nakedness, even in children, as being closely aligned to sin. Nakedness was therefore not to be indulged in, no matter what the circumstances. She would have preferred that bathing be done fully clothed, if only this were practical. Brenda learned her lessons well and soon shared her grandmother's views and opinions of nudity. So ingrained did this attitude become that when she attended university she had to move out of residence and take a small apartment, because she could not bear other girls to see her in various stages of undress. She still has not overcome this idiosyncracy, and despite being married for nearly a quarter of a century, continues to avoid being seen in a state of dishabille by her husband. He, in turn, has long since ceased to consider this peculiar and it is now a source of amusement more than anything else.

ORGASMIC DYSFUNCTION

A major (and understandable) source of dissatisfaction among many women is the inability to reach a climax though intercourse. When a woman emotionally invests a great deal of herself in what she has been led to believe should be a source of shared pleasure, it is a small wonder that she is unhappy when no return on her investment is forthcoming. She may begin to fret and wonder what she is doing wrong, to ruminate on what she considers to be a personal deficiency. The situation is not improved if her husband, too, begins to question her sexual abilities and responsiveness. This adds to her confusion.

If, at the same time, she knows or discovers that she is capable of reaching a climax through self-stimulation, the situation becomes even more inexplicable. Why can she reliably reach orgasm through masturbation but not through penile stimulation? Does the problem reside with her husband? Once she begins to ask these questions, the stage is being set for some high drama which frequently proves nonproductive for all concerned.

On the other hand, there are women who, although they rarely if ever reach a climax, seem reasonably content with their lot. They do not feel that orgasms are necessary for a reasonably satisfactory marital relationship. Why this is so is difficult to specify. It may simply reflect differences in sexual responsiveness or drive, or it may be a matter of learning; they have learned to expect little from a sexual relationship. But even though these women fail, in the accepted sense, to be sexually fulfilled, they quite obviously derive some measure of satisfaction from coitus which compensates for lack of orgasm.

Ocassionally a woman who has been functioning satisfactorily will develop an orgasmic dysfunction. The reason may have nothing directly to do with her husband but may simply be a consequence of some notions she has developed on her own. These may be irrational and have no basis in fact, but nevertheless they appear significant to her and are therefore of sufficient importance to effectively prevent her from engaging in and enjoying a normal sexual relationship.

The following three cases illustrate some of these points.

Case Report 5

Helen does not really like sex nor does she dislike it; she is indifferent; she can take it or leave it. Married for three years, she has never derived any great degree of pleasure from intercourse. She has never had an orgasm through intercourse but can reliably achieve this by masturbation, which she practices quite regularly. She loves her husband and the satisfaction that she gets from sex is the knowledge that it gives him pleasure. She is not overly perturbed about her lack of response and accepts that this is the way it is; some women have orgasms and some do not, and if you do not, then there is little to be done about it. You resign yourself to the way you are.

However, her husband feels differently. He thinks she should get more out of sex than she does, and in a real sense interprets her lack of response to a failure on his part. He feels that a husband should be able sexually to satisfy his wife and if he cannot, then perhaps there is something amiss with him; perhaps he is not the man he thought he was. When they have intercourse and his wife fails to reach a climax, he becomes upset and sometimes angry; this in turn causes Helen to become anxious and to try harder on subsequent occasions.

There is nothing in Helen's background to account for her lack of sexual response— no trauma, nothing out of the ordinary occurred in her sex education or instruction. Nevertheless, she feels inadequate as a woman and a wife—not intrinsically, but because of her husband's demands that she get the same thing out of intercourse that he does, a not altogether realistic expectation.

A characteristic of some women is an inability to become sexually aroused through "conventional" means, i.e., foreplay. The range of sexually arousing stimuli seems to be significantly restricted. Fortunately, however, these stimuli are not completely absent. For example, as a literary work *The Happy Hooker* falls short of being *Ulysses* or even *The Tropic of Cancer*. Nevertheless it would appear to have some slight merit, although perhaps not what was intended. With some women, at least, it has certain aphrodisiac properties. Some other novels, *Lady Chatterly's Lover, Fanny Hill,* have similar qualities. The sexual descriptions in these books seem to be able to arouse some women when all else, including their husbands, fails.

Case Report 6

Jessie was one such woman. This 32-year-old woman had been married for ten years and had three children. She had sex regularly with her husband, two or three times a week, but almost never reached a climax through intercourse. Her husband simply could not arouse her sexually no matter what he did nor how long the foreplay. Boredom rather than excitement was her usual response. Neither Jessie nor her husband found intercourse terribly fulfilling. However, like many women, contrary to what is commonly believed, Jessie was a confirmed masturbator and could rapidly have a series of orgasms through self-stimulation. She regarded this as perfectly normal and had no misgivings or feelings of guilt about this solitary sexual behavior. She found masturbation, if not ultimately satisfying, at least anxiety and tension reducing.

Fortuitously Jessie discovered that erotic literature had a tremendously stimulating effect. Her erotic material came initially in the form of *The Happy Hooker*. While reading this book she found herself becoming more and more sexually aroused, almost to the point of spontaneous orgasm. This experience had a very reinforcing effect, particularly so when she discovered that the effect had, in a sense, generalized and transferred to her husband. That is, for two weeks after reading the book she could become highly aroused when making love to her husband and actually had orgasms on every occasion. Unfortunately this happy and gratifying state of affairs continued for only this brief period of time and then disappeared.

However, despite the transient nature of the changes that had taken place, they provided Jessie with some hope for the future; the experience was proof to her that she could, at least under some circumstances, respond to her husband in a natural way. This episode radically altered her reading habits and she built up a sizeable collection of sexually oriented books; while some of these had the same effect as *The Happy Hooker,* none was quite so good nor had so lasting an effect. In fact, her response to this type of literature became weaker over time.

Furthermore, Jessie's new-found interest in salacious literature was disturbing to her husband, as the books presented problems in storage if they were to be kept out of sight of her children, and particularly her relatives who might prove less than understanding.

Case Report 7

Emily estimates that she had intercourse with her husband-to-be 40–50 times prior to their marriage. She felt no guilt about this and enjoyed the experience, reaching orgasm on most occasions. She was three months pregnant on her wedding day. Upon the birth of her baby, eleven years ago, Emily's responses to sex underwent radical changes. She no longer enjoyed sex and only rarely reached orgasm, and says that this had occurred only about once every two or three months since that time. Not only does Emily fail to reach a climax, she rarely becomes sexually aroused; if she does, the interest can suddenly vanish for no apparent reason. For the most part she goes through the motions of intercourse solely to satisfy her husband. When it has been completed, she frequently cries herself to sleep.

Emily loves her husband and is at a loss to understand what has happened to her. Her husband too is puzzled by her behavior and frequently accuses himself of being responsible, claiming that he is not man enough to satisfy her. These self-recriminations have become increasingly prevalent in recent years, and have taken on a bitter quality which only serves to increase the tension between them and to accentuate the problem.

It is perhaps not surprising that Emily became at least partially convinced that the blame her husband assumed was justified; perhaps her lack of sexual responsiveness was a reaction to him, since in the back of her mind was the notion that he had married her only because she was pregnant. Emily had an opportunity to test this hypothesis when her husband was out of the country for two months. She met a man to whom she was attracted, and although he did not know it, he was in fact a guinea pig. Over a two-week period they had intercourse four times and her response to this man was identical to that with her husband; she did not become sexually aroused in any meaningful way and consistently failed to reach a climax. This experience convinced her as nothing else did that her problem resided within herself. Unfortunately she was in worse straights than before; now she carried a burden of guilt because she had been unfaithful to her husband. And while she attempted to justify her behavior in terms of her original motives, she was not very convincing to herself. She had the additional problem of deciding, because of this gnawing feeling of guilt, whether or not to confess her transgression to her husband. There was the possibility that this would only add to the general misery.

VAGINISMUS

To the uninitiated it would appear inconceivable that a woman could be married for five or ten or more years and never have sexual intercourse with her husband. Nevertheless such a state of affairs can exist. Some women are incapable of having intercourse; they are unable to bear being penetrated. That is, whenever the husband attempts to insert his penis, their pelvic muscles contract making penetration impossible; if entry is forced, pain is so extreme that withdrawal is necessary.

There appear to be at least two distinct forms that this (vaginismus) can take: 1) the woman cannot tolerate insertion of any object; 2) intolerance is restricted to a penis. In the first group there are women who cannot undergo an internal examination, who cannot insert a tampax or accept any foreign object in the vagina, including their own finger. Women in the second group are not bothered by any of these, but "freeze" when their husband attempts to insert his penis, although they may well tolerate having his finger inserted. It is as if they suffer from a penis "phobia."

The causes of vaginismus are not always clear. In some cases it would appear to be a case of conditioning, of fear of being hurt by the insertion of some object. However, in many instances there is no readily apparent precipitating event and the woman concerned is unable to specify why she has this profound fear. Whatever the reason, it is a serious impediment to marital harmony and frequently accounts for the breakdown of a marriage. Not many husbands are prepared to live a life of celibacy to accommodate a wife whose responses to their attempts at coitus are crying, grimacing and pleas to "stop." Separation or divorce, or in some cases, extramarital entanglements are often the outcome. An example of vaginismus, the apparent etiology and the outcome is illustrated in the following case.

Case Report 8

Emma's mother was a strong believer in the power and efficacy of enemas. The slightest cough, sniffle or sneeze on Emma's part was sufficient cause for her mother to bring out the enema apparatus. From the time Emma was little more than a toddler, enemas became if not a weekly occurence, a frequent one. Any hint of constipation was also a signal for a treatment.

As Emma became older her attitude toward enemas became increasingly negative and she no longer complacently acquiesced to her mother's desire to purge her. From about the age of nine she refused to cooperate in this therapeutic procedure. The mother's response to this mutinous behavior was prompt and decisive; she had two older sisters forcibly restrain Emma while the operation was performed. This rough and high-handed treatment was accompanied by a good deal of struggling and pain. These forcible entries extended over the next four years, until Emma became too big and too strong to make their continuance practical or possible, much to her mother's dismay. She predicted dire results from this lack of purification.

Not surprisingly, Emma left home when she was 18 and able to support herself, and was married five years later. She has been married now for eleven years and has yet to consummate the marriage; the legacy of her experiences with the enemas is a total inability to tolerate penetration. Any attempt at intercourse causes her to become rigid, tense and unyielding, making penetration impossible. She becomes highly anxious and bursts into tears whenever her husband approaches her. Furthermore, she is unable to undergo an internal pelvic examination. Her response to this is similar to that of attempted intercourse, and on the one occasion when this was carried through to completion it was done under a general anaesthetic.

Emma's husband has adapted to his monastic marriage by finding sexual substitutes for his wife. This is not altogether satisfactory since Emma knows of his extramarital adventures, and although she is incapable of satisfying his sexual needs, is filled with recriminations for what she considers his disloyalty. He in turn experiences feelings of guilt, although these have become significantly less pronounced over the years. Nevertheless, the household is never free of tension and marital discord is the order of the day.

DYSFUNCTION AND SEXUAL IGNORANCE

A common assumption in current day thinking is that because we live in a relatively permissive society where sex is accentuated if not exploited, everyone on the verge of marriage possesses a vast store of sexual knowledge. It is further assumed that this knowledge has not been gained solely by reading books and magazine articles, that part of it, at least, has come from practical experience. While in the main this may be true, there are obvious exceptions. A good many young people enter into marriage with only the most rudimentary information about sex. It is as if they expect a "sex instinct" to take over and that everything will automatically fall into place.

Nothing could be further from the truth. Sex and intercourse, like any skilled behavior, must be learned. It is not something that comes naturally. To assume that one will perform in a sexually proficient and adequate manner in the absence of training or experience is a fallacy, and one designed to lead to a good deal of noncoital friction. The following case is an example of what can happen when two people believe that all that is required for intercourse is a penis and a vagina.

Case Report 9

Jill and *Peter* are both 19 years of age and have been married for four months. Neither had brothers or sisters, and both had been raised in homes where any mention or discussion of sex was forbidden and indeed punished. Jill's mother, who was having problems with her own sex life, provided no information on menstruation and when this natural function first occurred, Jill thought she was dying. Her knowledge and sophistication in other areas of sexual function was about on a par with her knowledge of menstruation. After 19 years the sum of her sex education consisted of strong negative feelings which she acquired overtly and covertly from her mother.

Peter was only slightly more knowledgeable than Jill about sex and sexual behavior. Raised in a sheltered and puritanic household, he was denied the company of boys his age and learned only the most rudimentary facts about sex. Both Peter and Jill were virgins when they were married and neither received any premarital sex instruction. Their wedding night was a comedy of errors; they did not know what to do. They had no idea of the simple mechanics of sexual intercourse and clumsily fumbled with each other, not knowing what to do next. The experience was a complete fiasco, leaving both of them frustrated and angry with each other. Jill was in tears and Peter sulked for the better part of the night.

Their subsequent attempts at intercourse have been little better. While they have mastered the rudiments of the act, it is unsatisfying to both; Peter ejaculates prematurely and Jill finds the whole thing distasteful and fraught with anxiety. Frequent bitter quarrels have highlighted their short married life.

SECONDARY SEXUAL DYSFUNCTION

Sexual dysfunctions in many women turn out on closer examination to be secondary to more basic problems. That is, these women may be inorgasmic or have little interest in sex or find sex aversive, but these are reactions to other aspects of their relationship with their husbands. The problem may be one of communication, of dislike for the husband for his manifest shortcomings, of disappointment in him because he has not lived up to her expectation, or for a variety of reasons. But whatever the cause their sexual response has dwindled or disappeared.

In situations like these it is not very productive to attempt to enhance or change the woman's sexual behavior in the absence of eliminating the primary cause. That is, the reasons for the sexual problem needs to be investigated and, if possible, remedied. The following case is an example of a sexual problem which is secondary in nature.

Case Report 10

Marion is a striking, well-dressed woman in her early 30s. She comes from a wealthy family and has had all the advantages that money ensures. Her marriage seven years ago to George was a signal for much rejoicing, since he was the only son of an equally wealthy family. It was truly a marriage made in Heaven. The first five years of nuptial bliss were uneventful in that the couple behaved as most married couples behave. That is, they discovered that each was something less than the other expected, something a little less than perfect.

During their sixth year together, George, in the course of his work, met and became amorously involved with a young woman who had a keen and abiding interest in sex. This liason continued relatively smoothly for about a year until a friend of Marion's, acting in her best interests, told her of George's infidelity. This caused something of an uproar in the household, which only abated when George promised to break off his relationship and never see the young woman again. True to his word, he did this. However, not six months passed before he became intimately involved with another young woman. Marion, much more sophisticated by this time, soon detected signs of extramarital activity. This time however, she did not confront George with his misdemeanours and, operating on the premise that what is good for the goose is good for the gander, promptly became sexually involved with a divorced friend of the family. George soon got wind of this and responded by hiring a private detective to report on his wife's activities. Once he had amassed a mountain of evidence of Marion's infidelity, he confronted her with it. Marion's reaction was not shame or guilt but indignation. That George would have a detective spy on her was too much! Stormy sessions followed this confrontation, with charges and counter-charges being flung out indiscriminately.

Eventually peace was restored, with each partner promising faithfully to put an end to their respective affairs. This they did. However, from that time on Marion lost all interest in sex with George. Where once she had been an active, interested, and aggressive participant in intercourse, having single or multiple orgasms on every occasion, she now found sex repulsive and unsatisfactory and began to seek ways of avoiding it. Watching the late-late show on the television became commonplace.

The foregoing examples bring to focus a number of factors relevant to the understanding of sexual dysfunction. Not all so-called "frigid" women are completely nonorgasmic; there are wide variations in this condition, and for some inexplicable reason, a woman who for the most part fails to reach a climax, can on occasion become highly aroused and achieve orgasm with little difficulty.

The direct causes of sexual dysfunction appear to be as varied as the number of women involved; there is no simple and straightforward explanation which can be routinely applied to all cases. Certainly the concepts of penis envy and Oedipal complexes serve little purpose in explaining sexual dysfunction. Emma is a case in point. It would appear more sensible to attribute her vaginismus to conditioning, brought about through constant and painful exposure to enemas, than to say that it represents an unconscious wish to .. "break off the penis and keep it." Explanations at this level of analysis serve little useful purpose in either understanding or alleviating the problem.

A more fruitful approach would be to consider the part played by learning and conditioning in the genesis of these disorders, since it could be argued that sexual behavior like other behavior is learned, and it is just as easy to learn wrong responses as it is to learn correct ones. Another important factor is that time is not necessarily a healer, and the injunction "not to worry and things will improve" serves only to make the advice-giver feel better—it has no effect whatsoever on the problem. This advice, so glibly presented and distressingly common, is in reality an admission on the part of those concerned that they do not really understand the problem and fail to appreciate the ramifications of what they are saying. The clearly observable fact that these problems can persist for years would appear to make this obvious.

It is not surprising that the average medical practitioner is unable to deal effectively with sexual dysfunction. These are not medical problems in the accepted sense, and by and large, medical training does not concern itself with behavioral problems of this kind; it is not part of the curriculum in most medical schools. Furthermore, many doctors when confronted with sexual problems become extremely embarrassed and find themselves unable to discuss them in any meaningful way. It is significantly easier to maintain an objective and professionally detached attitude while performing a pelvic examination than it is to discuss the intimate details of sexual disinterest or aversion. Physicians are educationally and emotionally equipped for the former; many are beyond their depth when it comes to the latter.

It is an unfortunate failing of medical schools that so little emphasis is placed on the teaching and examination of sexual disorders—not so much because these are medical problems, but because the family doctor is invariably the one that a woman first consults when she is experiencing difficulty with her sex life. Family physicians are well aware of this fact; they find themselves constantly faced with problems which they appreciate are grave, but for which they can offer no real solution apart from referring the patient to a specialist—a gynecologist or psychiatrist. The gynecologist, too, finds himself in an unenviable position in that he may have had little training in this area or if he has, is limited in the number and scope of sexual problems that he can cope with. To some extent, the same is true of psychiatry; there are just too many women requiring help for psychiatrists to deal effectively with them all.

INCIDENCE OF FEMALE SEXUAL DYSFUNCTION

It is perhaps no exaggeration to say that something on the order of 50–60% of married women are experiencing difficulties with their sex life, sufficient to cause other problems in the home. By difficulties it is meant that they derive no pleasure from sex, being either inorgasmic or lacking in sexual arousal; or they are indifferent to sex, even though occasionally reaching a climax; or they find sexual intercourse and the preliminaries to sexual intercourse aversive or repugnant. They are, in the common parlance, "frigid," an unfortunate and misleading term which nevertheless encompasses a variety of behaviors which characterize various aspects of sexual dysfunction. In general, the term frigidity as it is used in this book includes one or more of the following elements: complete or partial absence of sexual arousal, loss of sexual interest before reaching orgasm, disgust during foreplay, inability to achieve orgasm, absence of pleasure during foreplay, absence of pleasure during intercourse, discomfort during intercourse, pain during intercourse (dyspareunia), disgust during intercourse, inability to tolerate penetration (vaginismus). The central core of the problem is a greater or lesser degree of anxiety, and this is what interferes with normal heterosexual interaction.

It is impossible to specify the proportion of women who manifest problems in one or other of these areas. One can only make a general statement as to the overall number of women involved. Even this is unsatisfactory, since the proportion of women said to be frigid is determined by how frigidity is defined. If, for example, it is defined by the absence of a so-called vaginal orgasm, perhaps as much as 80% of women could be said to be frigid. If, on the other hand, frigidity is defined as the inability to achieve a so-called clitoral orgasm, then a much smaller proportion would be found. This becomes evident when the figures offered by different investigators are examined, and is the most reasonable way to explain frequencies which range from 5–80%.

VAGINAL AND CLITORAL ORGASM

There is probably no area in the realm of sexual behavior that has caused more problems and resulted in so much misunderstanding and confusion than the controversy over vaginal versus clitoral orgasm. The furor concerns the nature of a woman's sexual climax, the psychological and physiologic qualities of the female orgasm.

This polemic had its origin in psychoanalytic theory, with Freud a major contributor. The essence of the theory, as it relates to sexual orgasm and frigidity, is that in the psychosexual development of girls, sexual pleasure is originally centered in the clitoris (the female equivalent of the penis). However, as girls mature, the original love object, the mother, is exchanged for the father. This coincides with a change of the primary sexual zone from the clitoris to the vagina. That is, the vagina becomes sensitive and the center of stimulation, the organ for sexual climax. Whereas in the developing girl stimulation of the clitoris leads to orgasm, in the mature woman this sexual sensitivity is transferred to the vagina, and its stimulation by the penis leads to orgasm. A failure of this transfer to take place is the hallmark of immaturity, neuroticism and frigidity. The degree to which various contemporary psychoanalytic theorists subscribe to this theory varies, but it continues to play a prominent role in much current thinking. The relationship between frigidity and the transfer of sexual sensitivity from the clitoris to the vagina stems from the notion that the absence of a vaginal orgasm defines frigidity. It seems to be of little consequence if a woman is capable of one, two, or a dozen clitoral orgasms while having intercourse—if she fails to have a vaginal orgasm then she is frigid!

Unfortunately for psychoanalytic theory, there is little evidence to support this idea; it would appear to be more myth than fact. More than 20 years ago Kinsey (1953) and his associates noted that in most women the walls of the vagina contain few end organs of touch and are virtually insensitive when stroked or lightly stimulated; therefore, the vagina was probably much less important in achieving an orgasm than the exquisitely sensitive clitoris and its immediately surrounding areas. These findings have been elaborated upon more recently by Masters and Johnson (1970); they have pretty well substantiated that, from a physiologic point of view, one cannot differentiate between clitoral and vaginal orgasm, and the fears of inadequacy in women who have "only" a clitoral orgasm are groundless. Not that this is any big deal; this entire controversy is one of tilting at straw men. The vast majority of women who seek help because of orgasmic dysfunction do not do so because they fail to achieve a *vaginal* orgasm. Their complaint is that they do not have *any* kind of orgasm. We have yet to see a woman who was disturbed because she could not achieve a vaginal orgasm.

EARLY SEXUAL EXPERIENCE AND ORGASMIC CAPABILITY

In his monumental work *Sexual Behavior in the Human Female,* Kinsey (1953) has shown that a number of variables are at play in a woman's ability to achieve orgasm. Like other learned skills, it is something that requires practice or experience before it becomes fully developed. Using number of years married as a reflection of amount of practice, (and perhaps psychological conditioning) Kinsey has shown a steady increase in the percentage of women achieving orgasm on some occasions, and a similar increase in the percentage of woman consistently achieving orgasm through intercourse. These data are presented in Table 1–1, but should be summarized here:

By the end of the first year of marriage 75% of the women in his sample had experienced orgasm on some occasions. After five years this had increased to 83%; after ten years, to 87%; and after fifteen plus years, to 90%. The frequency of orgasm in relation to coital experiences is given as 63% in the first year of marriage, 71% by the fifth year, 77% by the tenth year, 81% by the fifteenth year, and 85% by the twentieth year. From these data it can be seen that 10% of women never, or only rarely, achieve orgasm during intercourse. On the other hand, those who do reach orgasm do so on the average of 63–85% of the time.

If failure to reach orgasm is the only criterion to define sexual dysfunction, then from these figures it would appear that a relatively small percentage of women are experiencing difficulties—which is not consistent with other estimates which suggest that something in the order of 50–60% of married women are unhappy with their sex lives. It seems likely that the explanation for this discrepancy lies in the observation that sexual dissatisfaction of various kinds, and from various sources, is not inconsistent with coital orgasm. That is, women who are indifferent to, and have little interest in sex, can and do achieve orgasm; women who are dissatisfied or unhappy with their sexual experiences may be quite capable of orgasm once they become sexually involved. It seems clear, then, that sexual happiness and sexual satisfaction are not perfectly correlated with the ability to achieve orgasm.

Kinsey has also shown that a marked relationship exists between a woman's premarital orgasmic experiences and her later, married responsiveness. Women who experienced orgasm (whether it be from dreams, masturbation, petting, coitus, or homosexual relationships) prior to marriage were much more likely to be orgasmically responsive after marriage than women who had not had this experience. During the first year of marriage, for instance:

Of those with premarital orgasmic experience, only 19% failed to reach orgasm with coitus, while 45–47% reached orgasm on nearly all coital occasions.
Of those who had never experienced orgasm prior to marriage, 44%—nearly half—continued to fail; only 25% achieved orgasm on nearly all coital occasions.

Taken at face value, it would appear that experience in orgasm before marriage is a good predictor of the ability to achieve orgasm postmaritally. It apparently makes little difference how these premarital orgasms are achieved, the end result is the same: an increase in the frequency of orgasmic responsiveness during postmarital coitus.

If we narrow the field, and look only at women with premarital *coital* experience, the picture is essentially the same:

If premarital coital orgasm was achieved at least 25 times, only 3-8% failed to achieve it postmaritally, and 50–57% were regularly responsive. If no premarital coital orgasm was achieved, 38–56% continued to fail postmaritally, and only 17–29% were regularly responsive.

It would appear that coitus *per se* is not as important in determining marital sexual adjustment as is the climactic outcome. The advantage of premarital orgasm is still marked if one considers those women who only petted or masturbated prior to marriage. During the first year of marriage:

Only 10% who had petted to orgasm failed in postmarital coitus, while 46–52% responded regularly with coital orgasm. 35% who failed to reach orgasm through premarital petting continued to fail in postmarital coitus, and only 32% responded regularly with orgasm. Only 13–16% who masturbated to orgasm premaritally failed in postmarital coitus, while 42–49% responded regularly.

For those who never masturbated at all, or had done so but failed to reach orgasm, the chances of success or failure for postmarital coital orgasm are roughly equal.

Kinsey quite rightly points out that these relationships may be more complex than they appear on the surface. It need not be true that premarital orgasmic experience is an important, and to some extent, necessary prelude to successful sex adjustment in marriage, that premarital orgasms lead to postmarital orgasms. It may well be that selective factors are at work to produce these correlations, and that women who engage in premarital intercourse, who pet and masturbate to orgasm, are women who would be sexually successful in marriage anyway. They are, in terms of sheer sexual responsiveness, different from women who do not engage in these premarital activities. But whatever the cause, it seems evident that a fairly reliable predictor of postmarital sexual responsiveness is premarital responsiveness, where ability to reach orgasm is an important criterion.

It seems clear from the studies of Kinsey and other investigators that the inability to achieve orgasm is prevalent among married women, and is an impediment to successful marriage adjustment. However, as was pointed out earlier, this is not the only problem nor need it be the most important. Something more than orgasmic failure is required to account for the discrepancy between those women who are nonorgasmic and those who are experiencing serious problems in their married life, problems which have their base in sexual maladjustment. While it is true that a marriage built solely on sex will not long endure, it is equally true that the absence of a satisfactory sexual relationship bodes ill for a married couple. Benjamin Franklin remarked that where there is marriage without love, there will be love without marriage. This is as true now as when it was first written.

Table 1-1. INCIDENCE AND FREQUENCY OF ORGASM IN MARITAL COITUS AS A FUNCTION OF YEARS MARRIED*

YEARS MARRIED	ORGASTIC COITUS AT LEAST ONCE (%)	FREQUENCY OF ORGASTIC COITUS (%)
1	75	63
5	83	71
10	87	77
15	90	81
20	90	85

*Data from Kinsey et al.: Sexual Behavior in the Human Female. Philadelphia. Saunders, 1953

PHYSICAL CAUSES AND VAGINISMUS

The vast majority of sexual problems are psychological in nature. However, there are certainly some instances where there is a physical or organic basis and these should be ruled out before any attempt at psychological intervention is made. When a woman complains of pain and discomfort during and after intercourse she should be examined for a physical cause. It may well be that a biophysical abnormality exists. Some physical problems have become less common in recent years since the advent of the pap test and regular internal examinations. And while lesions, defects, infections and tumorous growths are fairly readily observable during a thorough pelvic examination, such things as hormonal deficiencies, anemia, and central nervous system defects are not so readily detected and only extensive and intensive investigations make them apparent. Fortunately these account for relatively few of the cases of sexual dysfunction seen in the clinical practice. Nevertheless, inflammation and lesions of various parts of the genitalia, warts, cysts and polyps can lead to dyspareunia (painful intercourse); fortunately most of these localized pathologies can be satisfactorily dealt with by medical or minor surgical procedures, and they need not be a chronic hinderance to sexual participation and enjoyment.

Pain, although it can be graphically described, may be psychosomatic and may provide a convenient excuse for avoiding sexual advances. Only the most unfeeling and unthinking husband will persist in encouraging his wife to engage in intercourse when this is accompanied by moaning, grimacing, tears and involuntary muscle contractions, and the activity invariably followed by postcoital recriminations. Generally speaking, the sexual response of most husbands will extinguish after a few experiences of this kind. In situations like this, the pain may be real, but it is quite possible that the woman has been conditioned to respond in this way; she has learned to associate pain and discomfort with penile penetration and this now is her usual response. Perhaps on earlier occasions she has experienced pain during intercourse and although the reason for it no longer exists, the harm has been done; for women who have negative feelings and attitudes toward sex to begin with, not many unpleasant experiences are required to firmly establish a negative response.

On the other hand, it may be that claims of pain and discomfort are feigned, because the woman has learned that if she makes such claims her husband will leave her alone, few husbands wishing to be seen as a brute and a monster even in the eyes of their wives. This is an effective way of avoiding sexual contact and, as many husbands and wives are aware, its use is widespread.

The role of physical pathology is much less clear in vaginismus (muscle spasm) than it is in dyspareunia. Where there is or has been a physical cause, this is frequently associated with the aftereffects of dyspareunia. When a woman has been subjected to painful intercourse over an extended period of time because of some pathology, vaginismus may result and continue long after the physical problem has been cleared up. But these cases appear to be in the minority and where vaginismus is present it is likely that it has psychogenic origins. Nevertheless, whatever the source, vaginismus can effectively prevent intercourse. Involved are the pelvic muscles concerned with the perineum and the outer portion of the vagina. Rather than rhythmic contractions associated with the orgasmic response, these muscle groups contract spastically and with a great deal of force. The woman has no control over these spasms and any attempt at vaginal penetration, whether it be by a penis, a finger, a tampon or other object, will set them off and effectively block the entrance to the vagina. Intercourse attempted under these conditions is impossible, and persisted attempts extremely painful.

Case Report 11

Freda is a 25-year-old woman who has been married for two years and has yet to experience intercourse. The farthest she has progressed is to allow partial insertion of the penis in the vaginal opening for a brief period of time. But even this mild penetration is intolerable and causes acute pains, with the feeling of an attempt to put "something big into something small." Repeated attempts at intercourse during the first three months of marriage failed. In desperation Freda consulted a gynecologist, who diagnosed an intact and particularly tough hymen which he surgically excised. It was necessary to conduct the initial examination as well as the surgery under anesthetic; Freda could not otherwise tolerate even the insertion of a single finger. The effect of this operation on her sexual activities was nil; she continued to complain of severe pain whenever her husband attempted insertion, and if he persisted she would scream and cry until he abandoned the attempt in frustration. She claims that she is too small despite assurances by the gynecologist that she is physically normal. Her usual response is to "freeze up" whenever her husband approaches her. The frequency with which her husband approaches her has steadily declined and she now lives in constant fear that he will seek solace elsewhere.

Vaginismus need not be secondary to, or develop from dyspareunia. It can exist on its own with the etiology obscure.

Case Report 12

Sandra is a well-educated 29-year-old who has been married for seven years but never had intercourse. She can engage in foreplay for extended periods of time with no outward appearance of anxiety; she can participate in oral sex, both actively and passively, with no difficulty. However, as soon as her husband attempts intromission, her pelvic muscles go into spasm, making penetration impossible. (Even this has not made her unduly anxious or upset so much as frustrated.) Her husband continues to fumble around, attempting penetration, until eventually he ejaculates. The result of this is anger and frustration, she crying bitter tears and he raging at her for her sexual deficiency. This scenario has been acted out hundreds of times over the course of seven years with no change in the climax. A major problem with this young woman is a relative inability to become sexually aroused. Thirty or forty minutes of foreplay or extended oral sex results in only a moderate degree of arousal; she never reaches the point when she can say "Now is the time, now I'm ready." Sandra cannot explain her behavior; she has no idea of why she should feel this way. Certainly there was nothing in her background which would predict such a problem. Her own attitudes toward sex are healthy and normal and there was nothing discernible in her upbringing to account for it. She had never suffered any trauma concerned with sex; she had never experienced pain despite her husband's ineffectual and unfulfilled groping and probing.

The only hints are the facts that she has never masturbated and has never experienced orgasm, and that while she can not tolerate a penis, she can insert a dilator with little difficulty. The part that absence of masturbation played in the overall problem is far from clear, while her ability to tolerate a dilator indicates a vaginismal response specific to men. Her problem could best be described as a penile phobia. However, she never at any time has enunciated any fear of men; she is not concerned about being hurt as a result of intercourse, nor is she troubled about becoming pregnant; in fact her fondest hope is to have children.

Case Report 13

Even more inexplicable is the case of *Joan*. This 25-year-old woman has been married for five years, and has recently undergone a trial separation from her husband. His complaint, the cause for the separation which she echoes, is that they have yet to have intercourse. Nevertheless, she has recently had a baby! Both she and her husband are at a loss to explain this singular phenomenon. Unlike Sandra, Joan is extremely responsive to sexual advances by her husband; she becomes increasingly aroused by foreplay and exhibits all the usual signs, nipple erection, vaginal lubrication, breast swelling, rapid breathing. However, as soon as her husband commences to introduce his penis in her vagina she becomes rigid and the precoital signs disappear; no amount of further stimulation has any effect. Not infrequently her husband will ejaculate at this point and this probably explains her pregnancy. He has ejaculated right at the start, when his penis has been just inside the vaginal opening.

Joan's explanation for her vaginismus is that she is afraid of being hurt by her husband's penis. Despite assurances that she is completely normal and not too small, and has in fact never suffered pain from attempted intercourse, she continues to believe her husband's penis is too large for her. After the birth of her child, her family doctor pointed out to her that since it was possible for an eight-pound baby to pass through her vagina, she should certainly be able to accommodate a relatively small object like a penis. However, logical arguments like this have had absolutely no effect, and her response to intercourse remains the same.

AROUSAL DYSFUNCTION

There are women whose attitude toward sex can best be described as indifferent; they can take it or leave it. They manifest this indifference in an almost total absence of sexual arousal. They never, regardless of the criteria employed, display any of the more common signs which typically accompany female sexual arousal or responsiveness. This might be more easily interpreted if at the same time they derived no pleasure from sex, or if they never achieved an orgasm. But this is not the case. Many of these women will consistently reach a climax and obviously enjoy it, but will never initiate sex. Indeed, they frequently regard it as simply another wifely function. If the husband wants sex they will go along with him, without displaying any degree of enthusiasm but showing no signs of anxiety. If, on the other hand, he were to stop requesting intercourse, they would not miss it and probably never inquire as to his lack of attention in this sphere, at least in the context of personal deprivation.

There is no ready or easy explanation for the behavior of these women. However, a strong candidate would be that it is simply a matter of individual difference; women vary in their sex drives. One might expect that sex drive or sexuality is a normally distributed personality characteristic and that these women are at the low end of the distribution. But whatever the reason, they do not become sexually aroused and often tend to view sex as simply an adjunct to marriage, something in which they are expected to participate by virtue of the marriage ceremony, an activity dictated by the husband's whim. Intercourse is something that gives him pleasure and is therefore to be engaged in, like cooking appetizing meals. And if she derives some measure of pleasure by achieving a climax, then this is something of a bonus—in the same way that after preparing an excellent dinner, she too derives pleasure from eating it.

In a sense these women are less self-sacrificing than those who engage in sex for the sake of their husbands but derive no pleasure whatsoever from the act. The latter do not become sexually aroused and they never experience an orgasm. Theirs is a Victorian attitude that proscribes sex as being something a woman puts up with for the sake of her husband. She may find it aversive or she may not. A good many wives fall into the latter category. They will have sexual relations with their husbands solely on the grounds that he expects it and enjoys it. The only pleasure they derive from it is the knowledge that it gives him pleasure.

Apparently it never occurs to such women that they are being used, that sex is a mutual affair, and sexual satisfaction is not the exclusive prerogative of the male partner. If the husband questions his wife's role in the sex act and becomes irritated at her lack of response, she will frequently simulate pleasure and behave as if she is having an orgasm. In many cases wives are not very convincing—but they don't have to be. A husband will believe what he wants to believe, and if his wife goes through the motions of sexual arousal and climax, he is willing and eager, despite bad acting and in the face of minimal evidence, to believe her. It is something that does not bear too close scrutiny if the charade is to be maintained.

How long a woman is prepared to simulate sexual pleasure in the absence of reinforcement is a matter of conjecture, but it is reasonable to suppose that she will not do so indefinitely. The time will come when she gets the notion that there must be more to sex than she is experiencing, when through reading or discussion with other women she begins to think she is missing out on one of life's simple pleasures. She may then begin to reassess her relationship with her husband and to see him in an entirely new light. When this happens, the husband will find himself in great difficulty; in this day and age it is difficult to support the position that sex is for men only. She will demand that past wrongs be set right—which means his cooperation in a therapeutic endeavor. A wise husband will acquiesce or run the risk of being a cuckold.

SEXUAL AVERSION

In the absence of vaginismus and dyspareunia, the major complaint of women seeking help for sexual dysfunction is that sex is aversive; it is unsatisfying and frustrating. The natural history of these problems seems to be that the women entered marriage with little practical experience in sexual matters but with relatively open minds. However, for unspecified reasons they were never able to reach a climax. They engaged in intercourse fairly frequently, as most newly married couples do, but were consistently unsatisfied and left up in the air when it was over. At the beginning there was the hope and the feeling that this was not a major problem; perhaps it was the novelty of the sexual activity, perhaps orgasm would come with practice.

And so two or three or more times a week the couple would engage in intercourse, with the husband doing his level best to arouse his wife to new heights and she trying as hard as she could to achieve and maintain a high level of sexual arousal and putting all her efforts into achieving a climax. When this was not forthcoming, slowly the idea takes root that there is something amiss, that perhaps she is in some way abnormal and destined never to be sexually satisfied. With each ensuing failure this idea grows.

In conjunction with her increasing despair and frustration, a subtle change occurs in the way in which she views her husband; the romantic figure she married begins to lose some of his charm, his charisma, and there is a germ of an idea that perhaps he is in some unspecified way at least partially responsible for her inability to achieve sexual fulfillment, that the problem she is experiencing does not reside totally within herself. Furthermore, she begins to attend more closely to what is happening when they have intercourse; she recognizes that he becomes highly aroused and notes the obvious pleasure and satisfaction he derives from reaching a climax. She is also aware that foreplay has become less involved and of shorter duration and that her husband's ability to ejaculate has improved in that less time is required to bring this about.

These things, coupled with the fact that she is consistently unsuccessful in having an orgasm and is therefore chronically frustrated and physically uncomfortable and upset, begin to engender resentment in her and this is directed at her husband. This resentment grows and generalizes and while originally it was restricted to the sexual sphere, it now begins to include other aspects of his behavior. Fault-finding becomes more and more a way of life and occupies more and more of her time. In addition, and not surprising, her interest in sex begins to wane, with a concomitant reduction in frequency of intercourse. This is not only because of the fact that she derives little pleasure from it, but also because of the physical discomfort, and in many cases actual pain, that follows each and every unconsummated, unrelieved sexual experience. (Women, perhaps more so than men, experience physical discomfort from a failure to relieve the tension that accompanies high levels of sexual arousal.)

It does not take long for her husband to recognize this lessening of sexual interest and when it reaches the point where he feels that he is becoming deprived, he becomes more aggressive. Where at one time only subtle hints were required to convey to his wife that he is interested in sex, now it is necessary to make obvious overtures; eventually these become outright demands. At this point, his interest in sex is matched by her reluctance to have anything to do with it; she begins to seek reasons for not engaging in intercourse. The jokes about wives claiming headaches when they go to bed is firmly based on fact. This behavior in turn causes resentment in the husband, which in turn results in arguing and bickering both about sex and things not related to sex. Love has disappeared and the bedroom becomes a battleground. This snowball effect continues until the problem becomes magnified out of all proportion and only separation or professional intervention provides a solution.

One bizarre aspect of this whole sad situation is the attitude of the husband. Initially he has a genuine concern for his wife's problem. It then progresses through a somewhat less than true concern, keen interest, simple interest, slight impatience, a more intense impatience, annoyance, and finally anger. Towards the end the husband has succeeded in convincing himself that his wife's actions, her reluctance for sex, are deliberate and an attempt to humiliate and belittle him. This may not be a strongly held conviction, however, and if faced with the facts by a third party, he will admit that his wife probably has no control over her feelings and behaviors. Nevertheless, he lacks understanding of his wife's predicament, and shows a reluctance to face the fact that not only does she fail to get any enjoyment out of sex, but the entire act and its aftermath is fraught with anxiety, tension, frustration and acute physical discomfort.

Few husbands possess the insight, or perhaps the inclination, to sit back and ask themselves how long *they* would be prepared to continue sexual activities if the roles were reversed. How long would they endure going through the motions of intercourse in the absence of ejaculating? If all of the pleasures were visited upon the wife, and the whole process were solely for her benefit, one might conjecture that the only honest answer would be "not very long."

THE HUSBAND AS A FACTOR IN FEMALE DYSFUNCTION

It would be a serious error to leave the impression that in all the sexual difficulties which bedevil women the husband is always a passive onlooker, that he is completely and totally free of blame or responsibility, that he is an innocent victim of circumstances over which he has no control. While this is true to varying degrees in a great many instances, it is not universally the case. It is not uncommon for the husband, as near as can be determined, to be the precipitating cause of his wife's problem or to be the agent for exacerbating an existing condition which originally may have been relatively mild, but which has reached serious proportions. It is not unusual for a husband to send his wife for treatment while he remains in the background, refusing to come for interviews on the grounds that it is her sexual problem.

It is impossible to enumerate all the shortcomings of husbands and the ways in which they contribute to the sexual dysfunctions of wives. Nevertheless, there are a few common faults which can be mentioned. High on the list of priorities is an absence of meaningful communication. Husbands, even more than wives, can be extremely reticent in discussing problems they are having. Whether this is due to embarrasment, ignorance of the nature of the problem, lack of general sexual knowledge, a refusal to admit that a problem exists because this might reflect on one's own self image, or because of sheer bloody-mindedness, it is difficult to say. Frequently though, in our experience, one or more of these excuses has been involved. In the absence of effective communication there is very little a woman can do in attempting to remedy the situation. She can become only more frustrated, emotionally upset and angry, frequently to the wonderment of her husband. He may be genuinely surprised when, interviewed together, his wife complains bitterly that they never talk to each other. Too often husbands cannot see the forest for the trees.

A second imperfection, apparent in many husbands, is an almost total lack of sensitivity and consideration for their wives. They view their wives as chattel, someone to cook, clean house, look after the children and in general be on 24-hour call to satisfy their every whim. That their wives are independent human beings with needs, desires and individual aspirations, never crosses their mind. An example of this is Mr. and Mrs. G.

Case Report 14

Mr. G's notion of his wife's role was that she was there to make his life as pleasant as possible. He made all the decisions in the household and if his wife was consulted, which happened infrequently, it was after the fact. He would announce when and where they would take their vacation; he would arrive home with a new car, to the surprise and often dismay of his wife; he insisted the children attend a private school, and so on. Never did he sit down with his wife to discuss major decisions or plans; he arbitrarily decided what was to be done. He was also a firm believer in sex on demand—his demand. Perhaps a minor thing, but indicative of his general attitude towards his wife, was his behavior in the evening. Both he and his wife would be sitting in the living room, he watching TV and she reading. When a program ended, he would tell her, not ask her, to change to another channel. This she would do despite the fact that he was the only one watching it. It apparently never occurred to him to do this himself. Similarly, if during the evening he became thirsty, he would tell his wife to get him a drink of water, or if hungry, to make him a sandwich. This kind of behavior had been the norm all their married life and although his wife resented these unreasonable demands, she nevertheless acquiesced. In the course of one interview she remarked that there were times when she could have taken an axe to him. Nevertheless, she continued to be his obedient servant.

One of the first things we told her when she came for treatment was that she was to stop this slavish behavior. If her husband wanted the TV channel changed, then she was to tell him to change it himself. Similarly with getting him drinks and evening snacks. She was astonished and somewhat apprehensive at this advice, but accepted it.

At the following meeting she jubilantly recounted the details of her husband's response to her rebellious behavior. He was, to put it mildly, stupefied; he could not believe his ears. However, once he regained his composure, he did not argue the point and fended for himself. Furthermore, he never again made similar demands on her. The effect of this experience on Mrs. G was to give her new confidence and she began to challenge him on other matters as well, with a marked improvement in their interpersonal relations.

A third deficiency in many husbands is related to the second, but tends to be restricted to sexual relations. In these cases the husband is insensitive to his wife's emotions, moods and responses to sexual overtures. He expects her to be ready for sex at any time, just as he is, and is frequently at a loss to explain her lack of enthusiasm when he, with little or no preliminary advances, decides that it would be a good thing if they had intercourse. An example of this is Mr. R.

Case Report 15

This man apparently believed that an erection should not be wasted and so, in the morning when he invariably awoke with one, he would rouse his wife (who was even less interested in sex in the morning than at other times) and commence love-making. This was concluded very rapidly during weekday mornings, since each worked. However, on the weekends it was prolonged, lasting for as long as three hours. On these occasions he was quite impervious to his wife's pleas that she had an early appointment with the hairdresser, dentist or whatever. His only concern was what was immediately happening and he was oblivious to everything else. Needless to say, their married life was anything but tranquil.

And then there is the jack-rabbit. The husband's notions of sex and love-making is to demonstrate how quickly he can ejaculate and, having achieved this, how fast he can fall asleep. Frequently he has this skill honed to a fine edge and can do both in the space of ten minutes. It never occurs to him that it takes two to tango, that his wife has sexual needs just as strong as his, that require gratification. Unfortunately, many wives are unable to communicate this basic fact to their husbands and thus their sexual lives are ones of constant and chronic frustration.

The converse of this type is the husband whose penis is anesthetized. He can labor for an hour or more without reaching a climax. In women who are capable of multiple orgasms this may be an ideal state. On the other hand, in women who are inorgasmic and/or who find sex aversive and repugnant, this seemingly endless and fruitless friction is monstrous and almost guaranteed to insure uncharitable feelings and attitudes toward an over-indulged husband. There are husbands whose sex drive and amorous intent are directly related to the amount of alcohol they have had to drink. The drunker they become, the more they see themselves as Don Juans. They arrive home in a stuporous condition and expect their wives to fall over backwards with joy and anticipation of a frenzied hour in bed. They become angry and abusive if their advances are justifiably met with aversion and disgust. Nevertheless, this does not prevent them from repeating this scenario time after time.

Finally, there are those husbands whose sophistication with regard to sex in general, and coitus in particular, is virtually nonexistent. Their knowledge of the female anatomy and its function has been obtained second or third-hand, and usually from people as knowledgeable as themselves in these matters. They approach the marriage bed confident but ignorant, and intercourse becomes a matter of trial and error with frustration and anger the most likely outcome. By the time the couple have worked out the mechanics of coitus, which may take months, the damage has been done. The wife, although ignorant of sexual behavior herself, expects her husband to be aware at least of the basics of the act; he should know what goes where.

Consider two examples of the depths of ignorance attainable. First, the young woman who consulted her family doctor because of redness, swelling and general irritation of her navel. On inquiry it was discovered that both she and her husband thought that this was where his penis was supposed to enter. The mind boggles at the thought of their attempts at intercourse.

The second, and just as bizarre example, was the husband who sent his wife to us for the treatment of a sexual disorder. His reason for doing so was that she did not ejaculate! He was under the impression that when his wife had an orgasm there should be a forceful release of semen, just as in a man. That this did not happen was a cause of great concern. His wife shared his views in this biologic misconception.

There are, of course, many other deficiencies and imperfections in husbands which significantly contribute to their wives sexual problems. The ones mentioned are those which we have found to be common. Clearly, the husband is important in the sexual relationship and, as mentioned earlier, it is a chauvinistic mistake to view female sexual dysfunction as something for which the husband bears no measure of responsibility.

SUMMARY

Obviously sexual dysfunctions are not unitary phenomena. The forms they take, and the way in which they are expressed, vary. Much of this variability is explicable in terms of the learning history of the women involved. But individual differences also need be taken into account. Rape, for example, is perhaps the most traumatic sexual experience to which a woman can be subjected. Nevertheless, not all victims of rape develop sexual problems; some come through the experience unscathed.

Similarly with some other kinds of early learning experiences. The effects vary from woman to woman and there appears to be no observable or rational explanation for these differential responses. Even in the cases of secondary frigidity it is no easy task to pinpoint the reason why infidelity will result in a change in sexual responsiveness in one woman, but not in another. It is likely that the circumstances surrounding these transgressions— the general, overall quality of the marriage and the personalities in a very broad sense —contribute to this.

We have pointed out that the incidence of sexual dysfunction within the population is exceedingly high—much higher, we suspect, than is commonly assumed. Furthermore, the ramifications are grave indeed and bode ill for a great many people. While sexual problems may be the result of an unsatisfying and unhappy marriage, too frequently the reverse is true, with the breakup of marriage a serious consequence.

There is a strong tendency to view sexual dysfunction as simply the inability on the part of a woman to achieve an orgasm. Nothing could be farther from the truth. While orgasmic dysfunctions loom large, there is a variety of other problems equally or perhaps more serious. Dyspareunia and vaginismus are two such problems. Dyspareunia, while effectively interfering with intercourse, once dealt with may have no aftermath. Vaginismus, on the other hand, is a psychological problem which can, and frequently does, prevent intercourse, sometimes for years. Certainly from a male point of view this is far more serious than a woman's failure to reach orgasm.

There are also arousal dysfunctions where no amount of stimulation by the husband will prepare his wife for intercourse, even though she may at times reach orgasm. And there are women who have little or no interest in sex. They go through the motions solely to please their husbands but derive no pleasure from the act.

Much has been made of the virtues of the vaginal orgasm as contrasted with the clitoral. The supposition is that only by achieving the former has a woman reached full womanhood; anything else is infantile. Despite the fact that this distinction has been demonstrated to be a myth, the notion persists that there are two distinct types of female orgasm. The only function of this fairy tale is to create doubt and confusion in the minds of women.

A too-common assumption, particularly on the part of men, is that husbands are innocent bystanders so far as their wives' sexual problems are concerned. Unfortunately some women share this view. The fact of the matter is that husbands are frequently the source of the problem but even if not the source, a strong contributor to its maintenance. Husbands, as every wife knows, are not perfect in any sense of the term. They can be impatient, inconsiderate, insensitive, brutal and stupid. They can be all these things while maintaining the façade, of the patient, understanding, considerate and sensitive bedfellow. Their obtuseness is often beyond comprehension. Fortunately, though, husbands are frequently subject to the same laws of learning as their wives and it is possible to modify their behaviors in ways consistent with their wives' welfare.

2

Male Sexual Dysfunction: Description

Alas! Men, unlike women, cannot "fake" sexual performance; if a man does not achieve an erection or if he ejaculates prematurely, both he and his partner are acutely and distressingly aware of his failure. Only in the rare case of retarded ejaculation might a male "fake" orgasm. In the male, the problems and symptoms are of a binary nature: sexual success or sexual failure. Males too, can experience degrees of success and involvement in sexual intercourse, but not to the extent that women can. A man, above all else, must achieve intravaginal orgasm in order to feel that intercourse has been successful, whereas at least some women can obtain a degree of satisfaction and a measure of success without achieving an orgasm. So while male sexual problems may be less complex and not as heterogeneous as female sexual problems, they can be equally, if not more, distressing to the individuals afflicted.

Men and women differ in another important aspect: men seem less in need of a feeling of love, romanticism or even basic compatability when it comes to sexual behavior. It is not unusual for a husband to fight bitterly with his wife and then expect sexual intercourse shortly after. In fact, one of the most common complaints of women in sexual therapy is that their husbands are not romantic or loving, yet expect sexual intercourse whenever they are in bed together. Many women would be very content to "cuddle" with their husbands and even engage in foreplay without having intercourse, while to most men this would be unthinkable, and to some men, perverted. Male complaints are focused almost exclusively on their own failure to perform, with little attention paid to their partner's behavior. Men seldom complain of women being "animals" and only "wanting one thing," namely, sex. Even when a male complains of a woman being sexually over aggressive, his basic lament is not with the woman but with his inability to accommodate her in what he believes to be a satisfactory and satisfying way. Too often, though, his notions of what she wants and requires are erroneous and are based on his own rather narrow view of sexuality.

The types of male sexual dysfunction fall roughly into three categories: premature ejaculation, retarded or delayed ejaculation, and impotence or erectile failure.

TYPES OF DYSFUNCTION

PREMATURE EJACULATION

Ejaculation is a purely reflexive action of the body and is controlled by the lumbar portion of the spinal cord. It is mediated by the sympathetic nervous system and cannot be stopped once it is triggered. There are several problems which can be associated with ejaculation: premature ejaculation, retarded ejaculation and retrograde ejaculation. Premature ejaculation and retarded ejaculation are most important, and will be discussed in some detail in this chapter. (Retrograde ejaculation is a rare occurrence in which the male sperm empties into the bladder instead of passing out through the penis. This condition is associated in some instances with ingestion of tranquilizing drugs or with physical illness, and is almost always treated medically.)

As Masters and Johnson (1970) point out, there is no way of knowing how many men at some point in their lives experience premature ejaculation. Probably most men do. Premature ejaculation is, in fact, one of the most common sexual problems. Many men have only occasional episodes while others, in the absence of treatment, may be afflicted for life. It is not unusual for even the most sexually healthy male occasionally to lose ejaculatory control, but when loss of control becomes the rule rather than the exception there is cause for worry, and worry they do. There is disagreement on the exact definition of premature ejaculation, and interpretation varies from length of time before ejaculation during coitus, to number of strokes prior to ejaculation (Kaplan, 1974). Masters and Johnson define it in terms of the percentage of time in which the female partner reaches orgasm—less than 50% indicates prematurity. While this definition takes into account differences in sociocultural factors and individual personality traits, it is valid only in terms of the individual female response. A man who can delay ejaculation for only 60 seconds after intromission is not a premature ejaculator if his wife is very rapid in her response. On the other hand, a man who can thrust for 10 minutes would be defined as premature if his wife typically requires 15 minutes of intervaginal stimulation to reach orgasm.

We consider the male to be experiencing premature ejaculation if he ejaculates either prior to coital penetration or shortly after intromission. In some very severe cases, ejaculation occurs at the first hint of sexual arousal—even reading erotic literature can bring on the ejaculatory response. If the ejaculation occurs before the female can become sufficiently aroused to produce orgasm, she may become sexually frustrated by what she terms as her partner's failure. If the problem becomes chronic, then marital difficulties are highly predictable.

One problem in defining premature ejaculation is that there is also widespread disagreement among those experiencing it as to whether or not it constitutes a problem. There seem to be marked differences in social class attitudes toward prematurity. Although we have dealt with many lower-class male clients, most of our clients who have been particularly upset by this problem have been well educated upper-middle class males who have been very tuned in to their sexual partner's feelings and lack of enjoyment. Kerckhoff (1974) points out that such awareness and sensitivity is usually not present in lower class males.

In the lower classes, coitus is viewed primarily as a male activity, something many women feel they must simply "put up with." There is little indication that women should desire and enjoy sexual relations, even after marriage. Rainwater (1960) reports that in his sample of working class married couples: ". . . both husbands and wives feel that sexual gratification for the wife is much less important, so that, consciously at least, wives seem generally content if intercourse results in the husband's pleasure, even if not in their own. These couples see sex as primarily a male activity in initiation, interest, frequency of desire, and consistent gratification." Kinsey (Kinsey, Pomeroy and Martin, 1948) too has pointed out that: "At lower educational levels, it is usual for the male to try to achieve an orgasm as soon as possible after effecting genital union."

The amount of time to orgasm following penetration is of little concern when the focus of attention is almost entirely on male gratification. Only in cases in which premature ejaculation consistently occurs prior to penetration is it then recognized as a problem.

Certainly middle and upper class males are equally capable of being insensitive to their partner's feelings during sex. However, middle and upper class men and women are much more likely to be informed readers and exposed to changing attitudes related to male and female roles and sexuality. In informed couples, both sexual partners are sensitive to their own as well as to their partner's sexual gratification and more likely to identify premature ejaculation as a problem. And if a man ignores the problem, his partner will graphically draw it to his attention.

Premature ejaculation can have an acute or chronic onset, and it can occur as a singular problem or in conjunction with loss of erection. Some males also experience loss of sexual desire along with it. Cooper (1969) found that in cases of premature ejaculation in which there was a chronic onset (since adolescence) the prognosis was poor; acute onset and high levels of anxiety, on the other hand, were good predictors of successful treatment.

Cases of premature ejaculation are thought by some therapists to be caused by excessive sensitivity to erotic sensation, and treatment often involves the use of ointments applied to the penis to dull its receptivity. Many males have attempted similar approaches to treatment, including wearing of multiple condoms, inflicting a distracting pain by biting one's lips or pinching one's body, and flexing muscles—all these designed to distract localized arousal sensations. (Kaplan (1974) points out that such remedies are usually of little value, thus casting doubt on the excessive sensitivity hypothesis.)

The amount of frustration, anxiety, and anger generated by premature ejaculation is often considerable, and many couples attempt various ameliorative strategies to deal with it. Unfortunately, most of these home remedies are self-defeating. Doesn't it seem logical that if a husband ejaculates during foreplay that much of the foreplay should be eliminated? This is very often the strategy adopted by married couples, who then concentrate on female oriented stimulation and "quick" coital connection, before ejaculation occurs. They sneak up on it, so to speak. The husband will manually stimulate his wife to the point of orgasm, while she maintains a hands off policy. When his wife signals that she is ready, a furious scramble will ensue as he attempts union. He may be successful in this or he may not, but in any event the frantic effort on both their parts to achieve intromission is almost guaranteed to result in her loss of high sexual arousal, with his inevitable ejaculation before she regains her peak. Through this strategy a male tends to become even more unaware of the controlling mechanism of his own orgasm, and thus is even worse off. Masters and Johnson point out that another common strategy adopted by premature ejaculators is abstinence. However, as in the case of the "quick coital connector," this strategy tends to lead to a lessening of control and further frustration.

The man will abstain for a period of time which, in the absence of masturbation, will sensitize him to sexual stimuli; fewer or less obvious sexual cues are required to arouse him and less direct stimulation to cause ejaculation. There comes a point when his good intentions to abstain go out the window and he attempts intercourse—with predictable results. He ejaculates before he fairly gets under way, with frustration guaranteed to both himself and his partner. Fortunately, there are very effective therapy programs for dealing with most cases of premature ejaculation, which are discussed in Chapter 5.

DELAYED ORGASM, EJACULATORY INCOMPETENCE

The opposite condition of premature ejaculation is retarded ejaculation, commonly referred to as ejaculatory incompetence. In this condition a man has little trouble in obtaining or maintaining an erection, but has difficulty in ejaculating intravaginally. Penile thrusting may last as long as 30 minutes to an hour without ejaculation. Although this may be satisfying to the female partner (providing that fatigue, boredom or soreness do not set in), it is usually tremendously frustrating to the man and ends without relief. Some men embarrassed by this condition resort to faking orgasm, and then masturbate to ejaculation once their partner has fallen asleep. The condition has been described by Masters and Johnson (1970), who have seen 17 cases over an 11 year period. Friedman (1973) reports not finding a single paper in the literature devoted solely to the topic of delayed ejaculation. In our own clinical experience, we have seen only one case during the past five years. The case was somewhat atypical, since it involved delayed ejaculation in an exclusively homosexual 40-year-old male.

Case Report 16

Although uneducated, Mr. Q was very bright and personable. He had many of the classic background characteristics found in homosexuals, including a very close relationship with his "loving" mother and a very cold and bitter relationship with his "rejecting" father. For as long as Mr. Q could remember, he had experienced a problem of delayed ejaculation in homosexual relations and found it a source of considerable distress. When involved in either manual or oral genital sexual stimulation, he could not ejaculate after direct stimulation lasting as long as an hour. Often his sexual partner would become angry and ask Mr. Q what was wrong. Such admonishment would only serve to increase his anxiety and cause him to tighten his grip on a bedpost or chair in an attempt to force the ejaculation. Mr. Q gradually began to avoid sexual contacts as much as possible.

All of the possible etiological explanations of this case and others may be fascinating, but as yet not much is known about the problem. Masters and Johnson report cases in which religious orthodoxy and traumatic experiences were felt to be instrumental in its development. Friedman (1973) offered a psychoanalytically based explanation, seeing delayed ejaculation as an example of "success phobia." In success phobia, a person strives to succeed but when success is near, he or she quits because of the fear that their success will somehow result in retaliation from others and ultimately, their destruction.

The patient with success phobia has to maintain a good erection to portray that which he really lacks, a conviction of strength. However, in the demonstration of strength with his penis he is willing to go only so far, but no further, and stops just short of the culmination of success, ejaculation. This control is exercised at the very last point compatible with safty. (Friedman, 1973).

Quoting others Friedman continues

"thus through his symptom the patient with retarded ejaculation saves his life, preserves his penis, and supposedly emerges from intercourse a man"

The Friedman theory is an interesting albeit untestable one. However, as in the case of other sexual problems, regardless of the etiology of the disorder, specific conditioning and reality oriented programs seem to be effective in treatment. Thus, Masters and Johnson (1970) experienced success in 14 out of 17 cases of retarded ejaculation without attempting to deal with any underlying (unconscious) causes.

More recently, Kaplan (1974) has described retarded ejaculation as highly prevalent in contrast to Masters and Johnson's (1970) contention that it was relatively rare. Kaplan's experience and discussion of this problem seems to be the most knowledgeable in the field today. She described retarded ejaculation as occurring on a continuum; on one end is the individual who in the presence of specific anxiety arousing stimuli (a certain female partner or a certain situation) finds it difficult to achieve an orgasm, while on the other end is the male who has never been able to achieve an orgasm intravaginally. Admittedly, the extremely severe case is rare and most sexual clinics are more likely to see examples from the middle of the continuum.

IMPOTENCE OR ERECTILE FAILURE

The male erection is a reflexive action of the body which is controlled in the spinal cord and in higher centers of the brain. The erection is triggered through the parasympathetic nervous system which controls the supply of blood to the penis. As arousal increases, the arterials supplying blood to the penis expand, while the veins through which blood drains from the penis, constrict. The result of this parasympathetic action is that blood is trapped in the corpora cavernosa and corpus spongiosum surrounding the penis, causing the penis to stiffen and lengthen. When a man loses his erection following orgasm or because of psychogenic factors, sympathetic control is returned and the veins dilate, draining the penis of its reservoir of blood.

Impotence or loss of erection is almost always of psychogenic origin in men under age 55. Kinsey (1948) found that once men reach age 60 the incidence of impotence increases dramatically, and men 80 years of age or older have about a 75% chance of experiencing it. Some early beliefs attributed impotency in later life to excessive sexual activity in younger years. Kinsey found this correlation to be completely false, and compared this to a belief that excessive spitting in early years would result in a dry mouth in old age.

Although uncommon in the general male population, psychogenically caused impotence is a frequent problem presented to sex therapists. It is perhaps the most devastating type of experience for a man and is without question a source of considerable distress to thousands. As in the case of premature ejaculation, impotence can be a chronic problem developing over a long period of time or it can be an acute problem, falling upon a person as if he were struck by an uncharitable God. The acute cases in which there is a high degree of anxiety are comparatively successful in their response to treatment.

Some men are never able to experience an erection during sexual activity, but may awaken with an erection or find themselves with an erection when they are not consciously thinking about sex. Other men have no problem achieving an erection, but seemingly deflate when penetration is attempted. As one man described his problem "its like trying to stuff a marshmallow into a toaster." A second explained that it was like "trying to push a wagon with a rope." Regardless of the exact nature of the problem, most men respond to the situation with woeful embarrassment and severe loss of confidence. It is especially devastating to individuals who have prided themselves on their sexual prowess and consider it their major masculine attribute. Some men respond by trying to force an erection by flexing their stomach muscles or resorting to quick coital connections once an erection is achieved. The results are almost always the same: a limp penis, sore stomach muscles and a badly deflated ego. Erectile failure is an autonomic response of a vascular reflex mechanism and, therefore, cannot be controlled by stomach muscles or a strong desire to have an erection. The concept of mind over matter is not effective here. If the proper reflex mechanism is not triggered by erotic stimuli, or if it is inhibited by anxiety, then erection will not occur.

Erectile failure can occur in all men in all walks of life. Too much alcohol, ingestion of certain drugs, fatigue or anxiety can all cause acute erectile failure in men who previously had always achieved an erection. If there is overconcern and worry, a couple's response to his dismal failure may cause a repeat of the problem. An especially unproductive reaction is one which draws attention to the failure, and results in close scrutiny of the next performance for signs of potential success or failure. By concentrating on his penis, a man may become overly concerned with its flaccid state very early in a sexual performance and not concentrate on erotic sensations. This, of course, dictates against success. Concentration on the penis may also lead a man to attempt intercourse as soon as tumescence is achieved and before he or his partner are sensually ready. The frantic lunge usually results in loss of erection due to increase in anxiety and diversion of erotic attention.

Couples who can create a relaxed nondemanding atmosphere may cure the problem spontaneously. For the single man or the man with an insensitive sexual partner, the problem may become more severe and lead to complete erectile failure, anxiety, loss of sleep, loss of sexual desire, loss of weight and serious depression. Each sexual encounter is looked upon with anxiety and dread, and a man may begin to avoid sex altogether. The "bedtime headache," usually considered the female prerogative, is adopted by the man as an avoidance strategy.

CAUSES

The etiology of many male sexual problems is remarkably simple: e.g., a male is startled during intercourse and loses his erection—subsequent attempts at intercourse are flooded with anxiety, and failure again results. Learning theory lends itself very nicely as an explanatory framework for understanding such cases. A minority of cases, however, are much more complex and learning theory must be supplemented with other possible etiological explanations. It is the purpose of this section to discuss the simple as well as the complex etiological factors underlying male sexual problems.

TRAUMA

Rarely are males the victims of sexual trauma in the same way as females. Males, in real life, are not usually attacked and assaulted by females, as females may be by males, although this is encountered in fiction, e.g., William Inge's play *Picnic*. In fact, many males would welcome and fantasize such assaults. When a sexual assault is made on males it is usually carried out by older males, and rarely leaves the victim fearful of heterosexual encounters. The victim may develop a fear of males and more specifically of homosexual attacks, but such attacks are rarely reported as significant etiological factors in males experiencing heterosexual dysfunction. In addition, males who have suffered homosexual assaults as young boys or adolescents rarely end up being homosexual themselves. Saghir, Robins and Walburn (1969) found that most males participating in homosexual behavior reported having had homosexual relations with an adult while they were children, but in all cases their desire for homosexual relations preceded their initial involvement.

Males who have suffered incestuous sexual assults or more benign incestuous experiences often develop more perverse sexual problems, rather than sexual dysfunction problems. Incestuous involvement is commonly found, for example, in the background of transvestites, exhibitionists and sado-masochists. Psychoanalysts believe, however, that on an unconscious level the unresolved sexual love of one's mother (Oedipus complex) is a major contributing factor to male impotence: when a sexually dysfunctional male becomes involved in adult sexual relations, he tends to react as though he were in contact with his mother. "Since [he] is aware that such relationships are forbidden, [he] reacts by becoming sexually unresponsive. On this view then, both impotence and frigidity are seen as unconscious defensive manoeuvers aimed at avoiding active participation in a prohibited situation" (Meikle, 1972,). The unresolved Oedipus complex is not trauma in the usual sense of the word, but would fall in the category of more diffuse or insidious causes of sexual dysfunction. In probably 90% of all cases of male sexual dysfunction, the overriding complaint concerns trauma associated with failure to perform. Often this occurs during a man's very first attempt at heterosexual intercourse, or in some cases it could occur after a male has enjoyed a considerable number of successes. How the man reacts to his failure is important in determining his future sexual well-being. Commonly the reaction is one of deadening humiliation and loss of confidence.

A man's own concerned feelings about his sexual failure are sometimes exacerbated by his partner's reaction to the experience; if the female partner's reaction conveys belittlement and lack of understanding, the trauma can be greatly increased. An example is the case of Ken P.

Case Report 17

Mr. P was somewhat nervous on his wedding night, since he had never experienced intercourse, although he had participated in heterosexual petting. His bride, on the other hand, was more sexually experienced (which was not known by Ken, although most other men in the town knew this). Ken initially rose to the occasion, but as the evening progressed and intercourse became more imminent, Ken lost his erection and became increasingly anxious. His wife was not very accepting of his limp state and began to belittle him and compare his lack of performance to other lovers she had entertained in the past. Her final conclusion and focus of attention was directed at his small penis size, which by the end of the evening was reduced to the size of a thimble.

Subsequent attempts throughout their first year of marriage always ended in failure, serving only to reinforce Ken's already shaken image of himself. Ken was finally admitted to a large psychiatric hospital with symptoms of depression and anxiety following an attempted suicide.

Although Ken's case seems somewhat extreme, it is not atypical of the experiences of thousands of other men. Very often a traumatic failure occurs following overindulgence in alcohol, and surprisingly persists on subsequent occasions in the absence of alcohol. The key factor seems to be the extent to which an individual male worries about his failed attempt at intercourse. Very often a vicious circle of failure develops due to anxiety and more anxiety due to failure. Once failure has occurred, each subsequent attempt at intercourse is preceeded by almost obsessive concern about whether or not failure will again occur. The case of Mr. Jim V is a prime example of the vicious circle syndrome.

Case Report 18

Mr. V was 29 when he came for therapy; for treatment of his impotence—loss of erection. He was single, college educated, and a successful businessman whose employment allowed him to travel a great deal. He presented a picture of a very likeable and competent person, whose ambition and interpersonal skills had sent him on his way up the promotion ladder toward what looked to be a very promising career. By all indications he appeared a stable person who had come from a normal background characterized by parental love and concern. Mr. V's one downfall was that he seemed to put too much emphasis on his love-making ability. In fact, he stated that "if you can't have sex, you might as well give up." He talked at great length about his past heterosexual success and was very shaken by his current failures, which had occurred only three months prior to being seen. Indeed, he was now a stud with a broken limb.

Mr. V's troubles began in a motel room with an attractive woman of whom he was very fond and had dated on several previous occasions. On the particular evening which Mr. V refers to as the "disaster," he was drinking heavily and could not maintain an erection. He and his date were very distressed by his inability, although his date's initial anger turned more to motherly concern about "what was wrong with [him]." He also started wondering what was wrong, and attempted intercourse the next morning in order to gain back his self esteem. Again he met with failure and hurriedly left the motel in a state of near panic. Following this episode, whenever Mr. V had a date he worried about achieving an erection and performing coitus. On several dates he did achieve an erection early in foreplay, but then "hurried to have intercourse so [he] wouldn't lose it." The resulting act often turned into a comedy of errors, with stuck zippers and popped buttons, and always ended in failure. It wasn't long before Mr. V began to avoid dating. On occasions on which he did manage to have a date, he avoided physical contact so that he would not have to face the embarrassment of failure once again.

Mr. V's story is perhaps an even more typical chapter in the life of many males who have experienced a traumatic incident and sexual dysfunction. Even though Mr. V's original failure was most likely caused by overindulgence in alcohol, he was significantly enough shaken by this failure to worry about it—in turn, this led to more failure. By directing his attention to, and attempting to control, a function which was previously taken for granted, he disrupted the automatic nature of the erectile response. He was no longer concentrating on erotic thoughts; he was now concentrating on his own abilities whenever he was in a sexual situation. A more adaptive response, and one which the majority of men are capable of making, would be to recognize that the initial failure was purely and simply a result of too much alcohol (the brain is not the only organ rendered numb by alcohol), and that basically nothing was wrong. If Mr. V could have rationalized his failure in this way, the chances are that his disability would not have developed. What added to the problem at the time was his unjustified concern with failure, and this was reinforced by his partner's overly attendant behavior. Had they both laughed it off for the transient issue that it was, both would have benefited immeasurably the following morning.

For males, trauma can be both a cause and a result of sexual dysfunction. Anxiety, alcohol or demand for performance can all cause sexual dysfunction resulting in traumatic humiliation and shaken confidence. In addition, trauma can precede sexual dysfunction. Many men have suffered stresses within the job or even loss of the job, which had in turn caused worry and sexual dysfunction; also, some men facing their first sexual experience with either a prostitute or a date may have high levels of anxiety, generated by their concern which in turn leads to failure. Sexual dysfunction can also result from a variety of other traumatic situations, such as depression over the death of a friend or relative. Under such circumstances sexual desire is lost, but once the circumstance passes, sexual desire and sexual functioning return. (Although the vicious circle syndrome could result and sexual dysfunction could continue after the circumstance has passed.)

DYSFUNCTION AND EARLY LEARNING

Males, like females, are influenced by early learning experiences and again the type of parental behavior modeled is an important determinant of future adult behavior—sexual or otherwise. Males raised in an atmosphere of love and warmth will be much inclined to give this in their own marriage, while those raised amidst bitterness and strife will much more likely respond in kind in their own marriages. We have, as have many therapists, dealt with male clients who have related histories pathetically devoid of parental love.

Case Report 19

Mr. S had never observed his parents embrace, kiss, or show any physical affection toward each other or toward him. As an adult he, too, showed this same lack of physical involvement with others and in fact, found it extremely offensive to see others holding hands or embracing in public. Needless to say, he did not participate in these "stupid" behaviors himself, although he had on several occasions prior to marriage engaged in sexual intercourse. It was not surprising that he married a "frigid" woman, who also felt uncomfortable with physical involvement. Their marriage was unsatisfactory from the start, since neither enjoyed foreplay and only Mr. S desired intercourse, although only sporadically. When intercourse was attempted it usually ended in failure, since Mr. S found it difficult to achieve an erection and too often, when he managed this, experienced premature ejaculation. His attempts at intercourse were more out of a misguided sense of duty than true sexual desire. It was the role which he expected a husband should play even though his heart, and other parts of his anatomy, were not really in it.

This case was an extremely difficult one which involved active therapy for both Mr. and Mrs. S. The problem of treatment was greatly compounded by Mr. S's refusal to appreciate the need for sensate focus or any approach which did not directly involve problems of intercourse. He stated that he felt very uncomfortable with holding hands or with any noncoital physical contact, and despite rational explanation of the need for this type of procedure, he would not change his behavior. Although this case finally ended with the couple withdrawing from therapy after ten weeks, it illustrates the profound effect which early learning experiences may have on later sexual behavior. Possibly the lack of affection modeled in the home during Mr. S's childhood led to his own lack of feelings concerning sexual involvement.

Masturbation

Another important early learning experience for men is masturbation, which in some cases, may lead to certain adult sexual problems. It is not unusual for men to masturbate during adolescence; indeed, Kinsey (1948) found that over 90% of adult males had done so. Neither is it unusual for an adolescent to masturbate in circumstances necessitating very quick masturbatory sessions, sometimes ending in ejaculation without full erection. Adolescence may also be a time of very quick coital experiences, i.e., in the back seat of a car, with a prostitute or in a girlfriend's bedroom. The hurried ejaculatory experience may become habitual if repeated often enough, and lead to a premature ejaculation response in adult sexual functioning (Masters and Johnson, 1970).

Case Report 20

One man's introductory sexual experiences occurred while he was overseas in the armed services. Together with his colleagues he would visit a brothel where rigid time limits were observed. He explained that he would barely get started when the proprietor would pound on the door with shouts to hurry up, that his time was rapidly running out. With this kind of encouragement, he very quickly learned to ejaculate with unseemly haste. Unfortunately, when he got married his speed of response did not lessen, and his premature ejaculation became a chronic source of dissatisfaction between him and his wife.

Although males are subject to this kind of unique learning experience, they may be less likely than females to develop negative feelings about sex because of societal influences. Certainly, many men develop very negative feelings about sex and experience sexual problems because of the over restrictive and perhaps condemning attitude of their religious instructors. Most men, however, are able to rise above such influences because of the message they get from society: males are supposed to know all about sex, enjoy sex and perform superlatively. Males much more than females spend many hours of conversation recounting and fantasizing their own sexual episodes and boasting about loves won and lost. It would be difficult for a man growing up in our North American culture not to come under such an influence, adhering only to a narrow set of parental values. The double standard applied in our society to male and female sexual behavior is generally well acknowledged, although perhaps not so well accepted (Masters and Johnson, 1970).

DYSFUNCTION AND SEXUAL IGNORANCE

The double standard, with more sexual freedom for the male, is also a two-edged sword with the sharper edge facing the male. A man, it is assumed, knows of the intricacies of women and sex, although his means of acquiring such knowledge is often a mystery. Chernick and Chernick (1971) point out that the sexual education of many males usually begins at the local candy store, with 13-year-old males passing on their vast store of ignorance to the 11 and 12-year-olds. Because of the covert nature of sexual behavior, our society does not provide an open forum for intelligent acquisition of sexual knowledge; sex education in public schools is usually centered on reproductive behavior and not sexual behavior. The birds and the bees analogy is still prevalent. While this is a start at dispelling some ignorant beliefs and preventing the growth of others, it is certainly not the whole story. Even in some medical schools there is ignorance among students and faculty members about certain aspects of sexual behavior (Chernick and Chernick, 1971). Education does not always assure sexual knowledge about even the most fundamental type of behavior, as illustrated by the case of Mr. Lee M.

Case Report 21

Mr. M was a very bright 24-year-old graduate student who was at the top of his class in his professional school. He was referred to the sexual clinic for treatment of impotence. Mr M complained of extreme anxiety in sexual situations and had recently experienced loss of erection on two occasions. He was especially concerned about this because he was dating a girl with whom he was contemplating engagement and marriage. When asked to relate his failed sexual experiences, he became extremely embarrassed and lowered his head. "Quite frankly," he said, "I just don't know how to put it in. I've read a great deal about sex, but I still can't figure out who is supposed to put it in." Mr. M continued to relate that on his first attempt at intercourse he expected his penis to enter his girlfriend's vagina naturally and easily; when this did not occur, he became very upset and lost his erection. He did not wish to disclose his ignorance to his girlfriend and dismissed the incident as a result of his exhausted state. When he lost his erection on the next occasion, he became even more upset and immediately sought psychiatric assistance. Apparently he was too embarrassed even to experiment with different approaches to penetration for fear that he would "do something wrong" and his ignorance would be detected. It was explained to Mr. M by the therapist that any style of penetration which was comfortable for a couple was acceptable, and that it was not necessarily one person's role or the other's to guide penetration. In spite of this knowledge, Mr. M required several weeks of desensitization therapy before successful penetration occurred without loss of erection.

This illustrates two points: first, sexual dysfunction due to ignorance can occur even in the highly educated and bright person; second, because a male is supposed to know about sexual functioning, his problems may be compounded by the burden of this supposition. Being bright and being male is no guarantee of sexual knowledge.

Unfortunately, many wives have entered marriage as virgins and have expected their husband's knowledge and experience to carry them through their sexual education. When the husband has either very little to offer, or worse yet, has incomplete or incorrect knowledge himself, we may encounter something like this:

Case Report 22

Mr. and Mrs. T were college educated and in their early 20s when they sought assistance for sexual problems. They had been married for one year and during that time had never completed intercourse. The problem was that neither of them could achieve an orgasm, because of a profound fear of fainting. Mrs. T entered marriage with no prior sexual experience, and Mr. T had only experienced occasional petting. On their wedding night, Mr. T warned his new bride that intercourse might result in fainting. As a teenager, Mr. T had masturbated and on one occasion he had fainted following orgasm. He took pains to relate this story to his wife, with explicit details including a description of his mother finding him passed out with sperm all over his stomach. The picture he painted was frightening enough to establish a permanent pattern of orgasmic restraint whenever intense arousal was experienced by either party. One can only be amazed at the amount of self-control demonstrated by this young couple. As might be expected, however, the desire for sexual intercourse gradually extinguished over the year.

Mr. and Mrs. T were examined by a physician and assured that there was no chance that either of them would faint as a result of orgasm. This information was well received, but Mr. and Mrs. T continued to experience unsatisfactory sexual relations characterized by high levels of anxiety. Video desensitization therapy was successfully employed as an intervention strategy.

PHYSICAL CAUSES

Physical causes must be carefully screened out in every case presented for psychotherapeutic intervention. Masters and Johnson (1970) list more than 60 such physical causes, including anatomical problems, cardiorespiratory problems, drug ingestion, endocrine problems, genitourinary problems, hematological problems, infectious disease problems, neurological problems and vascular problems. Although there are these possibilities of underlying physical problems, it is generally agreed that most cases are of psychogenic origin.

Of those cases that are definitely linked to physical problems, over 95% result in impotence (Masters and Johnson, 1970). Only rarely are there physical problems underlying premature ejaculation or delayed ejaculation.

In some cases males can experience sexual dysfunction related to both physical and psychogenic factors. In addition to Mr. V.'s case, where the physical factor was overin-dulgence in alcohol, we have treated clients whose sexual failures have been brought on by prescribed medications. In these cases, the side effects caused by either alcohol or prescribed drugs were totally unexpected and resulted in the men's trauma and shaken confidence. If the physicians involved had explained all the possible side effects of the prescribed medication, possibly much consternation could have been avoided. Certainly the men involved would not have been so traumatized by their impotence when it first occurred, and thus could have avoided the beginnings of the "vicious circle."

Most men seeking medical assistance for sexual dysfunction count very heavily on physical causes as a source of their problems. In many cases the male ego is at stake, and the realization that the problem is possibly of psychogenic origin could cause further degradation. It is bad enough that one's masculinity is weakened, but to be suspected of a mental problem as well is too much for some men to accept. Every care must be taken to assure male clients that there is nothing terribly unusual about their problem and that in most cases it can be effectively treated. Unfortunately, many physicians dismiss cases of psychogenic male sexual dysfunction as hopeless. We have had more than one client come to us in a last ditch effort, full of despair, because their physicians said there was nothing that could be done and it was all in their heads. This is a very unfortunate situation which can result in an iatrogenic problem. Many of the men who came to us despite the words of their physicians, did so because of their own initiative in reading about sexual dysfunction, and their unwillingness to accept a life of celibacy. We can only hope that others who have listened to the unknowing and impatient words of an unin-formed physician will eventually seek help in a sexual dysfunction clinic.

SECONDARY SEXUAL DYSFUNCTION

Men, as well as women, often react to distressful situations and relationships with symp-toms of sexual dysfunction. These cases are diagnosed as secondary sexual dysfunction because the sexual problems are secondary to other problems. Once the other problems are solved, sexual functioning usually (but not always) returns. In males, there are two sources from which most secondary sexual problems develop: 1) specific attitudes or behaviors of the wife are damaging to sexual functioning; 2) stress and strains external to the marriage are placed on the husband.

In our clinical experience we have not found incompatibility or lack of love between husband and wife to be a prominent source of sexual dysfunction for males. Wives often report with amazement and disbelief that their husbands attempted intercourse after, or even during, periods of very bitter fighting. That men are well accustomed to having sexual relations with women toward whom they have no emotional attraction—or may even feel disdain—is evidenced by the success of the institution of female prostitution.

Partners' attitudes

While basic incompatibility may not be a cause of male sexual dysfunction, the particular attitude a woman has toward her partner's sexual performance may be very important. The woman who conveys an attitude of disgust and repugnance for the male genitals or for sex in general may dramatically affect her partner's sexual performance (Friedman, 1974). Some women accomplish this by being overly passive and taking no part in the actual sex act other than allowing penetration. Manual genital contact may be very limited or altogether prohibited. In spite of passivity or severely restricting the types of foreplay activity, some women none the less are outspoken in focusing on any flaw in their partner's sexual performance. A woman may even avoid sexual contact altogether by using the excuse that she is not satisfied sexually by her partner.

One older couple we saw in therapy reported that they had experienced twenty-five years of sexual problems due to the husband's premature ejaculation.

Case Report 23

The husband was a very successful government executive, and both he and his wife were college educated. During the initial intake interview the wife was dominant and outspoken, and repeatedly emphasized that if her husband's problem wasn't corrected she would seriously consider separation. The focus of her conversation was entirely on her husband's sexual inadequacy, and conveyed the impression that she was sexually a very "hot number" but had been held back all these years by her partner. When the focus of conversation shifted to the mechanics of their sexual behavior, an interesting picture emerged. During foreplay the wife would lie perfectly still and allow no genital stimulation. As soon as her husband ejaculated, while attempting intercourse, she would immediately turn from him and masturbate herself vigorously to orgasm. The husband was always a spectator of this belittling performance, and was made to feel that this was necessary because he couldn't satisfy her (either through coitus or manual stimulation). As therapy progressed, it became quickly apparent that the wife didn't desire any change in their sexual pattern. She detested being touched during sensate focus exercises, and did not wish to touch her husband in the genital area as part of therapy. In spite of the wife's reluctance to participate in therapy exercises, the husband did experience increased control in delaying ejaculation. However, as the husband became sexually more competent, the wife became more resentful and finally tearfully admitted that she had always hated sex and would need intensive therapy herself. Once the wife was able to admit that she, too, had a sexual problem, therapy progressed rapidly.

Not infrequently the opposite is true. We have successfully treated women for a sexual problem, only to discover that the husband has become either a premature ejaculator or is failing to maintain an erection. From discussions with such men it appears that they feel threatened by their wives' new-found sexuality. They begin to wonder if they can now fulfill her sexual expectations. Once this doubt creeps into their thinking, they can become victims of a self-fulfilling prophecy.

External stresses

Another important source of male sexual problems seems to be related to business strains and anxieties. A number of men we have seen in therapy fall into this category. Worry about job promotion or security, type of work, interpersonal relations, financial matters, excessive responsibility, or ability to work have all been mentioned as problems coincidental with the onset of sexual dysfunction. Sometimes the stresses in employment are insidious and build up over a long period of time, while in other cases, through a promotion or loss of job, they are instantaneous.

Whenever it is suspected that employment or some other external factor is a source of sexual dysfunction in a man, the interviewer must determine very carefully the overall history and pattern of sexual functioning. The problem may be complex and related to a number of sources, of which job stress is only one. A thorough therapist must explore all possibilities, including the employment picture. If this is suspected as a source of undue strain, then counseling and/or anxiety reducing therapy can be utilized. An example of this is Mr. L, a 46-year-old successful businessman in a highly competitive field:

Case Report 24

Suffering a temporary setback in his business, he became depressed and began drinking in the evening in order to feel better. The combination of depression and alcohol resulted in an inability to maintain an erection, and after four or five failures Mr. L abandoned all attempts at intercourse, telling himself that the situation would rectify itself once he got over the depression. However, once the depression lifted, he was greatly disturbed to discover that his first attempt at intercourse was a failure. Rather than repeat this, he again took to drinking in the evening so that he would not be expected to perform or, if there was no way to avoid intercourse, he would have a legitimate excuse for failure. This pattern continued for months and he only came for treatment when his wife threatened him with divorce.

SEXUAL AVERSION

A woman who expresses an aversion to heterosexual behavior is not usually thought to be homosexual, while a man who voices a similar aversion is almost always thought to be so. In spite of the changing role of women in our society, a woman would not be ostracized if she stated she did not like sex (meaning heterosexual sex). In fact, more eyebrows might be raised if a woman stated she *did*. For men, the picture is much different.

All men are expected to like sex (heterosexual sex), and if they do not, their attitudes are immediately suspected. As a matter of fact, many men with a low sexual drive report being brought up in very religious or moral environments in which sexual behavior was strongly discouraged and discussion of sex was suppressed. These men may report that they did not seek any sexual activity before marriage, and feel most comfortable with a pattern of infrequent sexual contacts in marriage. One such individual we treated believed firmly that any sexual contact beyond once a month was morally wrong.

However, although it is not often true that low heterosexual drive in men is associated with homosexuality, it is certainly a factor in some cases. And because of societal pressures toward heterosexual life styles, many homosexual men date women, and even get married. Sometimes they feel that by marrying a woman they will grow to like her sexually. All too often, this is not the way things work out, and the male with homosexual desires soon finds himself repeatedly revolted by sex with his wife. Premature ejaculation, or more commonly impotence, and infrequent sexual contacts are the resulting patterns. Many times the wife is completely unsuspecting of her husband's real desires, and may blame her husband's failure on herself. The homosexual male very often expresses disgust when asked about his feeling toward females. He may talk about women being ugly, dwelling upon the fat or grotesque women, or think of women in curlers. One homosexual client of ours reported that he would never have oral sex with a female because "that's where she pisses from and its full of germs." He saw no similar problem having oral sex with males.

SUMMARY

Although the exact incidence of male sexual problems in the general population is not known, there is no question that it is of considerable magnitude. As more sexual clinics are established and treatment becomes more widely available, a high incidence is becoming more apparent. Kinsey found that about 13% of the total male population could be defined as having an unusually low rate of sexual contacts. If it is assumed that a majority of males having few sexual contacts are avoiding sex because of problems, then one can use Kinsey's figures as an estimate of the incidence of male sexual dysfunction.

There are many psychogenic reasons underlying male sexual problems, which we have discussed. We have not discussed personality variables since this seems to be a "can of worms." Males from all walks of life—including government officials, editors of newspapers, businessmen, truck drivers and diswashers—have passed through our clinic complaining of sexual problems. Their personalities have been as varied as their professions, and at this point we have no data which can objectively identify a personality type, or even a constellation of personality variables, which correlates highly with sexual dysfunction. Subjectively, many of the male clients seem passive and dominated by their spouses. Since we see men who are dejected and think of themselves as sexual failures, this is not surprising. It is impossible for us to say if they are like this because of their sexual problems, or if they are like this in addition to having sexual problems. Since many men we have seen have had very long histories of successful sexual relations prior to experiencing sexual dysfunction, it is unlikely that looking for a personality type is a fruitful area to explore. It is interesting that in spite of many different causes of sexual problems, most problems can be treated by very similar procedures.

3

Assessment of Sexual Dysfunction, Female and Male

There are many variables which affect the efficacy of any given therapeutic strategy. For example, the client's desire to please or displease the therapist, or the client's conception of improvement. Because of these variables it is desirable to obtain assessment measures which are as objective, valid and reliable as possible. The search for such measurement procedures has been difficult because of the taboo and emotional feelings associated with the whole area of sexual behavior. In spite of the problems complicating assessment of sexual behavior, many fine efforts have been put forth by researchers, and some very promising assessment tools have been developed.

It is the purpose of this chapter to discuss and evaluate the development and current status of various assessment procedures now in use. In addition, since little is known of the generalized effects of sexual dysfunction therapy, we will also be briefly discussing this area. For example, does the elimination of heterosexual anxiety result in a decrease in general fears and anxiety? When sexual inhibitions have been modified, does this result in a more general release of inhibition? Does the client become more assertive in nonsexual situations as well? It is worth knowing whether treatment of sexual dysfunctions is specific to the target problem or whether there is generalization to other aspects of behavior.

Today, the assessment of sexual dysfunction is usually a much more careful and scientific endeavor than it was prior to Kinsey et al. (1953). There are no universally accepted methods of assessment, however, and many researchers and therapists have developed very different approaches to assessment.

In attempting to assess changes which may have occurred during treatment of sexual dysfunction it is advisable to adopt Paul's (1966) model for measuring efficacy of therapy intervention. This model, as pointed out by Obler (1973), "emphasizes multi-dependent variable measures evaluated in conjunction with subjective patient and partner reports of therapeutic effectiveness." Assessment should, therefore, include procedures from many different levels (i.e., attitudinal, behavioral, physiologic) and not be narrowly circumscribed.

For a clearer understanding of the various levels of assessment which may be used by clinicians and researchers, we have categorized assessment procedures into four general areas: 1) interview, 2) questionnaire, 3) behavioral, and 4) physiologic.

ASSESSMENT BY INTERVIEW

Personal interview is the earliest and most common procedure for assessing the presence and degree of sexual dysfunction. (Bergler, 1944; Menninger, 1938). There do not appear to be any workers in the field prior to Lowrie (1952) who suggested guidelines for conducting interviews. He quite rightly pointed out that interviews with individuals suspected of having sexual problems should not take the form of an inquisition, but should proceed on a friendly conversational basis using the question and answer method. He also proposed that interviews be conducted separately with each partner in order to thoroughly evaluate the sexual problem.

It was not until the early 1960s that any objective structure was given to interviews aimed at psychosexual problems. Masters and Johnson (1964) were the first to propose structured interviews which were to be conducted periodically with each partner throughout the therapy program. Although Masters and Johnson outlined specific questions to be asked during an interview, and a specific sequence for asking them they noted that the "choice of interrogative techniques (reflective, direct, etc.) should be based on the quality of comfort and ease of interchange which can be created between co-therapist and patient."

By outlining a structured interview, however, Masters and Johnson opened the way for a more objective means of assessing sexual dysfunction and a means of assessing change in sexual attitudes and behavior over time. Many of the questions which Masters and Johnson proposed as part of their interview procedure could certainly be asked at specified periods (pre therapy, post therapy, follow-up) as a means of assessing change. For example: "What is the usual incidence of intercourse now (times a week)?" or "How would you describe your sexual relationship with your spouse? Does it please you? Are you comfortable with it?" If the questions are asked by a person unfamiliar with treatment conditions (i.e., blindly) and are asked in separate husband–wife interviews, more objectivity can be added to the interview level of assessment. Quite clearly this objectivity is important where the primary concern is with determining the effectiveness of a particular kind of therapeutic procedure. It is less important where the goal is purely therapeutic.

Masters and Johnson rely heavily on interview procedures for their initial assessment of the problem and measurement of change. Their criterion for successful treatment of sexual dysfunction is determined by a report from their patients during an interview. Many other therapists and researchers dealing with sexual dysfunction have also relied solely on personal interview to determine whether or not their therapy has been successful (Brady, 1965; Cooper, 1969; Kraft and Al Issa, 1968; Lazarus, 1963; Madsen and Ullmann, 1967).

The initial interview with a client is one of the most important sources of information for determining the exact nature of the sexual problem. Although a comparison of pre–post interview responses is important and should be considered as a measurement of change, the initial interview should provide the therapist answers to diagnostic questions. Is this a medical or a psychological problem? Is this a case of essential or situational sexual dysfunction? Do both partners have sexual dysfunction problems? Are there any misconceptions which the couple has about sexual functioning? Has the couple tried to solve the problem on their own?

The first question is extremely important since some cases of sexual dysfunction do have an organic basis. In some cases, painful intercourse is due to actual lesion or disease process, and it is the responsibility of each therapist to determine whether or not the organic causes can be ruled out (Wolpe, 1969). A thorough medical examination should be conducted by a physician before psychological intervention is attempted.

Once the clinical therapist is assured that he or she is not faced with a case of organic sexual dysfunction, the next step is to determine if it is a case of essential or situational sexual dysfunction. Essential sexual dysfunction involves a learning history in which a woman or man has developed a negative reaction to sexual relations (and often sexual stimuli) in general. Situational sexual dysfunction, on the other hand, implies that a person does not respond satisfactorily in certain situations or with a certain partner, but does respond satisfactorily in other situations or with other partners. It is sometimes *very easy* to distinguish between the two. For example, a woman may report having had one or more traumatic sexual experiences as a child, or may report having received negative instructions concerning heterosexual relations, e.g., "sex is dirty and wrong." Our own clinical experience suggests that women who report sexual dysfunction in adult life very often also report never having observed their parents show any affection toward each other or them. A number of women we have interviewed reported never being kissed or embraced by their parents. An absence of physical affection in the family history of women with essential sexual dysfunction seems to be more common than reports of traumatic sexual experiences or reports of negative sexual instruction. In addition to a history which is predictive of essential sexual dysfunction, however, the most important distinguishing characteristic of this problem is a report that with *any* sexual partner or in *any* situation the woman would not derive pleasure from sexual relations.

As in the case of females, male sexual problems can be either essential or situational. Men more frequently than women have experienced sexual encounters with a number of different partners and, therefore, it is usually easier to determine during an interview essential versus situational sexual problems. To make this determination a therapist must very carefully inquire about the other sexual experiences and look for general signs of sexual discomfort. For example, if the problem of premature ejaculation has been experienced with a number of partners and in a number of situations, then by definition this is an essential sexual dysfunction problem. In some cases, however, a man may be impotent with his wife but not with other women, or he may be impotent in his home but not in a motel. In cases of situational sexual dysfunction the focus of therapy would be directed more at the situational functioning (i.e., the relationship with one's wife or the wife's approach to sex or the distractions in one's home) than at the man's sexual functioning *per se.* In our experience, the absence of an all-consuming love is rarely a cause of his sexual dysfunction. As mentioned earlier, men seem to rely less on love than do women as an integral part of sexual functioning. When a male's sexual problem is specific to his interaction with his partner, it is caused most often by his partner's attitude or approach to sexual behavior as discussed in Chapter 2.

We have not experienced any hesitancy on the part of men during interviews to discuss their premarital or extramarital sexual experiences. Women seem more reluctant to reveal such information during initial interviews and often only do so after a number of therapy sessions.

It is sometimes *difficult* to distinguish essential from situational sexual dysfunction when a woman or man has had no sexual experiences other than with the spouse. In these cases the therapist must probe very thoroughly the person's feeling toward the partner. If there seem to be disturbances in the marriage in areas outside of sexual relations, then it is likely that situational factors are important in contributing to the problem.

It is not uncommon to find that both partners have problems of sexual dysfunction. In separate interviews with each partner, the therapist must attempt to gain an understanding of a couple's attitude toward each other and toward sexual behavior. The therapist must also piece together a picture of a couple's approach to and conduct of sexual behavior. Careful questioning of a sexually dysfunctioned woman may reveal that the husband has a problem of premature ejaculation or loss of erection, or that the husband's approach to sexual behavior is uncomfortable or even painful to his wife.

In the initial interview, a therapist may discover that one or both partners have a misconception about sexual behavior which is affecting sexual relations. For example, one woman we interviewed believed that her uterus would be damaged if she had intercourse in any position other than the male superior position. Another woman believed that her breasts would become overly large if her husband caressed them. A young single woman (a third-year university student) worried for two months because she thought she was pregnant. On exploration it turned out that when kissing her boyfriend he had put his tongue in her mouth. She believed that this was the way women became pregnant, and that furthermore it was a fail-proof method. She was greatly relieved to discover this was an erroneous notion.

Careful interview can also turn up strange bedfellows and bizarre attempts at home remedy. One especially quick-thinking husband (with an apparently not so quick-thinking wife) convinced his frigid wife that a sure cure for her problem could be achieved if she would observe him and another female partner, a woman of some sexual skill and ingenuity, engage in intercourse. This somewhat unconventional modeling procedure produced only anxiety and guilt on the part of the wife because of her own comparatively inadequate performance. Surprisingly, the wife expressed no anger or jealousy since she was truly convinced of her husband's genuine interest in her problem. One can only ponder on other "therapeutic" endeavors suggested by her husband.

There is no doubt that misconceptions and weird attempts at home therapy can be corrected by patient and gentle instruction during the initial interviews. Although this may provide some benefit to the persons involved, very often a couple is still left with emotional response associated with sexual behavior, which must be removed.

Masters and Johnson (1970) emphasized repeatedly the necessity and advantages of co-therapists (male/female) when interviewing and treating sexually dysfunctioned cou ples. They have argued that females could relate more comfortably to female therapists while males could relate more comfortably to male therapists. Although their approach appears sensible and remarkably successful, there are no data available which would support the efficacy of a co-therapist approach as opposed to a solo-therapist approach; in fact, there seem to be a considerable number of studies in the literature reporting positive results in either case. Similarly, there are no data to support whether or not a same sex therapist/patient relationship would be any more effective in promoting improvement than an opposite sex therapist/patient relationship. It just does not seem to matter as long as the therapy approach is a sound one and the therapist or therapists conduct the therapy sensitively and sensibly.

There are a few guidelines, however, which successful therapists (male or female) follow when interviewing male or female clients. Women more so than men are accustomed to having a physician of the opposite sex. Consequently, it is not usually any more difficult for a female patient to relate her sexual problems to a male doctor than to a female doctor. However, this needs some qualification. Women do experience difficulty in relating their sexual problems to some doctors, but not because they themselves are shy or embarrassed, at least initially. What they complain about is that the *doctor* is discombobulated. He will frequently stammer and blush and respond with some inappropriate, facetious remark. When they observe him behaving in this way, they too begin to feel uncomfortable. In a different way, as Fordney-Settlage (1975) points out, males may have problems relating to female doctors because of "social sex-role stereotyping". That is, males do not easily see females as authority figures. With the increase in female physicians and psychologists this problem will undoubtedly be obviated in the future. Certainly, with such prominent and visible women in the field as Helen Kaplan and Virginia Johnson this may in fact not even be a serious problem today.

There are, however, some advantages and disadvantages which are present in therapy settings in which the client is of the opposite sex to the therapist. One very distinct advantage is that the client can learn to relate comfortably to a member of the opposite sex in a controlled interview setting; threatening heterosocial situations can be easily defined and alleviated. The interview relationship can serve as a desensitization procedure. Furthermore, by discussing difficult sexual matters with a therapist of the opposite sex, a client may learn to communicate more comfortably with his or her own sexual partner or with members of the opposite sex in general.

One possible disadvantage of a therapeutic relationship in which the client and therapist are of the opposite sex is that a flirting relationship may develop. The therapist must set a professional tone from the onset and make it clear that no relationship beyond the therapeutic setting is possible. In fact, some therapists openly discuss this problem with their clients before launching into therapy. Despite anticipation of this problem it is not at all uncommon for male clients to ask their female therapists out for dates, and what is even more destructive, for male therapists to attempt to seduce a female client, either under the guise of therapy or as an extratherapy activity. Under no circumstances should a therapist enter into a personal relationship with a client either within or outside the bounds of treatment.

One other problem sometimes mentioned by female therapists is that male clients sometimes use vulgar language during interviews purposely for the shock value. The experienced female therapist can easily deal with this situation by showing absolutely no shock and by confronting the client with his behavior if it seems to be interfering with therapy.

Regardless of the gender of the therapist, a male patient entering sex therapy has different concerns than female patients although there is some overlap. We have found that men more often than women are concerned about latent homosexuality, the size of their genitals, and their sexual identity (i.e., their feeling of masculinity). Women on the other hand, rarely report feeling less feminine as a result of sexual dysfunction problems; their concern is more often focused on feeling comfortable with sex or getting more out of it. Therapists should be sensitive to these sex role differences so they can help patients focus their goals in therapy and help alleviate anxiety.

The following section presents the basic ingredients of interview protocol which we follow in interviewing male or female clients.

STAGE 1: THE INTRODUCTION

Before the initial interview begins it is necessary that the physical setting is one of privacy and freedom from interruptions (Annon, 1976). While this is important for most clinical interviews it is especially important for interviews involving sexual histories. A number of our patients (both men and women) are very concerned about the confidentiality and privacy of the interview. Some do not wish to be seen in our clinic and confess that no one else knows of their problem. One female patient who was accompanied to our clinic by her husband did not want her husband to know why she was seeing a doctor. She had told him that she was just going for a checkup. Once she was in the privacy of my office (JPW) she stated that she was relieved that I was seeing her alone, since her husband knew nothing about her sexual problem. When her husband was interviewed alone (after it was agreed to share her problem with him) he was greatly relieved to find out that it was a sexual problem she was being seen for, and not cancer as he had feared.

We feel that it is important that the initial interview is always conducted alone with the sexual partner who is presenting the complaint. Usually couples appear in the clinic together for the first interview, but it cannot be assumed by the therapist that both partners are aware of the problem and are willing to work together (as illustrated by the above example). It is far less problematic if it is assumed by the therapist that the problem is embarrassing to the patient and unknown to his or her partner or anyone else.

Before asking a patient questions about his or her sexual problem, we have found it helpful to discuss sexual problems in general, including attitudes toward sexual problems and approaches to treating sexual problems. A discussion of these topics seems to help put the patient at ease by making him feel less isolated and peculiar and more hopeful that a solution can be found. A typical introduction that we might have with a male client seeking help for a sexual problem is as follows:

Hello, Mr. X. I am Dr._____. Before we start to discuss your situation I would like to explain some things to you so that you can get a better understanding of our program. First of all, we are set up here to deal with all types of sexual problems. For women this usually means problems of not having an orgasm or climax, problems in not liking sex, or even being afraid of sex. For men, the type of sexual problems we deal with usually include men who experience premature or rapid ejaculation, men who cannot get an erection or hard-on or who lose their erection, and men who have problems in not being able to ejaculate or come for a long period of time. All of these types of problems are very common. In fact, most men and women experience some degree of sexual problem during the course of their sexual experiences. We also deal with people who are attracted to members of their own sex, or attracted to children or even to animals. We deal with all types of behaviors which are causing problems in one way or another.

Many times people are embarrassed by their problem because they feel it is shameful or wrong. We try to emphasize to our patients that no sexual behavior is wrong, but that some behaviors may cause problems with some people. Many sexual problems are the result of faulty learning, and since behaviors can develop into problems because of learning experiences, they also can be corrected by different learning experiences. In many men, for example, loss of erection may be initially caused by fatigue, too much alcohol, or even tenseness or anxiety. The beginnings of a sexual problem cause worry which in turn causes a worsening of the sexual problem. The approach that we use in therapy for most sexual problems is to concentrate on the present situation and try to provide new learning experiences which will help to overcome the problem. This almost always demands that we work very closely in therapy with a person's sexual partner. In fact, if a person's partner does not wish to participate in therapy, then it is unlikely that we can help them. Do you have any questions about anything I have said so far?

This introduction serves several purposes. In the first place, it is intended to *disinhibit anxiety.* A person learns in this introduction that sexual problems are not unique or even uncommon; secondly, that the *therapist is accepting* of sexual problems and has dealt with many types of problems; thirdly, that there is hope and most likely a solution to the problem. All of these points contribute to a more open and free interview environment which promotes honest discussion.

STAGE 2: THE INTERVIEW

During the interview itself the therapist must maintain an accepting attitude throughout. Kinsey et al. (1948), and more recently Masters and Johnson (1966) and Green (1975), have emphasized this as an absolutely essential ingredient. If a patient detects hesitation or uneasiness on the part of the therapist then he or she may be severely inhibited in the discussion of problems. Green advises that a therapist practice a sexual interview with a colleague before embarking on therapy. There should be no hesitation on the therapist's part, and complete acceptance of all of the client's behavior. If the client detects any condemnation or even uneasiness on the part of the therapist, the client may avoid sensitive issues and the interview may not serve the purpose of accurately assessing the problem behavior.

One question commonly asked by psychology students and therapists in training is, "What language should I use in an interview? If a patient is uneducated and uses "street" language, should I also use street language?" Many therapists feel unprofessional using terms such as "fuck," "cock," "jerk-off" or "cunt" instead of the medical terms. Our own style in this area is to use the correct medical term along with the street term when a client uses street terms. This approach ensures that the client understands what the therapist is saying without sacrificing a professional milieu. Very often a client will not know a term used to describe a particular behavior, and the therapist must define the behavior precisely so there is mutual understanding. The following excerpt is from an interview with a 45-year-old male (Mr. L) who presented a complaint of premature ejaculation and loss of erection. Mr. L had only an eighth-grade education and a somewhat limited vocabulary. In the excerpt Mr. L is describing his sexual behavior:

Mr. L: Lately I've even tried kissing her down below to excite her.

Dr. W: And what was your wife's reaction to this?

Mr. L: She lets me do it for a little while, but she don't like it too much.

Dr. W: Mr. L, when you said that you kissed your wife down below did you mean that you put your mouth on her privates, on her vagina?

Mr. L: Yes.

Dr. W: This is a very common sexual practice which is usually referred to as oral sex or oral genital contact. Some people find this very enjoyable, while other people do not care for it too much. How do you feel about oral sex?

Mr. L: I don't care for it too much either.

Dr. W: How often do you attempt to have sex; sexual intercourse now?

Mr. L: About once a week.

Dr. W: And each time you attempt intercourse do you have a problem?

Mr. L: Yes.

Dr. W: Are you having an orgasm before you attempt to enter?

Mr. L: I don't understand.

Dr. W: Do you know what an orgasm is?

Mr. L: No.

Dr. W: An orgasm is when you come during sex. When liquid; sperm comes out of your penis. This is also termed climax or ejaculation. Do you come or have an orgasm before you enter your wife?

Mr. L: Oh yes, sperm comes out.

Dr. W: Are you getting a full erection, are you getting a real stiff hard-on?

Mr. L: No, not at all.

Following this interview, Mr. L was able to understand and use all of the technical terms describing sexual behavior, although he most often used street language. Our style was aimed at ensuring that there was no misunderstanding on either the therapist's or patient's part.

Before the interview is underway, a plan should be formulated for obtaining informa tion from a client. Masters and Johnson suggest and outline a very lengthy interview procedure, while others take much less time. We usually complete our intake interviews in three one-hour sessions, the first interview with the patient, the second interview with the partner, and the third interview with the couple. The first two interviews follow this outline:

1. Description of current problem and sexual behavior pattern in client's (or partner's) words.
2. Client's (or partner's) concept of the cause and maintenance of the problem.
3. Client's (or partner's) past treatment for the problem (including self-treatment) and success.
4. Client's (or partner's) concept of partners reaction to the problem, i.e., acceptance.
5. Client's (or partner's) past sexual experience and knowledge of partner's past sexual experience.
6. Client's (or partner's) evaluation of marriage outside of sexual area.

7. Identification of any other problems related or unrelated to sexual behavior.
8. Client's evaluation of partner's willingness to cooperate in therapy.
9. Therapist's summary of problem and suggested possible strategies of treatment which may be used.

The third interview summarizes for the couple the therapist's understanding of the problem and the outline for therapy. If therapy is indicated, then the cooperation of the couple as a team is emphasized and initial suggestions are put forth.

Through the interview procedure outlined above we are able to arrive at what we feel is an accurate assessment of the sexual problem. However, by planning the interview procedure carefully and standardizing the approach, a therapist can maximize the credibility of this level of assessment.

Very few therapists or researchers have outlined specific recommendations for interviewing males as opposed to females. Other than the few suggestions posited in this chapter, we are in agreement with the approach that very little difference in technique seems to be needed for interviewing male clients as opposed to female clients. A competent therapist who follows the important guidelines will have few problems.

The exact structure of an interview may vary widely from therapist to therapist but should reveal to the therapist information which is needed to make a diagnostic decision and therapy plan. The following interview is included to give the reader an understanding of our approach to interviewing. This is not the entire interview, which is very lengthy; rather, two important segments of the interview are presented here to illustrate part of the diagnostic process. In the first segment, information is obtained to determine whether this is a case of essential or situational sexual dysfunction, and what the exact nature of the problem is. The second segment of the interview attempts to establish what problems, if any, the husband may have.

SEGMENT 1.

Therapist (T):   Did you "freeze up" during sexual relations right from the beginning of marriage?

Client (C):   Yes.

T: What about before marriage?

C: I never had any sexual intercourse.

T: Did you have any sexual experiences with your husband before marriage?

C: No.

T: So going into marriage you had no experience with sexual behavior at all?

C: No.

T: Have you ever been able to actually have sexual intercourse?

C: Not really, because I just won't let his penis go into me. I just freeze.

T: Do you usually "freeze up" at the point of intercourse, or do you start to "freeze" before that?

C: No, just about at that point.

T: Would you describe yourself as being comfortable up till that point?

C: At times—and other times no.

T: Do you actually get stimulated to the point where you feel excited about sexual behavior?

C: Yes, at times. We could be playing a game of cards and I could feel that I want him right then, but by the time we get to the bedroom I freeze up.

T: Do you actually produce secretions? Do you get wet down there?

C: At times, but not that often.

T: So there are times that you do get excited.

C: Yes.

T: Have you been able to stimulate yourself to orgasm with your hands?

C: No.

T: Is that something you have never attempted?

C: Dr. P suggested that the last time I saw him. I tried it and I just don't know what it is, but I found it painful.

T: Are you able to insert tampax?

C: No, I never have.

T: That causes pain too?

C: I have never tried it, to tell you the truth.

T: Would you say that any type of insertion would cause pain?

C: I think so. The first time I went in for a pap smear I wouldn't let him do it.

T: Do you usually get hysterical when he tries?

C: Well, I went on Tuesday and I just kept tightening up and I wouldn't lie down on the couch. I began to cry.

T: When you are having sexual relations with your husband and you start to kiss and engage in other sexual behavior, is there a point where you all of a sudden "freeze up"? For example, when your husband touches you in the genital area?

C: Mostly I do, I just push him away when he touches me there.

T: What about breast stimulation, does that bother you at all?

C: At times, but mostly not.

T: What about the idea of touching your husband in his genital area, does that bother you?

C: No.

T: What was your upbringing like as a child, as far as sexual education?

C: They never told me anything.

T: Did they in fact impart the message to you that sexual behavior was dirty or anything like that?

C: No. They never said a word.

T: You never had any instructions at all, going into marriage?

C: No, not really.

T: Have you ever read any books on sexual behavior?

C: No.

T: What type of relationship did your parents have with each other? Were they openly in love with each other? Did they seem to have a loss of physical contact in your presence?

C: No, not really. Only once in a great while did they ever kiss or show any affection at all. My father travelled quite a bit and was away a lot. My parents seemed to get along but were not the affectionate type.

T: Did you ever have any bad sexual experiences before you were married? Were you ever in a situation where there was an attempted rape or anything upsetting sexually?

C: No.

SEGMENT 2.

T: Did your husband have many sexual experiences before marriage?

C: He had nothing either. He never had any sexual experiences with other women.

T: Can you discuss sexual matters with your husband?

C: Yes, in a way, but sometimes we more or less joke about it.

T: Do you feel you can communicate with him about problems whether they are sexual or otherwise?

C: Yes. I feel we can communicate about most things pretty well.

T: How do you get along with your husband outside of sexual areas?

C: We get along with each other very well. I love him very much.

T: Have you ever thought about divorce or separating?

C: No.

T: Is there anything in your husband's approach to sexual behavior that you would consider incorrect or inappropriate? Is the technique he is using correct as far as you are concerned?

C: I don't think he has any sexual problems.

T: Has he ever gone to anyone for advice about sexual problems?

C: Not that I know of.

There are a number of important points brought out by this interview for diagnosis of the problem. Several statements by the woman indicate an essential sexual problem of vaginismus. It should be noted that she has had unpleasant experiences associated with attempts at insertion under several conditions: intercourse, use of tampax, and gynecologic examination. Since these experiences were under very different circumstances and not always associated with the husband, a situational sexual problem can probably be ruled out. In addition, the woman does not feel comfortable touching her own genitals—which is a further indication of essential sexual dysfunction.

It is also important to consider carefully the instruction the woman received from Dr. P. In essence, he told her to go home and try to masturbate to orgasm. While the suggestion may, in fact, hold some therapeutic value, it is a naive approach without the proper structured program as outlined in Chapter 8. Indeed, it may provide the patient with yet another disturbing experience; yet we have found such short-sighted instructions reported by many of our patients in reference to their previous therapeutic experiences. One of the dangers of a behavioral approach to sexual problems is that on the surface this approach seems simple and effective when, in fact, behavioral technology requires careful and intelligent application with full knowledge of learning theory principles. It is, therefore, a deceptively seductive approach which, if applied incorrectly, can cause more harm than good.

The second segment of the aforegoing interview reveals that the husband may also be a victim of sexual ignorance and must be carefully interviewed. The fact that the woman is satisfied with her husband's approach to sex must be judged in the light of her own lack of experience. Since she has no knowledge of "good" and "bad" procedures, her assessment of her husband is not too meaningful. After interviewing her husband, it was determined that the problem was indeed a problem of essential vaginismus. The treatment plan involved sexual education (since both partners were naive), and detailed instructions for home practice sessions following systematic desensitization sessions in therapy.

INTERVIEW PROCEDURE FOR BEHAVIOR THERAPY

Although interview procedures may vary greatly from therapist to therapist, the interview procedures outlined by Masters and Johnson (1970) probably offer the reader the most comprehensive approach for interview technique of sexual dysfunction, no matter what theoretical orientation the interviewer may have. If the interviewer is planning a behavior therapy intervention, however, an addition to this procedure may be found useful. In building hierarchies for desensitization therapy, it is important to determine the specific stimuli and stimuli situations which are likely to evoke the most anxiety. The behavior therapist should pinpoint for a client the specific aspects of sexual behavior which bother her the most. It is wrong to assume that sexual intercourse is the most anxiety-evoking stimulus. There may very well be other aspects of sexual behavior which bother a client to a greater degree, as illustrated in the interview below with Mrs. L.

Mrs. L: I don't seem to enjoy sex anymore. I couldn't care if I had it or not. It is not like I haven't had it before, because I have. I've been married almost six years. It has been the last year-and-a-half.

Dr: What is the current rate of sexual intercourse?

Mrs. L: About 12 times a month.

Dr: Out of those 12 times, how many times would you enjoy it?

Mrs. L: Maybe two, three. Not very many, it is usually just to satisfy my husband and that is it.

Dr: At the beginning of marriage was there a higher frequency of intercourse?

Mrs. L: Oh, I'd say about the same. It may have been a bit higher during the first years.

Dr: You enjoyed it more at the beginning of marriage?

Mrs. L: Yes. When we were first married, neither one of us had really experienced a full sexual relationship with each other. We went to Dr._____ and he helped my husband out an awful lot. Like things that he could do to arouse me. After that we had a very good sexual relationship for a while.

Dr: Do you feel any anxiety when you approach sex now?

Mrs. L: Yes.

Dr: Are there certain things that bother you more than others in sex?

Mrs. L: I suppose breast stimulation more than anything. I'm really uptight about that. I just don't like it when my husband touches them.

Dr: How do you react if your husband touches you on the breasts?

Mrs. L: I get really jumpy. I don't even like it now when he touches me or puts his arms around me.

Dr: You said that out of 12 times you might enjoy sex two or three times?

Mrs. L: Right. I don't really enjoy it at first, not at all. My husband will keep persisting and then I find I am enjoying intercourse.

Through the remainder of this first interview, specific anxiety-arousing stimuli were elaborated on. In addition to breast stimulation, Mrs. L found touching her husband in the genital area very upsetting. Intercourse was not rated at the top of Mrs. L's hierarchy. This is only one step, however, in building an appropriate hierarchy for a client. Other tools (to be discussed) such as the card sort and Bentler scale (Bentler, 1968b), may also be found useful. Since hierarchy construction is such an important part of systematic desensitization, we will return to this topic in Chapter 4.

In short, patient self-report is very frequently cited in the literature as the sole means of determining the diagnosis and assessment of change in sexual dysfunction problems.

Unfortunately, both men and women have short memories and/or are not always candid in their reports. Nevertheless, there exist as many approaches to interview techniques as there are interviewers, and no procedure is right or wrong since individual personality variables of the therapist and the patient must be considered in each interview. The approach used by Masters and Johnson (1970), however, offers a comprehensive structured interview which may be adopted for most clinical situations involving sexual dysfunction in women. The general practitioner or researcher may also wish to use one of the many standard sexual history forms developed by various organizations. A very adequate sexual history form is offered by the Division of Family Study at the University of Pennsylvania. This copyrighted 32-item form is comprehensive and was developed by Dr. Kinsey and the psychiatric team at the Division of Family Study.*

An elaboration of specific anxiety-evoking stimuli is necessary in interviews in which behavior therapy is used. If, as in experimental investigations, the interview is to be used as a means of objectively assessing change over time, then we would suggest that the interviews should be 1) structured (the same questions asked in the same manner), and 2) done "blindly" without knowledge of the patient's treatment condition. A blind interview is done to control for possible therapist biases in eliciting or guiding responses in the direction he believes they should go.

ASSESSMENT BY QUESTIONNAIRE

Questionnaire and other paper and pencil methods have come into use in an attempt to add more objectivity to assessment procedures for sexual dysfunction. These more objective procedures seem to have taken two distinct lines of enquiry in attempting to assess sexual functioning: 1) concern for determining sexual experience, and 2) concern for determining sexual attitudes.

SEXUAL EXPERIENCE

The earliest paper and pencil assessment methods were concerned with determining male sexual experience. Podell and Perkins (1956) attempted to construct a scale of heterosexual experience using the procedures of Guttman (1950) Scaling. Based on the reported sexual experience of 100 college men, Podell and Perkins concluded that it was "feasible to order certain aspects of sexual behavior along a unidimensional cumulative scale." Brady and Levitt (1965) replicated the main results of Podell and Perkins, with the added finding that men with homosexual experiences have also experienced all aspects of heterosexual behavior. This finding appears to be very limited, however, since Brady and Levitt (1965) used 68 male graduate students for their sample. Certainly, clinical experience with homosexual clients would not support this finding.

The Podell and Perkins study and the Brady and Levitt study contain several design problems. Their results are based on relatively small sample sizes and, as pointed out by Bentler (1968a), their scales were not cross-validated nor were they tested for internal consistency. Bentler improved on these two earlier studies by using a larger sample size (N=175) and a cross-validation sample (N=108), and by statistically determining the internal consistency and scalability of his scale. Bentler (1968b) also developed a similar scale of heterosexual experience for females, and recognized the potential that his scale could be used for assessing changes in the sexual behavior which occurred as a result of therapy. The Bentler Scale is thus a valuable tool often used in therapy and research

*See Appendix A for information on ordering.

for assessing changes in sexual experiences. One potential problem in using the questionnaire method for obtaining information about sexual behavior is that, as mentioned before, some clients are not always truthful in reporting personal sexual experiences. Thorne (1966) and Udry and Morris (1967), however, have presented evidence to suggest that direct questioning about sexual behavior via a questionnaire is a reliable source of information. Udry and Morris obtained confirmation of a verbal report of women reporting coital experiences by analyzing urine samples of the women. The women were unaware of the purpose of the study, since they were told that the reason for collecting sexual data was that some researchers believe sexual excitement changes certain hormone secretion levels. Over a period of one month, 12 of 15 women yielded perfect concordance between laboratory positives and reports of coitus. Three women yielded a total of five discrepant reports which Udry and Morris did not feel was at all excessive.

Although the measure of sexual experience is important, for therapy purposes it is often the measurement of sexual attitudes which is more important. Many clients (women in particular) with sexual problems are often able to engage in, and have engaged in, a full range of heterosexual behaviors but do not enjoy doing so. For these clients it is important to assess attitudes toward sexual behavior and not just frequency or types of sexual behavior.

SEXUAL ATTITUDE

Feldman et al. (1966) were the first researchers to develop and use a questionnaire type of approach for assessing attitude toward heterosexual and homosexual behavior. Their procedure, which they termed The Sexual Orientation Method (SOM), was developed as a quick and accurate procedure for assessing changes during therapy in sexual attitudes of male homosexuals. The development of the SOM was strongly influenced by the semantic differential technique of Osgood et al. (1957). (Details on the construction of the SOM, as well as data on its internal consistency, unidimensionality, reliability, and validity are presented in the Feldman et al. article and will not be presented here.) Although SOM seems to be a statistically sound method of assessing sexual attitude, it has not been widely adopted by clinicians or researchers and is not widely reported in the literature. It appears from reviewing the literature that many researchers are interested in developing their own assessment procedures rather than using tools (even statistically sound ones) that others have developed. A number of authors have, however, used semantic differential type procedures for assessing sexual attitudes (Faulk, 1971; Marks and Sartorius, 1968; Paulson and Lin, 1970). Although the details of the various techniques may differ, Osgood's semantic differential appears to be a widely accepted and useful procedure.

Several authors have been concerned with assessing anxiety associated with sexual behavior. This area of assessment is especially important for behavior therapists using systematic desensitization and other anxiety reduction procedures. Obler (1973) developed a sexual anxiety scale (SAS) which he described as measuring cognitively experienced social and sexual anxieties. The scale, which is described as being reliable and valid, contains 22 items which range from anxiety experienced during contact with a member of the opposite sex to intravaginal penetration.

We (Wincze and Caird, 1973) have reported the use of a similar scale for assessing sexual anxiety changes which occurred during video desensitization therapy. In addition, we (Wincze and Caird, 1976; and Caird and Wincze, 1974) have used a card-sort method of assessing sexual anxiety. The card sort is a method in which potentially anxiety-evoking stimuli are described on cards and subjects are instructed to place the cards in categories of varying degrees of anxiety: i.e., 0=no anxiety, 1=slight anxiety, 2=moderate anxiety, 3=much anxiety, and 4=very much anxiety. An anxiety score is achieved by multiplying the number of cards in each category by the value of that category, and then summing the totals for all categories. By keeping a record of the value assigned to each card as well as the total value for all cards, a therapist or researcher can pinpoint areas of anxiety and total levels of anxiety. Table 3–1 presents a record of a card sort over time of a woman (Mrs. F) with heterosexual anxiety. The woman was undergoing video desensitization therapy, and as shown in Table 3–1, anxiety levels were reduced throughout the therapy procedure. In the card sort method, a higher score represents an increased level of anxiety. Since individual cards can be constructed for each client, tests of validity, reliability, and internal consistency cannot be determined for the card sort method. In our own research and clinical experience, however, the card sort seems to be useful as a means of determining changes in levels of anxiety. Subjectively, changes in card sort scores seem to correlate highly with client's reports of progress in therapy.

ASSESSMENT OF AROUSAL

One of the most overlooked areas in sexual dysfunction has been the problems of sexual arousal. Researchers and clinical practitioners have made the naive assumption that ability to achieve orgasm and ability to become sexually aroused are always highly positively correlated. While subjectively this would appear sensible, it is certainly not substantiated by our own clinical experience. We have found it very common for some orgasmic women to report lack of sexual arousal. Some women complaining of arousal dysfunction have reported orgasm rates as high as 75% during coitus. Looking at the other side of the coin, we have also treated women who have reported normal levels of arousal and were even frequent initiators of sexual contacts, yet rarely, if ever, experienced orgasm. Certainly there is a need to assess arousal dysfunction accurately if proper treatment programs are to be designed. Neither the presence nor absence of orgasmic experience alone allows the clinician or researcher to assume the presence or absence of sexual arousal. It is quite possible that arousal dysfunction could involve total lack of arousal across all situations and behaviors, or it could involve lack of arousal for specific situations and behaviors. A valid measurement of arousal would allow the clinician to diagnose the exact nature of the sexual problem.

The measurement of arousal would also be important for research aimed at evaluating the impact of sexual dysfunction therapy. Comparing changes in arousal scores pre and post therapy, or among several different therapeutic approaches, could be made with a valid arousal assessment scale.

Finally, valid assessment of arousal would be necessary in order to examine some theoretical issues. For example, it is very important to look at the relationship between anxiety and sexual arousal in order to gain a better understanding of the processes underlying some cases of sexual dysfunction. Are anxiety and sexual arousal reciprocal inhibitors, as Wolpe (1958) postulates? How do arousal and anxiety co-vary during treatment of sexual arousal or anxiety dysfunction? These and other questions could be attacked with the availability of an arousal scale.

Hoon, Wincze and Hoon (1976) have developed a sexual arousal inventory for the measurement of female sexual arousal which may satisfy some of the need. Their Sexual Arousal Inventory (SAI)* consists of twenty-eight items describing erotic experiences

*See Appendix A for information on ordering.

Table 3–1 CARD SORT SCORES OF WOMAN UNDERGOING VIDEO DESENSITIZATION THERAPY

Card number	June 7 (Pre test)	Sept 4 (Post test 1 follow-up)	Dates of Video Desensitization Therapy Sessions										
			Sept 10	Sept 12	Sept 17	Sept 25	Oct 9	Oct 18	Oct 24	Oct 29	Nov 4	Nov 6 (Post test 2 follow-Up)	May 20
1	0	1	0	0	0	0	0	0	0	0	0	0	0
2	0	0	0	0	0	0	0	0	0	0	0	0	0
3	3	4	0	2	0	1	0	0	0	0	0	0	0
4	3	3	2	3	3	4	3	0	0	0	0	0	0
5	3	4	4	4	4	4	3	2	2	0	0	0	0
6	2	2	3	3	3	4	3	0	0	0	0	0	0
7	3	3	3	3	3	3	2	0	0	0	0	0	0
8	2	2	3	3	3	3	1	0	0	0	0	0	0
9	2	1	0	0	0	0	0	0	0	0	0	0	0
10	0	0	0	0	0	0	0	0	0	0	0	0	0
11	3	3	1	3	3	3	1	0	0	0	0	0	0
12	3	3	1	1	1	0	1	0	0	0	0	0	0
13	0	0	0	0	0	0	0	0	0	0	0	0	0
14	0	0	0	3	0	1	0	0	0	0	0	0	0
15	1	1	2	3	3	4	3	0	0	0	0	0	0
16	3	3	4	4	4	3	3	3	2	0	0	0	0
17	3	2	0	0	3	0	0	0	0	0	0	0	0
18	1	1	1	1	3	3	0	0	0	0	0	0	0
19	4	4	4	4	4	3	0	0	0	0	0	0	0
20	3	3	0	0	4	3	0	0	0	0	0	0	0
21	3	3	4	4	4	4	3	3	2	0	0	0	0
22	3	3	4	4	4	4	3	2	2	0	0	0	0
23	3	4	4	4	4	4	3	0	0	0	0	0	0
24	4	3	4	4	4	4	4	4	3	2	0	0	0
25	4	4	4	4	4	4	4	4	3	2	0	0	0
26	4	4	4	4	4	4	4	4	3	2	0	0	0
Total score	60	61	52	61	65	63	41	22	17	6	0	0	0

which the respondent rates along a 7-point Likert arousal dimension. Respondents are asked to answer the following question for each item:

How do you feel, or think you would feel, if you were actually involved in this experience?

A rating of -1 equals "adversely affects arousal; unthinkable; repulsive; distracting," while a rating of $+5$ equals "always causes sexual arousal; extremely arousing." The SAI yields a total arousal score which can be compared to established norms. This test has concurrent validity with respect to sexual experience, activity and satisfaction, and has discriminative validity between women seeking therapy for treatment of sexual dysfunction and women satisfied with their sexual experiences. The authors also report that the SAI is easy to administer and score, has good test–retest reliability, may be used with single, married, or lesbian women, is available in alternate forms, and possesses exceptional internal consistency. In short, the SAI seems to have satisfied all the necessary psychometric properties for creating a valid and reliable scale. However, only time will determine its utility.

Recently Wincze, Hoon and Hoon (1977) have looked at an electromechanical means of assessing sexual arousal. Female subjects, while viewing various erotic video tapes, moved a hand lever to indicate their subjective state of arousal. This cognitive measure consisted of a potentiometer driven by a mechanical lever so that resistance changed according to where the lever was placed. The lever was connected to a Grass Polygraph and provided a continuous linear analog of the subjective state of arousal. Five out of six subjects showed significantly positive correlations with physiologic indices of sexual arousal. Further research is now being conducted by these authors and others, looking at the relationship between cognitive and physiologic indices of sexual arousal.

ASSESSMENT OF GENERALIZED ANXIETY, FEAR, AND ASSERTIVENESS

Commonly, women and men who seek treatment for sexual problems suffer from anxiety in other areas as well; they are anxious about sex, but they also display anxiety in a variety of other areas. One of our concerns has been to attempt to determine whether or not this anxiety is reduced concomitantly with a reduction in heterosexual anxiety. For this purpose we routinely administer the Willoughby Neuroticism Scale* (Willoughby, 1934). This is a 25-item questionnaire which is ranked on a 5-point scale (0–4). The highest possible score is 100, and a score in excess of 30 is interpreted as indicating general neuroticism. Clients complete this pre and post therapy.

As with anxiety, many women and men express fears for a variety of objects and situations, and we have attempted to determine if these are affected or reduced as heterosexual anxiety decreases. The measure we use here is the Fear Survey Schedule† (Wolpe and Lang, 1964). There are 76 items (e.g., insects, loud noises, operations, nude men or women) and these are rated on a 5-point scale in terms of the tension or anxiety each engenders. The scores we use are simply the number of items rated "Much" or "Very much" anxiety. This questionnaire is completed pre and post therapy.

In some cases at least, heterosexual anxiety might be related to a general absence of assertiveness—not perhaps directly related, but involved to the extent that it may exacerbate the problem. A reticence to communicate with one's sexual partner might be an example. To determine whether this aspect of behavior changes with an increase in sexual responsiveness would appear worthwhile investigating. To this end we utilize an Assertive Questionnaire§ described by Wolpe (1969). This contains 30 situational items

*See Appendix A for further information.
†See Appendix A for further information.
§See Appendix A for further information.

to be answered "yes" or "no," and the score is the number of items answered unasser-
tively. This, too, is given to the client before and after therapy.

Through our research we have shown that positive changes in sexual behavior following therapy do not produce improvement in functioning in other areas. Specifically,
clients did not show improvement on the Willoughby Scale, the Fear Survey Schedule
or the Assertive Questionnaire after successful remediation of their sexual problems. The
impact of desensitization therapy seems to be focused mainly on the behavior under
treatment with little or no impact on other problem areas.

ASSESSMENT BY BEHAVIOR RECORD

Lobitz and LoPiccolo (1972) and LoPiccolo and Steger (1974) have developed a measure
termed the Oregon Sex Inventory* (OSI), which combines the features of some of the
aforementioned methods by assessing both sexual experience and attitude. Using the
OSI, clients collect their own data by filling out a form which details their sexual behavior
on each day on which any sexual activity occurs. LoPicolo and Steger give the following
description of the OSI.

The OSI consists of 17 pages. Each page is headed by a brief description of a heterosexual act. The
total of 17 acts listed covers fairly comprehensively the entire range of "normal" heterosexual
behavior.

For each act, the client is asked to answer the same six questions: How regularly the act forms
a part of his repertoire, how often he would like it to, how pleasurable he finds the act, how
pleasurable he would like the act to be for him, and how pleasurable he would like the act to be
for his mate.

The scores on these six questions for each of the 17 acts are combined in a variety
of ways to form 11 clinical scales. Clients' scores on each scale can be plotted on a profile
sheet, which is scaled in relation to the means and standard deviations of scores obtained
by a group of 63 married couples with satisfactory sexual adjustments. Steger (1972)
reports that test–retest reliability and internal consistency reliability statistics yield significant coefficient values for each of OSI scale scores.

LoPiccolo has developed a revised edition of the Sex Inventory which includes illustrations of each of the 17 sexual acts along with the six questions just referred to. This
appears to be an excellent tool for use with clients of all educational levels.

Obler (1973) reports an alternative method for recording couples' sexual behavior by
instructing couples to keep a careful record of their successful and unsuccessful sexual
experiences. Couples are given forms which define for them successful and unsuccessful
sexual experiences (e.g., premature ejaculation success defined as the ability to withhold
ejaculation for a period of at least 2 min). Each partner keeps a private record for the
therapist. Obler feels that a pre–post success/experience ration comparison provides
"the most direct and stringent measure of treatment effectiveness."

In our research, we have used an abbreviated version of the OSI for measuring sexual
behavior changes (Lange, 1974). Our recording procedure consists of a "Weekly Sexual
Activity Check List" which both partners keep separately and return to the therapist at
the end of each week. As can be seen in Appendix B the Weekly Sexual Activity Check
List records the occurrence, anxiety, and arousal of 10 randomly selected sexual behaviors. Statistical analysis of the validity and reliability of this sexual behavior check list has
not as yet been conducted.

At this point, few other researchers have attempted to use behavioral records as a

*The inventory can be obtained at cost by writing to the author, Dr. Joseph LoPiccolo. See Appendix
A for information on ordering.

means of assessing sexual functioning. Keeping actual records of sexual behavior seems to hold great potential for the field of measurement and most likely will grow in use in future research. Because of moral and ethical considerations, however, it is unlikely that the use of trained observers and closed-circuit TV equipment will be used in the home to record sexual behavior, as has been the case in recording parent–child interactions (Patterson, Cobb and Ray 1973). Nonetheless, by encouraging couples to keep separate records, an acceptable degree of accuracy can be ensured.

ASSESSMENT BY PHYSIOLOGIC METHODS

Since the early 1800s there have been many and varied attempts to measure sexual behavior in males. Most of these were physiologic in nature. In contrast to the attempts to assess female sexual behavior, males have a much longer history utilizing less delicate stratagems. Some of the earliest devices for detection of male sexual arousal were produced by horsebreeders who were concerned with excessive masturbation in stud horses. Mountjoy (1974) points out that prevention of masturbation in stud horses is still considered important today "since autoerotic ejaculation will lower the sperm count and hence decrease the probability of fertilization." Because of the concern for the potential failure of studs to procreate, 49 devices for the prevention of masturbation in horses were patented between 1885 and 1919. For our purposes, it is important to note that some of these appliances had a remarkable similarity to those used for measurement of human male sexual arousal. One in particular, described by Mountjoy, is of interest since it involved electrical circuitry: as a horse's penis lengthened during tumescence, an electrical circuit was closed and the current generated from a dry cell battery passed through the engorged organ and caused, among other things, detumescence—probably to the dismay of the horse. Similar types of electrical apparatus were patented for human use to prevent masturbation in mental patients. From 1856 to 1910, well-meaning inventors produced 15 different antimasturbatory gadgets for the treatment of mental patients. The rationale for these was the prevention or exacerbation of mental illness. Again, for our purposes, their importance is that they represented early attempts at assessment of male arousal. Even though the intentions behind these early mechanical monstrosities were misguided, they were the historical forerunners of more modern types of assessment procedures. Electric circuitry which is closed by a male erection could easily be programmed to cause a recording pen to deflect, instead of delivering a shock or sounding an alarm. Unfortunately, this early technology was ignored or overlooked for a number of years, and it was not until the mid-1930s that interest in measurement of male sexual arousal was stimulated by other more scientific concerns.

Jovanovic (1971), in a review of the literature, reported that as early as 1936 researchers observed the occurrence of erections during periods of sleep. The early literature was descriptive, and was concerned mainly with simply recording the phenomenon. Using crude technical procedures, only the presence or absence of an erection during the sleep of male volunteers was recorded. The data reported total number of erections per person per night (3–5), the mean duration of an erection (25.3 min), and the total erection period per night (85.4 min).

More recently, advanced technology has led to a highly sophisticated analysis of the sleep-erection phenomenon. Fisher, Gross, and Zuch (1965) considered the relationship between erections and REM (rapid eye movement) periods of sleep. Using sophisticated EEG (electroencephalographic) machinery which was not available to early researchers, Fisher et al. (1965) were able to accurately record REM sleep. More importantly, Fisher developed a device which could record quantitative changes in the erection. Thus, the onset and degree of an erection and its total duration could be very accurately measured throughout a sleep session. The device was attached to the penis and recorded volume changes in a tube of water; as penis size increased, water was displaced up a tube. These investigators found that erections occurred only during REM periods of sleep, and that 95% of all REM periods were accompanied by full or partial erections. By waking subjects during periods of REM activity, they found that erections occurred even during dreams which were not sexual in content.

Karacin, Goodenough, Shapiro and Starker (1966) found that REM periods in which erections did not occur were often accompanied by dreams with high anxiety content. This is an interesting finding, since high anxiety is also related to loss of erection in the waking state. The whole field of dream research is a fascinating one, but for our purposes is important because of the technology which has been advanced in attempts to measure male sexual arousal. The device used by Karacin et al. (1966) was an important advancement in the field. Penile circumference changes were detected by a mercury-filled strain loop placed around the penis. As the penis circumference changed, the resistence of the mercury to a mild electric current also changed and was accurately recorded through a DC amplifier. Changes as minute as a fraction of a milimeter could be measured by this system.

Another very important influence in the study of male sexual arousal has come to us because of the interest in diagnosing and treating sexual deviancy. Freund (1957) was the first to use a psychophysiological device to measure the sexual orientation of males. His first paper on this topic was published in Czechoslovakia and not widely known in North American circles until 1963. Freund's early papers were concerned with the development of an accurate diagnostic procedure for discernment of homosexuality. His apparatus consists of a glass cylinder which when placed over the penis serves as a sensor, transmitting volume changes mechanically by air displacement. Bancroft, Jones, and Pullan (1966) took advantage of the technology developed by sleep researchers and developed a simple strain gage which they claimed was a technical advancement over the more cumbersome Freund device. Furthermore, Bancroft et al. recognized the potential of this accurate measurement system and applied it in the treatment of sexual deviancy. In one reported case, Bancroft et al. used electric shock as punishment for a 25-year-old male pedophiliac, contingent upon a defined penile erection in the presence of photographs of children. Photographs of adult females, on the other hand, were never paired with shock, and arousal to these stimuli was encouraged. The results of this study are somewhat unclear, and it is not known if this procedure was of any value in affecting the marginal positive results reported. The value of this study lies in the advancement of technology and in the potential use of an assessment device for treatment of sexual deviancy. Freund's and Bancroft's studies stimulated further interest in arousal measurement procedures.

Another influence on the development of physiologic assessment procedures has evolved with the growing interest in sexual dysfunctions. Masters and Johnson (1966, 1970) were the forerunners in this field, and developed diagnostic procedures as well as treatment approaches to these manifest problems. Their work began as early as 1953, but was not widely recognized until 1963. Their conscientious endeavors represent the best descriptive research on male sexual functioning and dysfunction. In spite of their detailed description of the physiology of male sexual functioning and response, they did not make use of physiologic measurement procedures. Most likely, this is because treatment and diagnosis are reasonably well defined without such information. A verbal description of premature ejaculation or loss of erection is usually sufficient for implementing a treatment program.

However, for understanding more about the process of sexual dysfunction in males, physiologic assessment may be an important area for future inquiry. Abel et al. (1975) for example, exposed male sexual deviates to audio tape descriptions of sexual behavior and found considerable variability throughout in penis circumference changes. By continually monitoring the physiologic changes occurring in the penis, these authors were able to identify very specific stimuli which triggered sexual arousal. Such ingenious methodology could also be applied to sexual dysfunctioning males to identify arousing stimuli and response patterns. This information may be important for treatment and understanding of sexual dysfunction. With the recent explosion of interests in this area and in new instrumentation, a great deal of effort will continue to be made. This will, it is hoped, result in the development of new and even more ingenious assessment procedures.

The study of the physiology of female sexual response is the newest and most intriguing level of assessment. It is only since the work of Kinsey (1953) and Masters and Johnson (1966) that the field has advanced. A number of devices have been examined which measure female sexual arousal (Jovanovic, 1971; Zuckerman, 1971), but until recently none have been satisfactory. The most promising devices in the field are focusing on changes in blood flow in the vaginal wall. According to Masters and Johnson (1966), "the transudation-like material which lubricates the vagina develops from the activation of a massive localized vasocongestive reaction." Vaginal lubrication is one of the human female's initial responses to any form of sexual stimulation. Several authors have reported the development of vaginal blood flow meters (Fisher & Davis, 1969; Sintchak & Geer, 1975; Hoon, Wincze, & Hoon, 1976; Tart, 1971). Geer et al. (1975) were the first to develop a photoplethysmographic device that was easy to use and seemed to be a valid measure of sexual arousal in women. Geer's device was a clear acrylic probe with an incandescent light source mounted on one end and a selenium photocell detector mounted on the side.

The probe measured the amount of light reflected off of vaginal wall tissue. The less light reflected, the more vasocongestion and hence the more arousal. The development of this device was largely influenced by the work of Masters and Johnson who noted color changes (blood flow changes) in the vaginal wall during periods of

Fig. 3–1. Diagram of photoplethysmographic probe for measurement of vaginal capillary vasocongestion. Probe is inserted by patient in a manner similar to inserting a tampon, and is positioned in first third of vaginal barrel.

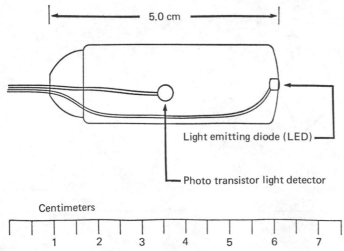

5.0 cm

Light emitting diode (LED)

Photo transistor light detector

Centimeters

1   2   3   4   5   6   7

sexual arousal. In Geer's study, women were exposed to erotic or neutral stimuli and reported their subjective feelings while physiological (blood flow) measures were continuously monitored. Geer found significant reflected light changes during the sexually arousing stimulus condition. Peter Hoon (Hoon, Wincze & Hoon, 1976) developed an improved probe device which used an infrared light source and phototransistor detector cell. Both of these technical improvements were included in order to eliminate potential artifactal flaws of the Geer device. In a well-controlled study, these investigators demonstrated that the infrared photoplethysmograph was valid since it was able to discriminate between sexually arousing, dysphoric, and neutral emotional conditions in women. In a second experiment, these authors demonstrated that sexually normal women can achieve greater levels of vasocongestion than can women seeking help for sexual problems (Wincze, Hoon, & Hoon, in press). This device thus holds promise as an objective and useful diagnostic tool.

The importance of physiologic measurement for the assessment of sexual response cannot be overemphasized. However, the applications and limitations of the various devices are still of serious concern.

While preliminary technical questions are still being asked of the new female "probe" apparatus, the technical specifications of devices for measuring male sexual arousal have been debated for a number of years. As discussed earlier, Freund's (1963) volumeteric procedure for measuring male arousal has been challenged by Bancroft et al. (1966) and more recently by Barlow et al. (1970) who have developed circumference change measuring instruments which the authors claim to be more comfortable and less cumbersome than the Freund device. Barlow's device is especially comfortable and the one which we use in our research. Our male subjects have never complained of discomfort while wearing the simple spring strain gage devised by Barlow, and many have remarked that they had even forgotten that the apparatus was attached to them. Although the circumference devices have a distinct advantage of comfort and simplicity over the

Fig. 3–2. Diagram of strain gauge for measurement of penile circumference change in males. Strain gauge fits comfortably around penis and is placed about midshaft of penis, with gauge on dorsal side.

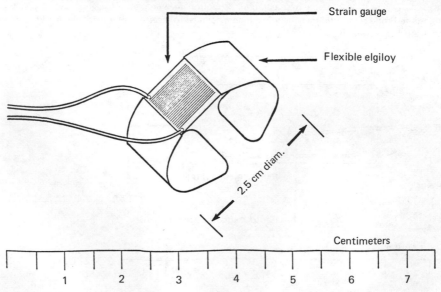

volumeteric ones, a recent study by Freund, Langevin and Barlow (1974) found the volumeteric measurement to be more sensitive to arousal changes than those utilizing changes in penis circumference.

Through the use of physiologic measuring devices a number of answerable questions have been generated. For example, Barr and McConaghy (1971, 1972) have looked at penile volume changes in response to appetitive and aversive stimuli. Their studies have added support to the theory of a general conditionability factor, since penile volume changes and galvanic skin response changes co-varied in different learning situations. Although these studies have little bearing on assessment, *per se,* they do point to the diversity and complexity of research which can emanate from objective assessment procedures.

In other inquiries, a number of researchers have posed the question, "What stimuli are more sexually arousing to heterosexual and homosexual males?" Four different groups of researchers have concluded, on the basis of greater penile volume and circumference changes, that erotic movies have more arousal value for males than either erotic slides or erotic audio tapes (Abel, Barlow, Blanchard and Mavissakalian, 1975; Freund, Langevin, and Zajac, 1974; Mavissakalian, Blanchard, Abel and Barlow, 1975; McConaghy, 1974; Sanford, 1974). Furthermore, lesbian movies and male homosexual movies are the best stimuli for differentiating between heterosexual and homosexual males (Mavissakalian et al., 1975)—heterosexual males show greatest penile circumference changes to lesbian movies, while homosexual males show greatest penile circumference changes to male homosexual movies. Interestingly, both heterosexual and homosexual males show about the same penile circumference changes to heterosexual films, which is not surprising since heterosexual films have both male and female participants and one can chose to concentrate on either sex.

One very intriguing study in the series above raises questions related to human ethology. Freund, Langevin and Zajac (1974) asked, "What effect does movement have on arousal?" These researchers found that movement is only an important variable in eliciting arousal if the erotic stimuli in stationary form already exceeds a certain threshold of erotic arousal value. Unanswered is the question of whether movement is arousing because it offers the opportunity to better perceive physical features, or whether there is some other erotic impact of movement *per se* (as in released action patterns of lower animals?) Further experimentation relying heavily on physiologic assessment procedures will undoubtedly shed some light on these and other questions.

Physiologic measurement of penile changes may also be an important method of evaluating therapy outcome. A number of studies have utilized physiologic assessment procedures (i.e., penile volume or circumference changes) as a method of increasing objectivity when evaluating treatment outcome (Abel, Levis, & Clancy, 1969; Bancroft, 1971; Barlow and Agras, 1973; and Conrad and Wincze, 1976). However, as Bancroft (1971) points out, "The implications of changes in erection during the course of treatment will depend on the importance of erections to the behavior being modified. It should not be assumed that changes in erection will reflect changes in behavior or attitudes." Thus, if changes in sexual attitude or overt sexual behavior are important to treatment outcomes, then evaluation of treatment on the basis of changes in erectile response alone is inappropriate. All levels of assessment may or may not be important, depending on the desired treatment outcome. Physiologic response changes are important when changes in erectile response have been a goal of treatment. For example, studies may show measured increases in erectile response in impotent men as a function of treatment.

PROCEDURAL SHORTCOMINGS

There are problems, real and potential, with physiologic assessment of sexual response. First of all, for the general practitioner, psychiatrist, or psychologist unfamiliar with the technology involved in physiologic assessment, it is inadvisable to pursue this area of assessment without first being carefully tutored in its use. The equipment involved is expensive and subject to frequent malfunctionings. Data reduction and interpretation from a physiograph strip chart is very time consuming and, therefore, impractical for applied settings. Because of this the use of physiologic recordings are as yet more appropriate for sophisticated research settings.

A second question of the utility of the psychophysiologic method of assessment is the validity of this technique. That is, does the erectile response or female vasocongestion response correlate with other indices of sexual arousal, namely, subjective report or attitude? Mavissakalian et al. (1975) have reported significant positive correlations in both heterosexual and homosexual males between erectile response and subjective report of arousal. Other researchers have also supported these findings, but there is an important question in all studies using psychophysiologic assessment procedures of whether or not the subject is faking the response. Freund (1963) demonstrated that some men can deliberately fake erectile response. That is, by concentrating on dysphoric thoughts in the presence of erotic stimulation, some men can inhibit erections. Conversely, some men are able to concentrate on erotic thoughts and obtain erections in the presence of unpleasant stimuli. Although the ability to "fake" erectile response is an individual skill, it is of considerable concern whenever this level of assessment is being used. Similar research with females has not as yet been conducted. Pragmatically speaking, many of the problems mentioned above are more important in the research laboratory than in the clinician's office. Determining improvements in sexual functioning do not usually require sophisticated equipment. Most clients are able to judge for themselves if they are functioning satisfactorily.

ETHICAL CONCERNS

Ethical questions may be raised concerning the measurement and assessment of sexual response in men and women. Kinsey's early critics were concerned about the ethics of questioning people about their sexual behavior. Would such questioning make people feel uneasy, and raise doubts about their own sexual functioning? Would there be any harmful side effects from the questioning? Would people become overly concerned about deviancy or inadequacy in friends if they were questioned about these behaviors? These and other questions have been raised over and over again in countless research and therapy programs since Kinsey's early work. One must always be on guard that a person does not become overly upset by such inquiries. In addition, ethical concerns must accompany every program dealing with sex, since the field is fraught with exploiters and quacks. Kinsey's group was troubled by imitators who apparently got their kicks by posing as legitimate sex researchers. Today there is a proliferation of "sex clinics" which are mainly money making operations and have no professional status.

Kinsey found that it was surprisingly easy to extract intimate sexual information from people without apparent stress or side effects. In interviewing our own clients, we have not found stress to be a significant factor if the proper environment for interviewing is created (as outlined earlier in this chapter). Certainly many patients find it difficult to talk about their sexual problems, but if the therapist is accepting, open, not pushy, and respectful, a great deal of anxiety can be disinhibited. The therapist must be fully prepared for the client who may be revealing problems for the first time. To the experienced therapist, assessment of sexual problems during interview or by questionnaire should be no more distressing than assessment of any other problem. Furthermore, there is no evidence that the questioning of persons about their sexual behavior, by a legitimate researcher or therapist, has a lasting or harmful effect on the person being questioned.

The use of physiologic assessment procedures may also raise ethical questions. While the female and male recording devices appear to be physically harmless, are they psychologically harmless also? Our experience to date with both male and female measuring devices is that there appear to be no psychologic harmful side effects. None of our clients reported being upset by the assessment procedures during the assessment or afterward. We have follow-up interviews with a number of clients as much as six months after participation in physiologic assessment sessions, with no report of any side effects or stress as a result of the procedures.

Recently, however, an article appeared in a number of newspapers which raises another question related to the ethics of such assessment procedures. Are such procedures dehumanizing? For example, at Harvard the dean of students refused to allow undergraduates to participate in a university study on the relationship of anxiety to sexual arousal. This study included the use of physiologic recording devices for measuring sexual arousal in men and women. Objections to the use of recording equipment were raised on grounds that it was dehumanizing and the after-effects of the research on individual students was unknown. The Harvard decision raises some ethical concern about sexual research programs using physiologic recording devices. Although it was an isolated decision, future therapy and research programs using physiologic assessment procedures must be weighed very carefully.

SUMMARY

The purpose of this chapter has been to inform the reader of various assessment tools available, including their limitations. This discussion by no means exhausts the list of available assessment procedures, although the most commonly used procedures and some of the most intriguing procedures have been included. Biologic assessment procedures of sexual response, such as secondary sex-organ and testicular function (serum testosterone levels and sperm motility), have not been discussed. These procedures have generally not been used in psychologic studies, and the relationship of bioassay procedures to other assessment procedures is clearly an area for future study.

In the final analysis, and from a strictly utilitarian point of view, the prime objects of rational methods of assessment and measuring behavior change are, first of all, to delineate the problem, to make sure that you are dealing with the correct problem and have not been misled or blinded to other areas of dysfunction. Secondly, it is most important that the therapist know the effects of the therapy, not only in terms of outcome but also during the course of therapy. This would appear so self-evident that it requires no restatement. However, the history of psychiatry, and to a lesser extent clinical psychology, is replete with reports of the efficacy of this or that kind of therapy based solely on "clinical" impressions, with no effort whatsoever to objectively (statistically) demonstrate these often extravagent claims. Obvious examples of this in psychology are the unsubstantiated therapeutic effects of the various types of group therapy. In psychiatry, one only has to look at electro-convulsive therapy and psychosurgery to witness the same sort of unwarranted generalizations.

From what is known of the effects of intermittent reinforcement, it seems reasonable to infer that in the absence of objective measures of change, therapists will be misled and an occasional "cure" will prove sufficient to maintain the therapist in his particular mode of action. People see what they want to see and believe what they want to believe, often in the face of what appears to be a mass of contradictory evidence. Nevertheless, we believe that therapists can, and eventually will, behave in more "rational" ways, and one method to promulgate this change is to strongly encourage the use of objective, reliable and valid methods of assessing changes in behavior.

This chapter has examined a number of different levels of assessment for sexual dysfunction. Assessment and diagnosis can be made on the basis of information from a number of different sources. It is important for the therapist or researcher to be aware of the different levels from which he or she can choose, and to be aware that each method of assessment possesses different degrees of reliability, validity and utility. With improved technology in computer science and electronic engineering, more sophisticated methodology and hardware can be employed for the development of assessment procedures. This whole area will most certainly show rapid expansion in research, which will lead to even more sophisticated procedures of assessment with greater accuracy and utility.

4

Female Sexual Dysfunction: Treatment

APPROACH AND RESPONSE

One thing is clear: there is no single therapeutic approach which is successful in treating sexual dysfunctions in all women. A procedure which may be highly effective with one woman, or one group of women, may be completely ineffectual with others. This, of course, is not peculiar to sexual problems and the same difficulties are encountered in treating many psychological disorders. Some depressives respond well to electroconvulsive therapy, while others derive little or no benefit from it. Some schizophrenics make startling recoveries in response to a particular type of drug, while others show no evidence of medication. Some phobics are completely free of their phobia after relatively few sessions of systematic desensitization, but others are not. The research literature is replete with examples of this sort and it is a familiar phenomenon to all therapists, regardless of their orientation or the procedures which they employ.

This variability of response to therapy among patients is probably not surprising given the diverse backgrounds, learning experiences, physiologic and biologic makeups of individuals. The ideal state would be that all members of a class of depressives or schizophrenics would respond in a uniform way to a particular treatment; that all phobics, regardless of the feared object or situation, would respond equally well to systematic desensitization. However, the ideal is rarely if ever achieved, and it must be recognized that the idiosyncratic responses of individuals are something which must be accepted as a fact of life.

Inexplicably and unfortunately, little attention has been directed towards those patients who fail to benefit from a particular psychotherapeutic procedure. The emphasis is on those who do respond, and despite the fact that in virtually every clinical research paper published there are a number of patients who do not change, or who get worse in response to the treatment, little or no attempt is made to discover why. How does one account for these failures? Too often they are simply viewed as nuisances who increase the variance of the results, thereby decreasing the probability of the overall finding being statistically significant. Not infrequently these people get "lost" or overlooked in the analysis of the data, and statistical significance of the grouped data become the *sine qua non* of the project. Differential responses within the group are ignored.

A similar problem exists in clinical practice. Regardless of the type of problem or the efficacy of the therapeutic procedures employed, various percentages of a group of clients will improve with treatment while the remainder do not. In a hypothetical case where the problem is one of simple phobias, as many as 90% might improve with the use of systematic desensitization, while 10% would not. It would be worthwhile knowing the reasons for this. What are the characteristics of this 10% which renders the treatment ineffectual? Possibly such knowledge could lead to screening procedures which would weed out the potential nonresponders; where more specific procedures could be devised. The particular characteristics of these people could be taken into account. To some extent this happens in the field of medicine: where the use of penicillin is contraindicated in some people, a different antibiotic has to be employed. The practice of psychotherapy is a long way from achieving this goal, but it is worth pursuing.

Fortunately, despite individual differences there is sufficient communality among people, or at least classes of people, to enable one to devise therapeutic strategies and procedures which are effective in the majority of cases. (If this were not so, the practice of psychotherapy would be even more chaotic than it is.)

There are three important reasons for developing new therapeutic procedures. The first is to devise a system which is efficacious for different types of problems. The second is to improve or enhance the recovery rate over existing therapies and over no treatment at all. The third is to allow for prediction of success and failure. One should be able to say in advance, with a high degree of certainty, that this patient will benefit from this treatment procedure—or conversely, that this patient has little chance of improving through use of this method.

The object of this book is to describe in some detail therapeutic procedures for the treatment of sexual dysfunction which are simple, of brief duration, and above all effective. At the same time, some suggestions will be made which will allow the therapist some measure of prediction of the potential efficacy of the treatment with given patients.

The treatment methods to be described have as their basis the general idea that the major factor which inhibits normal responses is anxiety. This is the central concept. The requirement for change, i.e., improved sexual behaviors, then becomes the removal or elimination of this anxiety. Since behavior therapy is not simply concerned with the removal of maladaptive behavior, but rather with the substitution of adaptive behavior, a response other than anxiety needs to be learned. This response is relaxation. That is, if the typical and usual response to sexual activity is anxiety, this anxiety needs to be eradicated so that the usual or most probable response becomes a feeling of calm and relaxation.

RECIPROCAL INHIBITION

This general principle is called reciprocal inhibition and the specific procedures are referred to as systematic desensitization (SD). While Wolpe (1958) is responsible for formalizing these procedures, the groundwork was laid by Watson & Rayner (1920) and Jones (1924). Most of the remainder of this chapter will be concerned with describing the use of systematic desensitization and related learning-based procedures in the treatment of female sexual dysfunction.

The principle of reciprocal inhibition, upon which systematic desensitization is based, has been defined by Wolpe thus: *"If a response inhibiting of anxiety can be made to occur in the presence of anxiety evoking stimuli it will weaken the bond between these stimuli and the anxiety"* (Wolpe, 1958).

In sexual dysfunctions, as in many other "neurotic" type disorders, there are responses which inhibit anxiety. Empirically, one of the most potent of these is deep muscle relaxation, first demonstrated by Jacobson (1938). Although there is a certain amount of controversy surrounding the role of relaxation (how and/or why it operates to inhibit anxiety, or indeed if it inhibits anxiety at all) in systematic desensitization (Cooke, 1966; Lomont & Edwards, 1967; Rachman, 1965), the fact is that empirically it works. People who have been trained in deep muscle relaxation consistently report a lessening of anxiety while in a relaxed state, improved sleeping habits, and a general change in their sense of well-being.

Originally Jacobson (1938) viewed and used muscle relaxation as an end in itself; by and large it constituted a therapeutic procedure, and involved as many as 200 training sessions. This was perhaps necessary for the purpose it served. However, in systematic desensitization, it is only an adjunct to the therapeutic procedure, albeit an important one, and therefore by necessity the amount of relaxation training is greatly reduced. Wolpe and Lazarus (1966) suggest that training be carried out over about six sessions (of 20 minutes each), with the patient then practicing at home for two 15-minute periods per day. The procedure we have adopted is, after the initial interviews, to spend about 20 minutes demonstrating the relaxation procedure, with the client going through the exercises with the therapist. The client is then instructed to practice doing these twice a day, for about 20 minutes on each occasion.

INITIAL INTERVIEW

During the initial interview the general principles of systematic desensitization are explained to the client in a way which she can understand. This means talking in everyday language without confusing her with psychological or psychiatric terminology. The explanation should cover relaxation, hierarchies, and the way in which the therapy will be conducted.

PREPARING THE CLIENT MENTALLY

One of the first things we attempt to do is to dispel the notion that the woman is alone with her problem. We point out to her that in all likelihood, 2–3 of every 5 couples are having sexual problems severe enough to interfere seriously with their marriage or sexual relationship; she does not have some unique thing wrong with her. The vast majority of women find this comforting, in a negative way. The fact that they do not suffer from a rare disorder gives them a certain amount of confidence that something therapeutic can be done for them.

Second, we attempt to explore possible reasons for her current problem. This part of the interview includes a history of her sexual behavior in the past and present and the changes, if any, that have taken place. It also takes into account her husband's or sexual partner's behavior and her feelings and attitudes towards this. If there are specific problems, e.g., no foreplay or extended foreplay, then these are discussed in some detail.

Having gained as much information as possible, we explain to the client that the basis of our treatment procedure is the general notion that very frequently women have attitudes and feelings towards sex which have, in one way or another been learned. What is required is for them to unlearn these and at the same time learn something new, a new way of behaving towards sex. The idea is that they have learned to respond to sex with anxiety, by becoming anxious and up-tight. To help them get rid of this anxiety is what the therapeutic procedure is all about.

As an example, we point out that, for some unspecified reason, a woman is unable to reach climax. She may be aware of this before she gets married, or she may discover it afterwards. Nevertheless, she continues to have intercourse without ever achieving orgasm. This results in frustration, and this frustration increases with every failure. Not only is there frustration, there is physical discomfort which lasts for quite a while after unsuccessful intercourse. (This is something many women have experienced and can understand.) We point out that women experience the same discomfort that men do when men pet for long periods of time and do not ejaculate. That, in fact, in many women this feeling is much more uncomfortable than in men. When a woman fails to have an orgasm she is frustrated, in pain and anxious. The next time she attempts intercourse, she becomes anxious because of her previous experience; she probably tries too hard and this works against her so that she probably fails again, with frustration, pain and anxiety the only result. And this process keeps repeating itself. It becomes a vicious circle. When this continues over a fairly long period of time, the woman begins to avoid sex and sexual overtures because she knows what the outcome is going to be. Furthermore, she begins to associate her misery with her husband; he becomes the source of her troubles. When this happens, the negative feelings about sex become transferred to him and this eventually makes for other problems which have nothing specifically to do with sex.

We have found that this kind of explanation is both understandable and welcomed by the client. Her problem is becoming less of a mystery to her. Most women are already aware of what the therapist tells them, although they may not have thought about it in these terms. A second objective is to suggest that the problem, severe as it may seem to them, is one which can be effectively dealt with. The feeling that they are not on a treadmill is an important motivational factor.

EXPLAINING THE THERAPY

The remainder of the interview deals with an explanation of what the therapy consists of, how and why it is done.

We explain to her the use and function of deep muscle relaxation and the relationship between relaxation and anxiety. That one of the characteristics of deep muscle relaxation is that it is incompatible with anxiety; you can't be relaxed and anxious at the same time. However, relaxation can inhibit or prevent only small amounts of anxiety. What is required is to break down the felt anxiety about intercourse, for example, into smaller pieces. We point out that usually women who are anxious about sex are not anxious only with regard to intercourse. They are anxious about a number of things or situations which lead up to intercourse. It is possible to make up a list of these situations and to rank them in terms of the amount of anxiety each would generate if they were actually experienced. A few examples are usually sufficient to make this abundantly clear to the client.

Having clarified this aspect of the procedure, we move on to teaching the client to relax discuss the hierarchy of sexual situations which bother her to varying degrees, and explain the rationale and method of treatment we will be using. This explanation is couched in fairly general terms and an example of this might be:

Once we have constructed the hierarchy and you have learned to relax, we can begin the treatment. This is simple and straightforward. All you have to do is relax in a comfortable chair and imagine, for brief periods of time, each of the situations on the hierarchy, beginning with the one which causes you the least anxiety. What happens is that when you imagine this first situation, and do this while remaining completely relaxed, any anxiety you might have felt about it rapidly disappears. It's been inhibited by the relaxation. When you no longer feel the least bit anxious about this first item, we move on to the second one on the hierarchy and do the same thing. When you no longer feel any anxiety in imagining this, we go to the third one, and so on all the way through the hierarchy until you can imagine the most anxiety-provoking item. However, by the time we get to this item, it no longer bothers you as it originally did. After imagining this a few times, you no longer feel anxious about it and your problem should be solved. That is, if *imagining* these situations does not make you anxious, neither will actually *doing* the things described make you anxious.

We assure her that although this is a relatively simple procedure, it is effective.

This, then, is an example of the type of explanation provided the woman. It may on occasion be somewhat more detailed, depending on the woman's level of sophistication and knowledge. The majority are satisfied with this; a few will ask questions or demand more detail. The therapist should be prepared for this and feel free to provide as much information as the woman wants. Too often, the clinician's attitude is that it is not necessary to burden or enlighten the client with detailed explanations. This seems to us to be an untenable position. After all, she above everyone should know exactly what will be done and why. This "doctor knows best" or "leave everything up to me and you will be all right" attitude is an archaic hangover from medicine, where all too often the patient is left in ignorance as to her problem, what is to be done about it and what the outcome or ramifications are.

In our practice we attempt to provide as much information as the patient can assimilate and we attempt to supply reasonable answers to her questions. We also point out that we offer no guarantees that we will be successful, and a principle that we consistently adhere to is to explain that we are not capable of "imposing" a cure on her; that we have no ready-made remedy, with her the passive recipient, that will solve all her problems. On the contrary, we stress that our role is to assist her in solving her own problems; that she must put some effort into this and not simply rely on us to work miracles. At the same time, we stress that when working together there is a high probability that a change for the better can be effected. We consider it important to be honest and straight-forward with our clients, but at the same time stressing the positive aspects of the therpeutic procedures. There is no question that motivation and the proper "set" or expectation of improvement is highly important in any therapeutic endeavour; of itself it won't result in change, but without it the therapist is faced with an almost Impossible task.

At the conclusion of the first interview the woman is taught relaxation techniques and is given a battery of questionnaires which she takes home, completes, and mails back. (These have been described in Chapter 3.) She is also instructed to prepare a written list of sexual situations that bother her and to bring this with her for the second session. We also arrange for her sexual partner to accompany her to the second interview.

RELAXATION TRAINING

For relaxation training the client is seated in a comfortable chair facing the therapist. As a preliminary, the therapist explains that the vast majority of people are unable to achieve complete relaxation even though they may think they are relaxed. The ability to relax must be learned, and although there are individual differences in the ability to do this and the depth of relaxation achieved, everyone can learn to do it provided they go about it the right way and conscientiously practice the exercises. The major problem in relaxation is to learn to discriminate between being relaxed and not being relaxed. Obviously one can tell the difference in being very tense and not being tense, but what is required is the ability to make finer and finer discriminations between these states. Improvement in discrimination comes about from practice; the more one practices the easier it becomes. We explain that the procedure consists of tensing individual muscle groups, concentrating on how these feel when they are tense, gradually releasing the tension and concentrating on how the muscles feel as this is being done, and finally how they feel when all the tension has been released.

The therapist then demonstrates this, with the client copying each step. Our practice is to begin with the lower extremities and work up. The muscle groups we concentrate on are the feet, legs, stomach, chest (breathing), hands, lower and upper arms, shoulders, neck, face, tongue, and jaw. Details are provided in Appendix B.

Having demonstrated these exercises once, the therapist explains that it is a simple but effective method of learning to relax and that all the client need do is to practice the exercises twice a day, for about 20 minutes on each occasion. She is told to do this while sitting in a chair and to be as consistent as possible with respect to the times of day that this is done. The object of these instructions is to get her into a routine which (it is hoped) she will have little trouble maintaining. We also explain to her that once she has mastered relaxation by following these exercises, it becomes possible to achieve this state without the exercises. That is, by simply imagining and concentrating on various muscle groups, she will be able to relax at will and in situations removed from her usual surroundings, i.e., in her home or in the therapist's office.

In the vast majority of cases the instructions we provide, coupled with the home practice, is sufficient to achieve relaxation in the patient within a week or so. We have not found it necessary to attach any mystique, such as an atmosphere suggestive of hypnosis, to our demonstration and instruction. The instructions are presented in a straightforward conversational way, without the suggestion that the woman can feel herself becoming more and more relaxed, or that she can feel the tension leaving her body, or any of the other ploys used to induce hypnotic states. Very occasionally we may use hypnosis with a woman who finds it impossible to relax in any other way, or we may employ it with women who are unable to clearly visualize the hierarchial scenes, but these are exceptions. Before resorting to hypnosis to induce relaxation, we use an audio tape containing a detailed description of the relaxation procedure, and the woman follows these instructions in her own home. Usually even the most recalcitrant woman responds to this.

Occasionally a woman will report that she has a great deal of difficulty in falling asleep at night and frequently takes medication for this. In these instances, we recommend that she practice some of the relaxation exercises when she goes to bed—at least those that are possible while lying down. Since one of the reasons for difficulty in falling asleep is tension, the ability to relax should help the problem, and many of the women who practice this report that it is beneficial. It also serves the function of teaching her to relax in the presence of stimuli which may ordinarily engender anxiety, i.e., her bedroom and bed.

This concludes the initial interview and a second appointment is made for the following week. This second session is concerned with assessing the effects of relaxation training, interviewing the partner alone and then with the client present, and constructing the hierarchy of sexual situations which will be used in desensitization.

SECOND INTERVIEW

INTERVIEW WITH SEXUAL PARTNER

As mentioned earlier, treatment of a woman's sexual dysfunction must take into account a consideration of her partner's role in the problem. For this reason, no matter what type of therapeutic procedure is to be employed, it is our practice first to discuss the problem with the man alone, and then with both partners together. In the interview with the man alone we are concerned with his views on the problem. How does he see it? What are his reactions and what effect is it having on the marriage (or relationship) in general? Are there specific things that turn his partner off? What are her responses to sexual overtures, both general and specific? What, if anything, does she do to avoid sex? How does he approach sex (what specifically does he do while he and his partner are attempting or having intercourse)? How much does he know of sexual behavior and how much does he think his partner knows? How long has the problem been present, and how did it develop (full-blown, or over an extended period of time)? Is it getting worse or remaining static? Does he consider himself an important factor in the problem, and if so, in what way? What has he or his partner (or both) done in attempting to alleviate the problem? Does he have any information or suggestions as to the source of the problem? How frequently do he and his partner have intercourse, and what changes have taken place in the frequency? What are his partner's views on birth control and pregnancy? How would he describe the problem, e.g., aversion, indifference, disgust? Does he consider the problem to be a serious one? Is there good communication between him and his partner? To what extent will he cooperate in helping to solve the problem?

These are the major areas we explore with the male. What we attempt to do is acquire as much relevant information as possible. Frequently the man will mention things that the woman has forgotten or neglected to tell us. In general, the object is to get as clear a picture of the sexual relationship as possible. We are also interested in significant inconsistencies between what he says and what his partner says.

During this interview we encourage the man to ask questions and we attempt to clarify the picture for him. We explain the nature of his partner's problem and why we think she behaves the way she does. We attempt to dispel any doubts he may have as to the reality of the problem, pointing out that his partner has no control over her antisexual behavior, and that it is not something which will go away "if only she would put her mind to it" (a not uncommon view in husbands). We explain in detail the nature of the treatment: what we will be doing, what his partner will be doing and what we expect of him—including a holiday from sex while the treatment is being conducted. This occasionally elicits groans of apparent anguish which we frequently find astonishing and inexplicable but which probably reflects the perversity of human nature. Why do men who have been having dramatically unsatisfactory sex complain so bitterly at the prospect of being deprived of it? It becomes even more confounding when the partner agrees with them. One couple, for example, postponed treatment because they were going for a week's holiday and could not possibly abstain from sex during this period, despite the fact that both found it extremely unsatisfying, frustrating and a cause of brutal quarrels.

The joint interview with both partners is concerned with laying down the ground rules for the behavior of each during the treatment period, what they are to do and what not. The therapeutic program is reiterated, and great emphasis is placed on following instructions implicitly. The couple is again encouraged to ask questions both of the therapist and of each other. If any peripheral problems or areas of concern are expressed, attempts are made to resolve these. The therapist also explains that successful treatment of the problem requires a good deal of effort on *their* part; the therapist will be able to assist them, but they must be prepared to cooperate and expend some energy in the process. They cannot sit back and wait for something miraculous to happen.

HIERARCHY CONSTRUCTION:

A cursory reading of the literature on systematic desensitization suggests that constructing anxiety hierarchies is a simple, straightforward task. That is, if it is explained to the client what is required she will be able, without too much difficulty, to methodically list 30–40 sexual situations which cause her varying amounts of anxiety. Then all that remains to be done is to list these in hierarchic order. Nothing could be further from the truth. In practice, one of the most difficult aspects of desensitization is the construction of a hierarchy which is a true reflection of how the woman feels and which zeros in on the problem.

A number of factors contribute to this difficulty. There is, first of all, the problem of securing a sufficient number of discrete sexual situations which can be rank-ordered in terms of their anxiety evoking potential. Despite the fact that the woman may have had the problem for years, she is frequently at a loss to describe the situations which cause her anxiety. This is not surprising since she tends to view the problem as one exclusively concerned with intercourse. This is the activity which she considers to be the major, if not the only problem. Frequently her response to the question, what is the problem and what aspects of sexual behavior bother you? Is "Intercourse; if I didn't have to go through that everything would be fine." It is only when it is pointed out to her that intercourse is only the end product of a whole series of other sexual behaviors that she begins to recognize and associate the preliminaries to intercourse as part of her problem.

A second troublesome factor is finding and describing anxiety arousing situations which can be rank-ordered so that the difference in anxiety evoking potential between items is fairly consistent. It is usually not too difficult to find situations which result in a great deal of anxiety, i.e., intercourse, and situations which cause only minor amounts, i.e., sitting in the same room with her partner. With a little probing, most women can supply these. The problem arises in filling in the gaps between these two extremes.

A third problem is simply arranging these items, once they have been elicited, in proper and accurate hierarchic order. Following Wolpe and Lazarus (1966) we make use of "subjective units of disturbance" (SUDS), where a SUD is the subjective difference between items on the hierarchy. Having made up a list of 30–40 items which cause the woman anxiety, we say to her: "What I would like you to do is read through this list; imagine, as clearly as you can, that you are in each of these situations, and select the one which would cause you the greatest amount of anxiety." The woman does this and we say: "All right, we will give that one the value '100.' Now do the same thing again, but this time find the situation which would cause you the *least* amount of anxiety." When this has been done we say: "We will give that item the value 'one.' Now we have the two extremes, and what I would like you to do is go through the entire list and try to give each of the other items a value between one and 100, in terms of how anxious you would feel if you were actually involved in each of the situations described. Remember, each item can be given any value between one and 100."

On the face of it this would appear to be a relatively simple task. In practice, though, it doesn't work out this way and one frequently ends up with a bimodal distribution, a hierarchy in which there are large gaps in the middle with items clustered at the extremes. To be useful and effective, additional items are required to close this gap. This can usually be accomplished by questioning the woman and suggesting to her possible additional items.

There are a variety of dimensions which are relevant. Time, for example, is one. A woman will usually feel more anxious as the time for intercourse approaches. Anticipation twelve hours in advance is less traumatic than anticipating it two hours hence. This in turn will be less than when she is preparing for bed. This is also the case with respect to menstruation. Imagining intercourse and situations related to intercourse at the beginning of menstruation are usually less anxiety evoking than the same situations imagined during the last menstrual day.

Frequency of intercourse is another such variable. Many women will react differently to the same situation if it occurs once every two weeks rather than twice a week. That is, if they imagine having intercourse after two weeks abstinence, they may feel less anxious than if they imagine the same thing after having had intercourse 2–3 days previously. But to confound the problem, the reverse may be true.

A third dimension is circumstance. The less likely that the sexual activity will lead to intercourse, the less anxiety it evokes. Having her breasts fondled when her husband is soon going to work, or when company is expected, is less anxiety arousing than if this were done when there was nothing to prevent the act being carried through to completion. A woman may have no compunction about sitting on her partner's lap at a party, but would never consider doing this when they were home alone.

These, then, are some of the dimensions along which particular situations may be varied in order to insure a hierarchy which will be appropriate and where the items are fairly evenly spaced in terms of SUDS.

Unfortunately the difficulty does not stop here. Even after the hierarchy has been completed, the therapist may discover, to his dismay, that when the list is being presented during the desensitization sessions, items which are ranked fairly low on the hierarchy, in fact evoke a great deal of anxiety; conversely, items which are high elicit very little. This inconsistency appears to arise from at least two sources. The first is that the response to the same sexual situation, for a given woman, varies from time to time. (On one occasion, imagining having her breasts touched causes a good deal of anxiety. On a second occasion, the same thing results in little anxiety.) This can be clearly demonstrated by presenting the items typed on individual cards and allowing the woman to arrange these in terms of the anxiety each evokes, on a number of occasions over a period of two or three weeks. Different orders of sorting result over sessions. It seems likely that two variables are the way the woman feels at the time she is doing the ranking (happy and optimistic versus sad, depressed, and pessimistic), and the context in which she imagines each situation. She may feel confident and imagine the situation as she would like it to be, or she may be in despair and imagine the situation as it actually exists (and with which she has had a good deal of experience).

Whatever the cause, situations like this arise. The therapist must be prepared for them and add, delete, or alter the order of items as the situation demands.

It is our practice to have at least thirty items on a hierarchy. This is more than the norm and some may be redundant. Nevertheless, it is our feeling that it is better to be redundant within the hierarchy than to run the risk of sensitizing the client by presenting items which evoke inappropriate amounts of anxiety.

A sample of hierarchies is illustrated in Appendix B.

THIRD INTERVIEW

DESENSITIZATION FORMAT

The first thing on the agenda for the third meeting is to have the woman complete the card sort, as described in Chapter 3. This is repeated at the start of every session, and provides an ongoing assessment of her anxiety level as therapy proceeds.

Following the card sort, the session is devoted initially to determining the degree of relaxation the woman is able to achieve. This is done in the room where desensitization will be conducted. Our procedure is to have the woman recline in a lazi-boy type chair in a semi-darkened room which is free from outside noise and distraction. We ask her to get comfortable and to concentrate on relaxing her muscles, beginning with her feet and legs, and working up her body. In essence, this is a replication of what she has been practicing. Next we request that she think of something pleasant—for example, that she is lying in a field on a warm day watching the clouds drift by. After a few minutes, we ask her how she feels; does she feel warm, calm and relaxed? In the vast majority of cases she will report in the affirmative. From her statements of how she feels and from our own observations, it's possible to decide that she is or is not relaxed. Our experience has been that when a woman reports that she is calm and relaxed, then she very likely is. There is no reason to believe that she is less able to determine this than she is to recognize that she feels anxious and tense.

The actual desensitization procedure is simple and straightforward. If we are convinced the woman can relax reasonably well, we explain that what we would like her to do is to visualize or imagine as clearly as possible each of the hierarchic situations as these will be described to her. She will be doing this for increasingly longer periods of time. She is told to remain completely relaxed and calm while doing this. If she feels that she is becoming tense, anxious, or nervous she is to immediately raise her right index finger. Under no conditions is she to continue imagining these situations if she feels herself tensing up, since this will add to the problem.

Once the instructions are clear, the woman is asked to close her eyes and to concentrate on becoming completely calm and relaxed. We allow one to five minutes for this, depending on our subjective impression of how well she is relaxed. With practice, the therapist can make a fairly reliable judgment by observing the patient's legs, hands, and face. Mentally compare the facial expression of the patient with that of someone sleeping, where the facial muscles are relaxed and the features loose with the mouth slightly open. Obviously if she is sitting with her hands clenched and frowning, she is not relaxed.

When the patient is in this relaxed state, the first item on the hierarchy is presented. Taking the first item from a possible hierarchy, we would say: "I want you to imagine, as clearly as you can, that it is 8:30 in the morning. Your husband has his coat on and is preparing to leave for work. You lightly kiss him just prior to his going out the door. Try to get as clear a picture of this as you can. If you begin to get anxious or tense, simply raise your finger."

If the woman does not signal anxiety, we allow her to imagine this scene for 15 seconds. At this point, we say: "All right, now stop thinking about that; think about clouds drifting by, and relax." After about 30–60 seconds, the instructions to think about the hierarchic item is repeated. This time, in the absence of anxiety, the woman visualizes this scene for 30 seconds and then is instructed to stop, think of the clouds etc., and to relax. This procedure is repeated four additional times, for 30 seconds, 45 seconds, 60 seconds and 60 seconds, so that the minimum amount of time spent imagining the scene is four minutes.

If at any time during visualization of the scene the client signals that she is becoming tense or anxious, she is immediately told to stop thinking about the scene and to concentrate on the peaceful, nonanxiety arousing situation. When she is once more relaxed, the item is again presented. This procedure is repeated until she can imagine the hierarchal scene for the prescribed periods of time (15, 30, 30, 45, 60, 60 sec) without becoming tense or experiencing anxiety. Usually, we allow 30–60 seconds between presentations, but this could depend on how long the woman requires to achieve relaxation after having become tense or anxious.

Within the general systematic desensitization paradigm, the amount of time we have the woman imagining each item is long. Wolpe and Lazarus (1966) mention 5 seconds as the usual time, but this can vary from 1–2 seconds to 15 or more, depending on the reaction of the patient to the item and on the complexity of the scene. Our system, because we have a larger number of items in the hierarchy and hence a reduced number of SUDS between items, allows us to present each item for a much longer period of time. That is, the amount of anxiety generated by each individual item is less with a longer hierarchy.

Having successfully confronted the first item on the hierarchy, we allow about a minute, while the woman thinks about the nonanxiety scene, before beginning the next item on the hierarchy. The same procedure is repeated and this continues until all the items on the hierarchy have been dealt with. As a rule, we cover four or five items on each occasion, but again this depends on the individual woman. If she experiences no anxiety while imagining the items, it's possible to deal with five items. On the other hand, if she repeatedly signals anxiety it may be possible to deal with only two.

Problems Encountered

One of the problems encountered here is how a woman interprets and tolerates anxiety. Some woman will signal anxiety when they feel the least twinge; others will continue to visualize a scene even though they are experiencing some small amount of anxiety and tension. In the absence of physiologically monitoring their autonomic responses, there would appear to be no way around this obstacle. Fortunately though, in practice this is of little significance apart from increasing the number of sessions required to complete the hierarchy.

Occasionally a second problem is that of getting "hung up" on a particular item. Repeated presentations of a certain item may continue to elicit anxiety, even with brief exposure. This may arise, as mentioned earlier, because the way a woman feels about a particular situation has changed since the hierarchy was established. At this point the therapist can do one of two things: 1) He can proceed to the next item, and if no difficulties are encountered with this, reintroduce the troublesome item at a later date. 2) He can break down the problem-item into smaller segments, establishing a new mini-hierarchy with this item in its original form as the most anxiety evoking item. This is sometimes referred to as "branching off."

For example, the item might be: "You are in bed with your husband, he is caressing you and inserts his finger in your vagina." This act could be conceivably viewed as the end product of a series of other behaviors and a mini-hierarchy might then be:

1. You are in bed with your husband. He is caressing your stomach.
2. You are in bed with your husband. He is caressing you over your pubis. Your legs are together.
3. You are in bed with your husband. He is caressing you over your pubis. Your legs are apart.
4. You are in bed with your husband. He is lightly caressing your genitals.
5. You are in bed with your husband. He is lightly caressing your genitals and you can feel his finger at the entrance to your vagina.
6. You are in bed with your husband. He is lightly caressing your genitals and you can feel the tip of his finger in your vagina.
7. You are in bed with your husband. He is lightly caressing your genitals. His finger is partially inserted in your vagina.
8. You are in bed with your husband. He is lightly caressing your genitals. His finger is completely inserted in your vagina.

By reducing the complexity of the original item it is usually possible to overcome the problem.

One way of minimizing the occurrence of this problem is to establish a new hierarchy at the beginning of each treatment session, using the original items. Although it is time consuming, this can be done by having each item on the original hierarchy typed on a three-by-five card and allowing the woman to sort these, in terms of their anxiety evoking characteristics, prior to each therapy session. While this reduces the probability of encountering problems of the kind described, it is no guarantee they will not arise.

Our practice is to conduct the therapy sessions at least twice a week and preferably three times a week. Empirically at least, this schedule has proven to be the most effective as well as the most efficient.

ADJUNCTS TO SYSTEMATIC DESENSITIZATION

It is useful to have the woman practice desensitization at home between therapeutic sessions. Give her typed descriptions of the hierarchical items which have already been dealt with in a therapeutic hour, and instruct her to review these by herself in the same way it was done by the therapist. This is really a procedure for reinforcing her earlier nonanxious behavior.

We instruct her to imagine each of the items (beginning with the least anxiety evoking) while in a completely relaxed state, and to continue to do so until she can do it with utmost ease and no sign of anxiety or tension. Having done this, she is to proceed to the next item and repeat the process, and so on. To ensure that the client will not become inappropriately anxious while doing this exercise, we begin it only after the second therapeutic session, and the items which she is to practice are the ones from the first session. She is always practicing items which have already been presented by the therapist.

Most women can do this without too much difficulty, although occasionally one will report that she finds it impossible to function on her own. One solution is to enlist the aid of her partner, having him present the items to her in the same way the therapist would. Initially this may prove embarrassing to one or the other or both but usually, with perseverance, this will disappear.

One of the virtues of having the man involved in this aspect of the treatment is that it brings him face to face with the issue. By going through the hierarchy with his partner he not only has a much better appreciation of the general problem, but also of specific situations which cause his partner anxiety. This frequently comes as a revelation to him. This makes him more sensitive to what she is experiencing and also provides a basis for discussion of the problem; it frequently leads to an examination of their relationship, both sexual and nonsexual. This in itself is worthwhile, since a lack of communication is often one of the characteristics of couples experiencing sexual problems.

A variation on the above procedure (Madsen and Ullmann, 1967) is to involve the man in a more active role in the entire therapy program. That is, he is present during construction of the hierarchy and becomes responsible for the desensitization proper; he presents the items to his wife. The authors suggest that there are additional advantages to this procedure. These include: allowing the partner to invest something of himself in the therapy; reducing or alleviating his anxiety as to what is actually transpiring between his wife and the therapist; increasing the degree of generalization from therapy to nontherapy situations with a concomitant change in his sexual behavior *viz a viz* his wife.

Madsen and Ullmann also suggest that there be no proscription against intercourse during the time therapy is being carried out. They suggest, in essence, that sexual behaviors between the partners parallel the advances being made in dealing with the hierarchy. That is, the couple engage in sex to whatever degree the client strongly desires, but anything she objects to be avoided. In theory this is a good suggestion; in practice it does not always work out in the anticipated manner.

We proscribe a hiatus in intercourse, and sexual advances in general, while therapy is being conducted. Our reason for this is to avoid the possibility of resensitizing the wife to sex; this has happened in our practice. The problem that arises from Madsen and Ullmann's suggestion is inherent in the procedure. They advocate that the couple engage in sexual behavior only to the extent that the wife finds this pleasurable, discontinuing if she begins to feel anxious or upset. While this procedure may present no problem for the woman, it frequently results in a great deal of dissatisfaction for the man.

The situation is one where the couple are engaging in sex play, with the male not unnaturally becoming increasingly sexually aroused, while his partner suddenly withdraws, explaining that she is becoming nervous and tense. For the man, this can be extremely frustrating and annoying. At this point there are a number of possible courses of action:

1. He may insist on continuing and carrying the act through to its conclusion.
2. He may discontinue, angry and frustrated.
3. His wife may smother her feelings, assure him that everything is fine, and continue through intercourse.
4. He may accept the situation and cease his sexual advances with neither overt nor covert recriminations.

The last of these possibilities is the only appropriate one; however, it is the one least likely to occur. All the other options will only exacerbate the problem. If the man ignores his partner's pleas and carries on, she will become anxious and angry—which will not only cause immediate problems, but may also nullify any therapeutic progress which has been made. Furthermore, once the act is completed, the man may feel guilty and to alleviate this, berate her for being less than a woman, cold and unfeeling. She will react to this charge and so on *ad infinitum*. If he adopts the second approach, his anger and frustration will be readily apparent to his wife and this prepares her for a similar reaction in retaliation. The third option is the one frequently taken. The woman grits her teeth while disavowing that there is anything wrong, and accedes to intercourse. At this point in time men are easily fooled (or hear only what they want to hear), and so they uncritically accept what she says, continue the sex act and are genuinely surprised when, at the conclusion, their partners are in tears and refuse to speak to them unless perhaps to graphically point out their abysmal lack of sensitivity.

All of this, then, is the reason we strongly suggest that the couple not engage in sex play or intercourse while the therapy is being conducted. However, there are exceptions to this rule which are invoked when the possible advantages outweight the possible disadvantages. The next section examines this issue.

IN VIVO DESENSITIZATION

In vivo desensitization is a procedure whereby the hierarchic items are presented in a real life situation rather than through the medium of imagination. Instead of the woman imagining her partner kissing her or engaging in some other activity, the couple actually do this in the privacy of their home. The preliminaries are exactly the same as in the usual desensitization–relaxation training, hierarchy construction, and explanation of the theory and rationale behind it. However, in addition, great emphasis is placed on rigidly following directions.

Prior to embarking on the therapy, partners are interviewed together, with the discussion focusing on the problem: why the problem exists, how it is maintained, what is required to remedy the situation, and the man's role in the therapeutic procedure. It is pointed out, as convincingly and as forcefully as possible, that any deviation from the prescribed procedure is likely to have a deleterious effect; it will exacerbate the problem and prolong the treatment. It is explained to the man that while we appreciate the frustration that is bound to result from the treatment, this is transitory and the long term gain more than compensates for the immediate inconvenience. We emphasize the difficulties he has experienced in the past, that in the absence of change these will probably worsen, and that he must be fully committed and acceptable of a certain amount of inconvenience and discomfort. The object is to make the man graphically cognizant of the nature of the problem, emphasize the importance of his behavior towards his partner, and to secure a commitment from him that he will do nothing which would be detrimental to the therapy.

This may appear to be harsh and belaboring the obvious, but men in the heat of passion do not always behave in rational ways, and from our experience the more this is reinforced the fewer difficulties will arise.

The actual procedure involves the couple being seen by the therapist approximately once a week. At this time they are given five cards, each containing a description of one item from the hierarchy. These are numbered in terms of their anxiety evoking potential. They are instructed to practice the behaviors described, beginning with the lowest ranking, and to continue this practice until the woman feels completely comfortable and free of anxiety. As in the usual desensitization procedure, they are instructed to approach each of these in a gradual way, i.e., for increasingly longer periods of time (15, 30, 30, 45, 60, 60 sec) unless the woman begins to feel nervous or anxious, at which point they stop the behavior, wait until she again becomes relaxed, and then continue. Once the anxiety for that behavior has been eliminated, they move on to the next and so on until all five items (behaviors) can be carried out in the absence of anxiety. Under no conditions, no matter how sexually aroused they may become, are they to proceed farther than the descriptions on the cards. It sometimes happens that the woman will be in a particularly good mood, become aroused and hence overly optimistic, and either overtly or covertly encourage her husband to continue his sexual behavior past the point where she has begun to experience anxiety. From here it's all downhill and a familiar pattern: not wishing to disappoint, she allows him to proceed, becoming increasingly anxious and filled with self-recriminations at the end. The possibility of this happening must be recognized when this procedure is used.

Usually a week is sufficient to complete the five items, at which point the couple returns for a meeting with the therapist to discuss progress and any problems which may have arisen. They are complimented on their progress and given the next five items with the same instructions. This procedure is continued until all the items have been dealt with.

To assist in this home practice program, we have prepared a mimeographed booklet which the couple can refer to at home. It explains the entire procedure, including the theory and rationale, and contains data sheets where practice sessions can be recorded and problems noted. This booklet is particularly helpful in situations where it is not possible for the woman to attend the clinic on a regular basis; where a woman has difficulty in imagining or visualizing the described scenes; where hypnosis is impossible or ineffective; where imagining the situations results in no anxiety; or where there has been an obvious failure of the imaginary procedure to generalize to real life situations.

VIDEO DESENSITIZATION

We have developed a variation on the usual verbal desensitization procedure which has proven highly effective (Caird and Wincze, 1974; Wincze and Caird, 1973, 1976). The hierarchy is presented *visually* instead of having the woman imagine a *verbally* presented situation. While completely relaxed, she is shown the situation on a television monitor and requested to imagine that she is the actress and her husband the actor on the screen.

There are precedents for this approach. Visual aids, in the form of slides, movies, and video tapes have proven effective in reducing fears when these have depicted models engaging in the feared or phobic behavior (Bandura, Blanchard and Ritter, 1969; Bandura and Menlove, 1967; Hill, Liebert and Mott, 1968; O'Connor, 1969; Woody and Schauble, 1969, a,b). However, none of those studies dealt with sexual dysfunction; furthermore, the paradigm was one of modelling and not desensitization. The major distinction between these two procedures is that in our use of video tapes, specific attempts are made at counter-conditioning through deep relaxation.

The study by Obler (1973), mentioned earlier, incorporated visual aids as an adjunct to the usual desensitization treatment. However, since the investigation was confounded by a variety of treatment variables, it is impossible to determine whether or not their use significantly affected the outcome. The study by Wincze and Caird (1973) left little doubt that the use of video tapes is highly effective in reducing heterosexual anxiety in women, and this was reflected in improved sexual attitudes and performance. Nine out of ten women contacted 3–18 months after treatment reported much or very much improvement in their sexual activities.

PROCEDURE

Video desensitization is virtually identical to the usual desensitization described in the previous section. Interviews, relaxation and hierarchy construction follow the same format. It is only after the hierarchy has been established that the procedure changes. We select the video film, from a library of 140 films, which corresponds to each item on the hierarchy. The tapes themselves were produced by the authors, employing professional actors. They range in heterosexual complexity from a couple standing in a living room talking, to nude intercourse. That is, they include most aspects of normal heterosexual interactions. Many are duplicate situations, but one will have the male the aggressor, while a second will show the woman initiating and assuming the dominant role. Each of the scenes is four minutes in length and they are on 10 minute Sony video cassettes, two to each cassette.

The therapeutic procedure whereby these hierarchic scenes are shown to the woman is essentially the same as in the usual systematic desensitization. She reclines in a lazi-boy type chair, about six feet away from a 25-inch TV monitor in a semi-darkened room, and becomes completely relaxed. It is explained to her beforehand that she will be seeing a couple engaging in normal heterosexual behavior of the kind that comprise the hierarchy, that each of the individual scenes will be shown in segments, and that each segment will be on the screen for increasingly longer periods of time. She is to imagine herself in the position of the woman on the screen, and to imagine the man to be her partner. She is to remain completely relaxed and calm. If she begins to feel anxious or tense, she is to signal by raising her finger and the film will be stopped. Under no circumstances is she to continue to view the scene while tense and anxious.

As in the desensitization described earlier, the film is shown for 15, 30, 30, 45, 60, 60 seconds with about 30–60 seconds between segments, provided no anxiety is experienced. If at any time she signals anxiety, the film is stopped, rewound, and that particular segment repeated until all anxiety associated with that scene has been dissipated. The therapist remains in the room, operates the cassette player, and answers any questions that might arise in the course of the session.

Once a particular scene has been viewed completely without anxiety, the next scene on the hierarchy is shown. Usually there is a 1–2 minute break between scenes. This is necessary in order to change cassettes and it also allows the woman an opportunity to concentrate once again on relaxing. She is instructed to close her eyes during the times the film is not on the screen and to think about clouds drifting by or some equally soothing and calming situation. This procedure is repeated until all the scenes have been viewed. Usually the presentation of four or five of these constitutes a therapeutic session, although there is some variability here. Frequently, despite the care in constructing the hierarchy, the early situations are tolerated with little or no anxiety while the later, more sexually explicit ones, do cause some tension and anxiety and hence progress is slower.

Occasionally, problems arise in using some presentations, and women have to be screened. For example, one woman we had been working with for a long time on genital touching procedures, reported that she felt perfectly comfortable with this procedure and was eager to view a video tape of female masturbation. The video tape chosen was a widely distributed tape on this subject, entitled "Shirley." Halfway through the film the woman client was observed to be gripping her chair tightly, and the tape was turned off. The client began crying, having experienced a very strong anxiety reaction both to the woman in the film and to her masturbatory behavior. The client stated that the woman in the film was disgusting and she was now convinced that masturbation was too. We no longer use this film, although we have spoken to other therapists in the field who find the film useful.

EFFICACY

What makes the video procedure so effective as an anxiety reducer? It seems likely that one important factor is that the woman is seeing a couple engaging in sexually intimate behavior which quite obviously they are enjoying. The actors show no obvious stress or anxiety and the entire situation is one of relaxation and enjoyment. A second important difference may be that the visual presentation brings home, as the imaginary one cannot, the reality of the situation: that sexual behavior is normal behavior and should not be fraught with anxiety. Third, the films serve an educational function. They demonstrate to the woman what heterosexual behavior is all about; it obviously is not simply a matter of coitus. Intercourse is only the culmination of a long series of behaviors, which are in and of themselves pleasurable. This has come as an astonishing revelation to some women. Finally, many women can readily identify with the woman on the screen; they can project themselves into the situation much more easily and realistically than is possible through imagination alone.

Rationally, it would appear that the effectiveness of this procedure derives from modelling (Bandura et al., 1969; Bandura and Menlove, 1967) and/or reciprocal inhibition, depending on the circumstances under which the procedure is carried out. If the films are shown without any attempt to inhibit anxiety by relaxation, then any therapeutic change might be attributable to modelling. If, on the other hand, the woman views the scenes while relaxed (following the usual SD paradigm), then the effects are likely due to reciprocal inhibition. We have employed both of these procedures.

There is subjective evidence to give these suppositions a certain validity. Women have remarked that the couple are quite clearly enjoying themselves, that what they are doing seems perfectly natural, and that they themselves are not shocked or disgusted by this display of intimate sexual behavior (although they may have expressed some trepidation at the start). They have commented on the fact that they can easily put themselves (and their partners) in the place of the actors, despite the fact that there may be no physical resemblance whatsoever. And they have expressed the view that they have really learned something from the films. The cumulative effect of these factors is impossible to determine but, subjectively at least, they appear to contribute to the overall result.

Some of the problems encountered in standard desensitization are met here too, but these can be dealt with as previously described.

VARYING VIDEO DESENSITIZATION

As in the verbally presented desensitization, there can be variation in the video procedure. One such variation is to have the partner sit with the woman in the treatment room and operate the cassette player. (This might be utilized where the woman being treated is deaf or where there is a language barrier (Caird and Wincze, 1974).) The only major modification required here is to explain in detail to the partner what his role is, what he is to do, and how to operate the cassette player. Where we have used this technique, the therapist's role becomes one of discussing with the couple (before and after each session) problems which they may have experienced, and selecting in advance the tapes to be used during each session. The usual injunction not to engage in sexual behavior during treatment also obtains here.

Another variation, which has met with limited success, resembles that described earlier for the *in vivo* desensitization procedure. In this instance, following Madsen and Ullmann's (1967) suggestion, the man assumes the role of primary "therapist" and the couple are instructed to practice at home the behaviors they have witnessed during the therapeutic sessions. Recognizing the inherent dangers of this, as explained earlier, it is strongly and repeatedly emphasized that during their home practice sessions, they proceed no further than what they have been exposed to visually. They are provided with written descriptions of each filmed situation which they use as guidelines and as a reminder just how far they are to proceed. Once again the therapist becomes an advisor rather than an active participant in the on-going therapy.

Even where this kind of treatment has worked, some qualification is required. Where the woman and her partner follow the instructions, and where they complete the therapy sessions and the home practice, the results are reasonably good but not impressive (Lange, 1974). The major reasons for failure are complex. A strong candidate for the villain is a couple's negative attitude towards a type of therapy where there appears to be no therapist. Such couples tend to terminate therapy before completion.

PATIENT-THERAPIST RELATIONSHIP

At this point one should consider the context of the "healing professions": the accepted role of the "healer" *viz a viz* the role of those seeking help. These roles have been shaped and defined by tradition and have become part and parcel of European and North American culture. They have grown and been fostered by the medical profession, including psychiatry. The essence of this belief is that there are those who require help or assistance of one kind or another, whether it's purely medical or psychiatric. Then there are those whose job it is to provide this assistance with a minimum of discomfort to or active involvement of the patient. That is, a potential patient presents herself to a doctor, the doctor in turn decides what the problem is, prescribes and supervises a course of treatment, while the patient becomes the passive recipient upon whom procedures are imposed. This is what clients expect and how they view the role of the doctor or therapist.

Deviations from this standard practice are therefore difficult for patients to accept; it requires a whole new way of viewing the therapists' role and clients' responsibilities. It comes as a shock to recognize that she, the patient, is a person responsible in varying degrees for her own behavior, and must demonstrate this in concrete terms, putting forth some effort on her own behalf. She cannot rely on the doctor or therapist to impose a cure while she sits back, passively, awaiting a solution to her problems.

This latter attitude is frequently and graphically demonstrated by women who plaintively exclaim, "If there were only a pill I could take to cure my sexual problems!" Alas, if it were only possible. It also seems likely that interacting with this phenomenon is the mystique attached to the therapist. By virtue of being a "professional," the assumption (often unwarranted) is that something significant and perhaps magical will come about. After all, unless the therapist was effective, then he or she would not be doing what he or she is doing. It is quite clear that the placebo effect operates in pyschotherapy just as it does in physical medicine.

It is for these reasons that we believe many women stop treatment prior to completion. They expect an intimate relationship with the therapist, and believe that through *his* ministrations a cure will be effected. When this is not forthcoming, when their expectations are not met, they rapidly become disillusioned, disgruntled, and convinced that the whole thing is a waste of time.

While these appear to be the major sources of difficulty in using this strategy, it is possible that the criticisms of the Madsen and Ullmann (1967) procedure, raised in an earlier section, also contribute to failure—particularly in those cases where the couple complete the required number of therapeutic sessions.

We have learned from our research into sexual dysfunctions that women (and their partners) are not always truthful in reporting what goes on at home, what progress they believe they are making, and if they are following the therapist's instructions. Undoubtedly some falsification results from a desire to please the therapist. However, in others, lack of motivation leads to neglect of the instructions and deliberate falsehoods to conceal this. Another possibility is that the sexual partners may not be accurately reporting or carrying out the therapist's instructions, simply through misinterpretation or lack of understanding. For example, one couple repeatedly reported a failure of the woman to achieve climax in the female superior position. However, this was not surprising when we learned that the woman was lying on her back on top of her partner!

Another possible explanation for failure using the home program may be that it is simply a bad model, even if applied correctly. The use of home practice alone may result in the therapist being led astray as to the true nature of the problem. That is, he may be missing the target. But whatever the reasons, this kind of approach does not appear fruitful and an educated guess would be that any therapeutic endeavour which attempts to dispense with the therapist will meet with only minimal success.

GROUP TREATMENT AND MASSED PRACTICE

Other procedures which we have tried are treating women in small groups, and compressing the treatment time from 2–3 weeks (spaced practice) into a two-day period (massed practice). Both of these procedures have been used in the treatment of phobias (Paul, 1966; Ramsey, Barends, Breuker and Kruseman, 1966; Suinn, 1968, Robinson and Suinn, 1969; Suinn and Hall, 1970). Degree of success has varied. In general, the group treatment has proven effective (Paul, 1966), while the massed practices approach has shown to be less so (Ramsey et al. 1966). However, none of these studies was concerned with sexual behavior and the results were equivocal enough to warrant further investigation.

ADVANTAGES AND DISADVANTAGES

There are clear-cut advantages in using groups and in reducing the treatment time involved. There are also disadvantages. An obvious advantage is that it is possible to increase the number of women a single therapist can deal with in a given period of time. Considering the magnitude of the problem, in terms of the number of women affected and seeking treatment, this is an important consideration. Probably the majority of therapists in the area of sexual dysfunction have long waiting lists, and in fact find it impossible to treat all the women seeking help. Therapeutic groups would appear to be a way of solving this problem or at least mitigating it. An example of the current inefficiency of present practices is the report by Masters and Johnson (1970). They report treating 790 cases over an 11-year period, and this includes 448 males; only 342 females were treated—an average of 31 per year. While we point this out, it is not intended to denigrate their work or to detract from its value, but simply to stress that a more efficient system is required. In the final analysis, the value of any therapeutic procedure stands or falls on its availability to those requiring it.

The same problem arises with other forms of therapy, including systematic desensitization; there are limits to what a single therapist can accomplish. Therefore, any procedure which promises to alleviate this problem is worth considering.

A second advantage in treating groups is that it brings together women who share a common problem. This demonstrates concretely that theirs is not an isolated case; that there are other women experiencing the same difficulties in their sexual lives. There is a certain heuristic value to this. Unlike men, women in a group of this kind rapidly form friendships (at least temporarily) and are much less restrained in discussing their problems among themselves. In contrast to men, women appear to feel much less threatened by their problem; they do not, at least in discussing their sex lives with other women in the group, view their particular problem as reflecting on their womanhood. They seem better able to cope intellectually with their sexual difficulties and they are obviously more frank than men in their discussions. From a male point of view, it's astonishing the degree to which they will confide in comparative strangers and compare notes about their own and their partner's sexual behavior and shortcomings. This communality of interest appears beneficial during the actual desensitization procedure. There is less tension and anxiety manifested while viewing the scenes, and some of this undoubtedly results from their discussion between scenes. There is quite likely social pressure as well which inhibits the display of anxiety. (This may or may not be beneficial.)

This free interchange between members of the group is not universally true; some women remain isolated from the rest of the group and do not become seriously involved at a verbal level. However, these tend to be exceptions.

A disadvantage of this group procedure is that it is impossible to present individualized hierarchies. Our solution to this problem has been to devise a "general" hierarchy of 42 scenes, based on the frequency with which these resulted in anxiety in a test group of women. That is, we selected 55 scenes which, on the basis of previous experience, were the most commonly used. A description of each of these was typed on a 3" × 5" card and we had a group of clients (N-10) individually sort them in terms of the amount of anxiety (SUDS) each would engender if the woman were in the situation described. This provided us with ten hierarchies, each containing the 55 items. There was a good deal of similarity among these and from them we constructed a single composite hierarchy arranged in terms of the frequency with which each appeared at a particular place in the 10 hierarchies. Since there was redundancy in terms of SUDS, among these, 13 scenes were dropped and the remaining 42 constituted the hierarchy used in the group treatment. No difficulties were encountered in use which was probably attributable to the number of scenes used and therefore the low SUDS difference between adjacent scenes.

A study was carried out using this general format (Reith, Caird and Ellis, 1974, 1975). The women were randomly assigned to one of five groups: 1) Group massed practice (GMP); 2) Individual massed practice (IMP); 3) Group spaced practice (GSP); 4) Individual spaced practice (ISP); 5) Control–crossover.

Individual treatment means that each woman was treated singly by an experienced behavior therapist. Group treatment refers to treating women in groups of four. In massed practice, the treatment was compressed into two consecutive days. In spaced practice this was carried out over a three-week period involving two weekly sessions for a total of 6. The control group was interviewed, given the pre-test questionnaires and the relaxation training, and then told that they could not be seen for treatment for three weeks. At the end of this period all were reassessed and randomly assigned to one of the four treatment groups.

The format for treatment for the GMP women consisted of their reclining in lazi-boy type chairs, formed in an arc, about 10 feet from a 25-inch television monitor. The therapist with the TV playback machine was in a control room, connected to the experimental room by a two-way intercom; the women were clearly observable through a one-way screen.

Following a five-minute period when the woman become comfortable and relaxed, the first scene on the hierarchy was shown, again in segments of 15, 30, 30, 45, 60, 60 sec. The instructions for signalling anxiety, and the procedures in this eventuality, were the same as previously described.

The procedure for IMP was identical, except that the women were treated singly.

In the GSP, the format mirrored the GMP with the exception that treatment was spread out over 6 sessions. In practice, approximately 7 scenes were shown on each occasion, regardless of how long this took, although this never exceeded an hour and three-quarters —and then only during the final two sessions where the behavior displayed on the screen was highly intimate and involved, and resulted in some anxiety in a few of the women.

The ISP followed the traditional desensitization procedure, the major difference being that the number of sessions was, as in GSP, carried out over a three-week period with eight scenes being viewed during each therapeutic session.

The massed programs were usually conducted on the weekend, with 22 scenes being viewed on the first day and 20 on the second. Each session lasted from 10 AM to 4 PM, with a break for lunch.

The two main findings, so far as therapeutic outcome is concerned, are that improvement, in terms of increased sexual contact and enjoyment, was greatest in the GMP and ISP groups, 87% and 89% respectively. Less improvement was demonstrated in the GSP and IMP groups, 57% and 60% respectively. We consider these results important, since they suggest that sexual problems can be dealt with in groups, using a much abbreviated treatment time, with an outcome as good as that obtained using individual spaced practice, the most common procedure currently in use. If these results can be replicated it would clearly be a forward step in the treatment of a pressing problem.

An additional and unanticipated finding in this investigation was that of 20 inorgasmic women treated individually, using spaced practice, 15 were orgasmic at a three-month follow up. Since the investigation was primarily directed at reducing heterosexual anxiety, with little attempt made directly at improving orgasmic functioning through masturbatory training, these results are impressive.

A possible explanation for this finding is that the women were much better educated and came from a higher socioeconomic background than those in the earlier investigations (this study was carried out in Vancouver, BC). The women included teachers, nurses, and the wives of professional and business men. It is interesting that over and above the increase in sexual satisfaction, many of the women reported that the video scenes were "instructional" and had lead to fuller and more varied sexual behaviors.

LIMITATIONS OF SYSTEMATIC DESENSITIZATION

The assessment procedures we use involve measuring assertiveness, generalized fears and degree of "neuroticism." Desensitization does not result in long-term changes in these measures, despite the fact that heterosexual anxiety is reduced and sexual performance improved. In general, it would appear that it may be most effective only with the target behavior of heterosexual anxiety. However, the data are conflicting on this point. Some women become orgasmic even though the treatment was not directed to this end. Again, the socioeconomic level may be a factor to consider in this result, as we have seen from the work of both Kaplan and Masters and Johnson.

Another problem in the use of desensitization is that the woman undergoing treatment must be able to visualize clearly the described scene—or, if the video procedure is used, be able to effectively put herself in the position of the woman on the screen. Not all women are capable of doing this. And while hypnosis might be used here, it adds to the time and complexity of the procedure and certainly would not be feasible in a group treatment situation.

An additional obvious disadvantage in using the video technique is simply that video tapes depicting various stages of heterosexual behavior are not at this time widely available. Obviously every therapist cannot produce films, as the production cost is impressive, to say the least. In addition, there is the cost of the equipment necessary to show video films. (The cassette player which we use costs about twelve hundred dollars, plus about four hundred for the monitor.)

Given that the stimulus material was available, a partial solution would be to use 8MM film and a projector which uses film cassettes. This can be purchased (in 1976) for approximately two hundred dollars. However, the problem of suitable film remains. While there is no shortage of stag films, these are clearly not appropriate and would probably have the opposite of the desired effect. A possibility would be to edit sexual films, selecting those portions which depict the desired behavior and eliminating the more novel material.

Another alternative (Obler, 1973) would be to use 35MM slides. In that study, the author used slides in cases where the client experienced difficulty in imagining a particular item. This, however, was only an adjunct to standard systematic desensitization and did not provide the basis for therapeutic intervention. Nevertheless, even with this minimal use of visual material, success of treatment was impressive; 11 of 13 women and 7 of 9 men became sexually functional, with a concomitant reduction in heterosexual anxiety; these gains were maintained at an 18-month follow-up. A second investigation (Lehman, 1974) describes in some detail a procedure using slides to initiate orgasm and improve sexual functioning in general. The results of the treatment in five women were that two experienced their first orgasm, a third reported a loss of guilt feelings over masturbation, a fourth discovered an increased pleasure in masturbation which generalized to sexual behavior with her husband, and the fifth woman lost her feeling of disgust and "nausea" over masturbation.

The seeming disadvantages of this video technique may be less serious than they appear. A great deal, probably the majority, of the work being carried out in the treatment of sexual dysfunctions is being done within universities or foundations of one kind or another. The research, of which therapeutic change is a logical by-product, is being financially sponsored by government or private funding agencies. This makes it possible for the researcher–therapist to deal with financial problems in ways which would not be possible if he or she were acting as a private practitioner. It allows one to produce one's own films and to purchase the equipment necessary to make use of them. The crunch comes when the psychiatrist or gynecologist or psychologist in private practice wishes to do the same. Then the cost becomes prohibitive, and by necessity one will be compelled to make use of less-sophisticated material. However, Obler's study indicates this may not be significantly less beneficial.

SUMMARY

A major variable which affects success or failure in the treatment of female sexual dysfunctions is individual differences—which, unfortunately, cannot be controlled for in any meaningful way. The importance of these differences cannot be overestimated. However, recognition that they exist makes it possible to devise therapeutic strategies which might minimize their influence.

In this chapter we have discussed various procedures for reducing heterosexual anxiety. The major focus has been on systematic desensitization and its variations, including video desensitization. Certain procedures are necessary for effective interviewing, so that the client is mentally prepared to receive the maximum benefit from therapy. Relaxation training is important.

Hierarchy construction is all important, but can be difficult. The therapist cannot rely on common sense as a guide in this, and only by close questioning of the woman can an accurate hierarchy be achieved. Even then there is no guarantee that it will not require modification during therapy sessions.

The details of systematic desensitization proper have been outlined in such a way that it should be possible for someone relatively naive in the area to use it as a guide to therapy. Some of the pitfalls one may expect to encounter have been enumerated, and it is hoped this will make the therapist's job a little easier.

Some of the procedures we have discussed are only minimally effective. For example, having the husband act as the primary therapist. We have offered possible reasons for his lack of effectiveness. The sexual partner is important, however, in relation to a woman's problem, and there are definite things the partner should and should not do.

A fruitful approach, from a therapist's point of view, would be to treat women in groups and to concentrate the therapeutic program in two days of marathon sessions.

5

Male Sexual Dysfunction: Treatment

The treatment of male sexual problems has many of the same therapeutic components discussed in Chapter 4 for the treatment of female sexual dysfunction: complex sexual behaviors are broken down into simpler components and practiced in hierarchic steps, relaxation is taught, communication of sexual feelings is encouraged or reestablished, education in matters of sexual behavior takes place, pressure to perform sexually is relieved, and anxiety is reduced. These major factors make good therapeutic sense for both treatment of male and female sexual problems. Above and beyond these common essential ingredients are a number of other components which may be crucial in the treatment of gender-specific sexual problems.

Desensitization seems more commonly used for the treatment of female than for male sexual dysfunctions, but evidence for its effectiveness in treating males is also available (Wolpe, 1958; Lazarus, 1965; Friedman, 1968; Kraft and Al-Issa, 1968; Garfield, McBrearty and Dichter, 1969). Indeed, we use this procedure efficaciously. The more common use of desensitization with women may be because female sexual problems often involve sexual anxiety similar to phobic reactions. Many women clients are fearful of men in general, of the male penis, or of penetration, to such an extent that their reaction resembles a phobia. Adult males, on the other hand, are rarely fearful of females in general, or of female genitals, or of penetrating (although the first frank look at a woman's genitals has proven a great shock to many an adolescent). Males are most often fearful of failing to adequately perform sexually. While desensitization is used with the performance fear, *in vivo* practice sessions are usually quicker and more effective with men.

This chapter will discuss treatment of male sexual dysfunction, and Chapter 6 will discuss problems and obstacles to treatment. Both chapters should be read carefully, since treatment is invariably plagued by obstacles. The vicissitudes in dealing with men can be as troublesome as those encountered in women.

INTERVIEW: SETTING THE STAGE FOR THERAPY SESSIONS

Following careful assessment procedures, the therapist should have a solid basis for describing the sexual problem and mapping out a therapy program. In a behavioral approach to therapy, the emphasis is placed on the "here and now," and the therapist obtains more specific problem-oriented information once the course of therapy is explained to the client. For example, if sexual anxiety is the major problem, then the therapist must extract detailed information from the client concerning all aspects of his anxiety experience. On the other hand, if technique is a problem, then the therapist must obtain details of a couple's approach to, participation in, and behavior after sexual relations.

In addition to obtaining more detailed information at this time, the therapist should outline for the clients the approximate time course of therapy and other possible therapeutic options. We feel that it is also important to advise clients that very often people resist the therapy because it is uncomfortable. Some people skip appointments, while others fail to practice assignments. Clients are encouraged from the onset of therapy to discuss their feelings of discomfort directly with the therapist, rather than to subtly sabotage the therapy effort.

Clients are also told at this time that they must not engage in sexual activity beyond that which is suggested by the therapist. Sexual intercourse is prohibited until the therapist feels that it is appropriate for the couple to progress to this stage in relations. Many couples tend to disregard these instructions and end up participating in, or attempting, intercourse during practice sessions. To guard against this, the therapist must warn his clients against such temptation. Furthermore, clients must be specifically and clearly informed *why* intercourse must be postponed until the therapist feels they are ready. The major reason for this instruction is to help the couple avoid yet another disturbing sexual experience, which may heighten anxiety and prolong treatment. Secondarily, abstinence from intercourse also serves to reestablish important preliminary sexual behaviors, and reduces pressures to perform.

Following the introductory interview, the therapy program can be started.

HIERARCHY CONSTRUCTION, RELAXATION TRAINING AND DESENSITIZATION

We have found that it matters very little whether a client is a male or female when applying a desensitization procedure. The considerations and techniques of hierarchy construction, relaxation training, and desensitization format are basically the same for men as for women. One very important difference, however, is apparent in the content of hierarchy scenes. Males are sensitive to the demand characteristics of sexual involvement, and often report female sexual aggression as the key stimulus for evoking anxiety and sexual failure. Some males feel very comfortable in their own performance as long as their female partner is an impassive participant. A slight hand movement on the back of the neck, a sound of encouraged sexual pleasure, or a verbal expression of sexual desires, have all been identified as female aggression by a number of our male clients. Any one of these seemingly benign behaviors by a woman has triggered loss of erection in some of our male clients. Because of this important consideration, hierarchy scenes are often constructed in an order which recognizes male/female sexual aggression as important stimuli. Following is an example of a complete hierarchy used in video desensitization therapy with a male client complaining of loss of erection. The client was a 40 year-old, middle-class businessman with a high-school education. He was unmarried, but had a steady girlfriend who participated in the therapy process with him.

Hierarchy, Mr. B: Scenes 1–7: Male aggressor
1. Male and female fully dressed; male puts arm around female and kisses female.
2. Male and female fully dressed; male fondles female's breasts over clothing.
3. Male and female fully dressed; male kisses female and fondles breasts inside of brassiere.
4. Male and female in underwear, talking to each other in bedroom.
5. Male and female in underwear in bedroom; male embraces female and kisses her.
6. Male and female in underwear lying on bed; male fondles female's breasts.

7. Male and female in underwear lying on bed; male fondles female's breasts and caresses genitals over panties.

Scenes 8–20: Female aggressor

8. Male and female fully dressed; female caresses male's penis over clothing.
9. Male and female fully dressed; female caresses male's penis inside fly.
10. Male and female in underwear in bedroom; female caresses male's penis inside underwear.
11. Male and female nude in bedroom, talking; female holds male's hand.
12. Male and female nude in bedroom; female kisses male.
13. Male and female nude in bedroom; female embraces male.
14. Male and female nude in bedroom; lying on bed touching each other on legs, back, stomach—sensate focus.
15. Male and female nude in bedroom, lying on bed; female caressing male's back and buttocks.
16. Male and female nude in bed, guiding male's hands over her body; breast and female genital touching.
17. Male and female nude in bed, embracing, and male fondling breasts and female genitals; female encouraging male's touching.
18. Male and female nude in bed; female touching penis and masturbating male.
19. Male and female nude in bed, mutual genital caressing; female encouraging intercourse.
20. Intercourse.

Mr. B was a typical client complaining of loss of erection. His anxiety was minimal when he was the aggressor, but it increased sharply when the female became the sexual aggressor. Mr. B had the most difficulty with scenes 8 and 9, the very first aggressive movements of the female fondling the male penis. Once Mr. B was able to comfortably view scenes 8 and 9, he did not signal anxiety during the remaining scenes. Mr. B reported obtaining an erection with his girlfriend for the first time in over a year, following completion of his seventh therapy session (at this point in therapy he had completed scenes 1–17). He continued to show progress throughout therapy, and at a six-month follow-up, reported no further problems.

TREATMENT OF SPECIFIC PROBLEMS

LOSS OF ERECTION AND LACK OF AROUSAL

As discussed in Chapter 2, psychogenically caused impotence resulting in loss or lack of erection is one of the most common and devastating male sexual problems. Fortunately, there are a number of treatment approaches boasting of high therapy success rates. Systematic desensitization was the first behavioral approach for treating this problem (Wolpe, 1958). A number of other researchers have followed Wolpe's lead, and have presented supporting evidence for the effectiveness of this therapeutic strategy for the treatment of impotency (Friedman, 1968; Jones and Park, 1972; Kraft and Al-Issa, 1968; Lazarus, 1965, 1969; and Obler, 1973). For the most part, systematic desensitization is used in conjunction with other procedures, and there are few controlled tests of its efficacy. Usually, it is combined with thought stopping, sexual reeducation, practice in sexual assertion, practice in graded sexual behaviors, and strict instructions to refrain from sexual intercourse during the therapy program. Garfield, McBrearty and Dichter (1969) and Lobitz and LoPiccolo (1972) have presented comprehensive treatment programs for impotency which combine a number of behavioral procedures in a "package."

The behavioral "package" approach seems to be highly effective, and indeed the Masters and Johnson (1970) treatment approach for impotency is also a "package" program. Most contemporary sexual therapy programs which claim to be efficient and effective for the treatment of impotency, whether they are strictly behavioral in nature or more eclectic, have three essential ingredients:

1. Reeducation: This can be new knowledge about communication, sexual technique, sexual attitude or sexual functioning.
2. Redirection of sexual behavior: Almost all therapists inform the male not to concentrate on his erection. He is told not to attempt intercourse, and that it does not matter if he achieves an erection or not. It is only important that he and his partner are comfortable with what they are doing sexually.
3. Graded sexual exposure: In both Masters and Johnson type programs and behavioral programs, a hierarchy of sexual behaviors is constructed and presented to the client. Clients may practice graded sexual behaviors either in imagination, as in systematic desensitization, or they may practice the behaviors directly with their partners. Our own program for most impotent male clients combines both visualization (either video presentation or imagination) and direct practice.

The results for the most part are very encouraging, and the outlook is especially so if a male has a capable and willing female partner to work with.

One other technique that is often used in cases of male impotency is the technique of "stuffing." In this procedure, the female sits astride the male, who is lying on his back, and his flaccid penis is placed or stuffed into the vagina. The purpose of this procedure is to demonstrate to a couple that penetration is possible even if the male does not obtain an erection. Moreover, since penetration can occur without erection, performance anxiety is lessened, which may in turn lead to erection. Clinicians recommending this procedure often report that erection occurs during containment following stuffing, thus leading to increased confidence on the part of the male. To make the insertion more comfortable, a water-base lubricant is advised for couples using this procedure.

PREMATURE EJACULATION

Systematic desensitization has not been extensively used as a mode of therapy for premature ejaculation, however, there are a few studies which have reported its successful application in the treatment of this frustrating problem (Ince, 1973; Kraft and Al-Issa, 1968; Obler, 1973). Since ejaculation is a sympathetically controlled function, the use of desensitization to lessen anxiety and sympathetic arousal is a logical treatment approach. Desensitization usually includes hierarchy items such as approaches to sexual behavior, participation in sexual behavior, and also sexual failure. Anxiety over sexual failure, i.e., premature ejaculation, is usually the most readily identified problem and usually is rated high on the hierarchy. Examples of sexual failure hierarchy items are:

1. You are involved in sexual foreplay with your partner and she begins to stimulate you in the genital area. You suddenly lose control and ejaculate in her hand. Your partner turns away from you. She is angry.
2. You are about to have sexual intercourse with your partner and as you attempt insertion you have an orgasm.
3. You are about to have sexual intercourse with your partner and as you attempt insertion you have an orgasm. Your partner says in a disgusted voice, "Can't you ever hold back?"
4. You are about to have sexual intercourse with your partner. You insert your penis and as you begin to move your hips you lose control and have an orgasm. Your partner says, "You can never satisfy me."

Few therapists use systematic desensitization for the treatment of premature ejaculation without adjunct procedures. A typical therapy program attempts to define for the man and his female partner what premature ejaculation is. Many couples are surprised and enlightened to learn that the definitions of prematurity vary widely and, in fact, some couples even discover that what they felt was prematurity may be considered normal. One couple we dealt with, for example, presented a complaint of prematurity only to discover that the problem was more properly defined in terms of a female orgasmic dysfunction. The male was engaging in intromission for periods of up to 10 minutes before ejaculating, but since his partner wasn't experiencing an orgasm the couple defined the problem as premature ejaculation. In defining for the couple what prematurity means, the focus and goals of treatment can be clearly understood by the couple and the therapist. This goal may differ from couple to couple.

The next step in a comprehensive program usually involves a reorientation of the couple's approach to sexual behavior. In almost all cases of prematurity that we have dealt with, the couple has adopted a number of self-treatment procedures (outlined in Chapter 2) which are self-defeating. These self-defeating behaviors usually are vain attempts to distract attention from arousal and orgasmic sensations. The therapist directs the couple to reverse their thinking and concentrate specifically on preejaculation sensations. The ejaculation should be enjoyed rather than dreaded, the sensations leading to ejaculation should be attended to rather than ignored, and sexual contacts should become more frequent rather than avoided. This last point is especially important, since there is considerable clinical evidence that abstinence from sexual contacts usually increases loss of ejaculatory control.

Couples sometimes express doubts that such a redirected focus of attention is possible, especially if they have found some of the self-defeating behaviors to work in terms of delaying orgasm. However, when carefully questioned about enjoyment of sexual contacts, including distraction, the male readily admits that it isn't very enjoyable and hasn't really worked, since he is still seeking help. The therapist should also emphasize that control can only be achieved if a man is in touch with all his bodily sensations.

Many couples also believe in the myth that sex can only be fulfilling if both partners reach simultaneous orgasm during coitus. A male, therefore, may attempt to hold back, letting himself ejaculate only if he detects his partner's approaching orgasm. Few males ever consider continuing in coitus after they reach orgasm. Most males feel that once they reach orgasm, the sex act is over; even if they wish to continue, they feel they are physically unable to. Ejaculation does reduce sexual motivation in a man. Detumescence, however, is a slow process in some males and a firm erection may be maintained following ejaculation. There is no reason why many men cannot continue active coitus following orgasm. Even if detumescence occurs during coitus, the penis can still be contained in the vagina, and sufficient pelvic movement can continue to bring the female partner to orgasm. Men must be told two facts: 1) orgasm for both partners does not have to occur simultaneously during intercourse, and 2) intercourse can continue following their own orgasm.

In some men, the penis becomes very sensitive following intercourse and they may find continued intromission irritating or painful. However, even this irritation varies greatly, and the experience on one occasion should not preclude other attempts at continued coitus following orgasm.

Once males are told to practice continuation, it often proves to be a rewarding experience. A great deal of the pressure to perform is removed with the knowledge that they can still bring their partner to orgasm even if their own orgasm occurs very quickly after penetration.

The third part of a comprehensive treatment approach usually involves practice in genital stimulation, concentration on physical sensations, and application of the Semans procedure (Semans, 1956) or the squeeze procedure (Masters and Johnson, 1970). The

Semans procedure, developed by James Semans, focuses the client's attention on his penile sensations during genital stimulation and ejaculation. The procedure demands that the client and his partner stimulate each other in the genital area until the male experiences sensations which are premonitory (warning) to ejaculation. The man at this point removes his partner's hand until the sensations totally disappear. This procedure is repeated over and over until the man feels that he can control his ejaculatory response for an adequate period of time.

Masters and Johnson have developed a variant of this procedure by instructing the client to squeeze the head of his penis (or have his partner squeeze) in addition to pausing when ejaculation seems near. The squeeze occurs by placing the thumb on the frenulum and the first and second fingers on the superior (upper) surface of the penis. The man or his partner then squeezes the head of the penis very hard for a period of time, and then pauses until the preejaculation sensations disappear. The amount of time suggested for the application of the squeeze may vary from therapist to therapist. Masters and Johnson suggest a squeeze for three to four seconds, but other therapists in the field advise anywhere from 10 to 45 seconds. It is not clear if the squeeze adds anything to the Semans procedure—both procedures seem to work very well if practiced conscientiously.

Once control is achieved by direct genital stimulation, then practice in penetration is suggested. Couples are usually advised to practice coitus using the female superior position, since less pressure is on the penis in this position and hence less chance of loss of ejaculatory control.

There are several commercial films demonstrating the squeeze technique which are graphically good, but the language used in these films is best for the college-educated client. We have used both commercial films and video tapes which we produced for demonstrating the squeeze technique. These films are usually of value for understanding the procedure; however, as mentioned in the previous chapter before showing them the therapist should explore very carefully both the client's and his partner's attitude toward exposure to films of sexual activity. If the couple are not properly prepared for viewing the films, the scenes can be misinterpreted as pornography or considered disgusting. The films should be introduced as medical illustrations and the contents explicitly explained beforehand.

PREMATURE EJACULATION COMBINED WITH SECONDARY IMPOTENCY

A man who has repeatedly experienced premature ejaculation and has engaged in self-defeating treatment for a period of time, will very often develop loss of erection. In the most chronic stage, the male will ejaculate without achieving an erection. The therapist is then faced with the problem of which dysfunction to treat first. Fortunately this is not a difficult choice, since there is a great deal of commonality in the treatment of both dysfunctions: reeducation, dyad communication, relaxation, graded sexual exposure and practice.

When both impotency and premature ejaculation are combined, the therapist is usually faced with a serious problem of long standing duration, and it is advisable to spend time on reeducation and communication with the couple. Often self-defeating behaviors and communication problems have developed into patterns which lead to continual disappointment. Therapy must concentrate on sexual reeducation and redirection through techniques such as sensate focus. Through this approach the male may begin to experience erections before attention has turned at all toward premature ejaculation. If, however, sensate focus exercises lead to ejaculation, then therapy may concentrate on ejaculatory control.

In our experience, men complaining of both impotency and premature ejaculation are especially unassertive with their sexual partners and with women in general. The initial joint interview with the therapist is often completely dominated by the female, who complains and answers for her partner. Even when urged to respond for himself, the male often gazes at his partner first to check her nonverbal communication.

As therapists, we have experienced frustrations with unassertive people. It is easy to fall into the same communication pattern as the wife, and begin to ignore the male client. The therapist may find himself or herself addressing all of the questions to the more dominant, assertive female partner and explaining the therapy to her, and asking her approval about therapy procedures and scheduling. Naturally, the therapist must not fall into this trap. From a very early point in the therapeutic relationship, the therapist should identify this pattern as a potential problem. He should then program not only assertive verbal training, but assertive sexual training as well. Also, the therapist should punctuate this training with an effort to value the unassertive person's opinion, and reinforce any assertive behavior.

Because of the usual chronic nature of dual dysfunction complaints, therapy often proceeds slowly, with an initial concentration on reeducation and dyad communication before focusing more directly on sexual behavior. The most immediate suggestion a therapist can make to such a couple is to encourage, in fact, demand of the couple that they do not attempt to engage in sexual behavior until advised to do so. Even if the couple hasn't attempted sexual relations for a number of months, this instruction is often met with eager acceptance.

The treatment outcome for males presenting dual dysfunction is not as encouraging as for singular dysfunctions. The reason is mainly because a dual dysfunction usually represents a more long-standing trouble, and one which is more likely to be complicated by severe interaction problems. If couples stick out the treatment regime, and if therapists are clever and possess inexhaustable energy, such couples can be treated in long-term therapy. The mere presence of a dual dysfunction, however, does not necessarily dictate a poor prognosis and long-term intensive therapy. Annon (1976) suggests that before involving any couple in long-term, expensive sexual therapy, a brief approach should be attempted. Each client must naturally be judged on his own merit and not *a priori*. Some clients whom on first glance appear recalcitrant, may latter become the most responsive and rewarding people to work with.

PROBLEMS OF DELAYED OR RETARDED EJACULATION

The understanding of ejaculation problems may be helped by conceptualizing the ability to control ejaculation along a continuum, with both ends of the spectrum out of control: those who cannot delay ejaculation on one end, and those who are unable to ejaculate on the other. While Kaplan (1974) sees delayed ejaculation as a more common problem than do other therapists, the chronic case of total inability to ejaculate intravaginally is undoubtedly rare. Most experts agree that these more chronic cases are often merged with deep neurotic problems. Masters and Johnson (1970), Friedman (1973), and Shusterman (1973) point to cases of deep-seated fears associated with delayed ejaculation. Whether or not it is necessary to remove such fears or work through such fears for amelioration of the delayed ejaculation is not known. However, there are scattered cases reported in the literature of successful treatment of this problem using behaviorally oriented approaches (Annon, 1976; Cooper, 1969; LoPiccolo, Stewart and Watkins, 1972; Masters and Johnson, 1970).

There seem to be two schools of thought in treating this problem behaviorally. The problem may be approached, on one hand, more or less as one would treat the lack of orgasm in a female. That is, one assumes a great deal of performance anxiety, and treatment follows the line of graded sexual exposure and desensitization (Ranzani, 1972). On the other hand, the problem may be approached as one would approach premature ejaculation, and advise the male to participate in genital stimulation sessions with his partner in order to direct physical stimulation and heighten sensations. Unlike the treatment for premature ejaculation, however, there is no pause or squeeze when sensations near a peak. Rather, stimulation is continued through to orgasm. LoPiccolo and Annon both suggest the use of imagination as part of this procedure. That is, as orgasm approaches, the male is instructed to imagine intravaginal intercourse with his partner. Masters and Johnson do not couch the processes of their treatment approach in conditioning terminology, but do argue that through repeated masturbation of the male by the female, the female will become associated with pleasure. This association (classical conditioning?) presumably will disinhibit the male from holding back in future sexual encounters.

Further suggestions for treatment involve gradually including the female in intravaginal orgasm by moving from manual stimulation to insertion of the penis just prior to orgasm. Eventually insertion occurs earlier and earlier in the procedure, and the female thrusting becomes demanding to the point where orgasm is occurring intravaginally on a regular basis. As mentioned earlier, the use of water-base lubricants will heighten sensations and avoid irritations.

Questions certainly remain as to the best treatment approach for this problem. Since heightened anxiety is agreed upon as a factor in premature ejaculaion, it seems logical to assume that complete apathy may be operating as a factor in delayed ejaculation. Case histories of males with this problem, however, usually contain evidence of high degrees of anxiety. Our current understanding of the physiological and cognitive controlling mechanisms of this problem is certainly far from clear. In heroin addicts and methadone-maintenance patients, one of the most common complaints is delayed ejaculation and loss of libido. Studies have shown that in methadone-maintenance patients, there is a marked reduction in serum testosterone levels compared to normal controls (Cicero, 1975; Sagar, 1976). Similar studies have not yet been conducted with males not on drugs who are also experiencing delayed ejaculation. This might be an interesting area for future research.

Adjunct Treatment Procedures: Video Tapes

With a number of male clients we have used video tape programs, both for purposes of demonstrating techniques such as the "squeeze," and for purposes of desensitization. Males much less frequently than females signal anxiety during desensitization procedures. Some male clients report that it is difficult to imagine demand characteristics experienced in real life situations while watching video tapes (in spite of our instructions to try to visualize themselves in the video scenes). The anxiety reactions reported by males have, as mentioned earlier, always been associated with aggression on the part of the female models. Males never signal anxiety over specific sexual acts, as females do.

It is difficult to say if males who have benefited from video desensitization procedures have benefited from anxiety reduction or from graded exposure and modeling. Certainly there is not the same level of anxiety in males as is evident in female clients. Women seem to work through their anxiety during video desensitization with repeated exposures. Men rarely require repeated exposures and tend to race through the hierarchy. Our experience has been that while video procedures are good adjunct treatment techniques for males, coupled with graded *in vivo* practice, used alone the procedure has not been successful.

Men seem to benefit greatly from the technical demonstration films. One advantage in working with a man is that sexual films rarely produce the anxiety reactions seen in women. They are, of course, more likely to have viewed stag films and have received peer support for this. Most of our female clients have not had similar experiences with pornography.

Biofeedback

Technical advances since 1970 have led to the development of feedback instrumentation for displaying penile changes (Laws and Pawlowski, 1973; Pawlowski and Laws, 1974). Research now looks at biofeedback of penile changes as both a feasible and useful adjunct treatment of male impotency (Herman and Prewett, 1974), although we are still in the initial stages of exploration in this area. The control procedures necessary for good scientific studies of biofeedback processes in human organ systems make research very difficult. It is almost impossible, for example, to completely rule out cognitive and striate muscle mediation in most studies. In purely applied terms, however, the penile biofeedback studies by Herman and Prewett have opened the door for new therapy approaches. The practical usefulness of penile biofeedback will be determined by rigorous research over the next five years.

INAPPROPRIATE TREATMENT PROCEDURES

Almost all of our male clients have engaged in self-treatment or have sought prior professional treatment for their sexual problems. All too often they have experienced only marginal help, or no help at all; at times their experiences have been bitterly disappointing and have shaken their confidence in themselves and in their doctors. It is hoped that this section will provide some guidelines for avoiding fruitless treatment approaches. We can advise on what *not* to say to clients seeking help, and what *not* to do for them.

Nerve Pills

Many of our less-articulate male clients have been told by doctors that their sexual problems are results of their nervous conditions. The remedy is almost always tranquilizing drugs or "nerve pills" (as clients are so likely to say). When one's "nerves" are bad and one is receiving "nerve pills," the conceptual understanding in the client who accepts this explanation is low and unpredictable. A client may believe that his nerve endings are damaged or that his brain is functioning incorrectly. At any rate, the client told that he has a nervous condition is left with little understanding of his problem, and no practical solution.

There may be many men presenting sexual complaints whose problems are secondarily related to general anxiety and who derive some benefit from tranquilizing drugs. All too often, however, this is a short-sighted solution, leaving the client untreated and perhaps more worried than before. The trouble with the prescription of medication for male sexual problems is that it is often done routinely and without detailed sexual histories being taken. There is no question that many physicians feel uncomfortable or inadequate asking questions about a client's sexual behavior and, therefore, are content to deal with the problem quickly and superficially. Clients very often detect the therapist's cursory treatment of them and are left with bitter experiences. Some therapists do not even attempt to treat the problem with drugs, and simply tell their clients that nothing can be done. This is one of the most devastating tactics a physician can employ, and serves no useful purpose. A number of our male clients were told this, but continued to search for a solution. The physician should have said, "I'm sorry, but *I* can do nothing for you. However, there are therapy procedures to help men with sexual problems, and I'll refer you to a doctor who can help you."

Condoms or Anesthetic Ointments

A number of our male clients attempted to reduce their penile sensations by applying anesthetic ointments to the penis or by wearing several condoms. This was their treatment for premature ejaculation. Most of the men who have tried this approach have hit upon it themselves, or through friends or advertisements in men's magazines. One such advertisement, for example, advises men that they can "linger longer" by using Linger Cream. Such products are of little value since, as pointed out earlier, the most effective treatment focuses the male's attention on his arousal sensations rather than trying to blot them out. Female partners often object to the use of condoms, because of the artificial sensations.

Sex With Therapist

There have been a number of reports in newspapers exposing the unethical practice of some therapists who have suggested or carried out sexual relations with their clients. The rationale behind their client-oriented sexual activity is couched or bedded in therapeutic terms. A therapist might argue that he or she alone is sensitive enough, or aware enough of a client's emotional and sexual hang-ups to deal with the sexual problem. Certainly it is obvious that a client could greatly benefit from a sensitive and intelligent approach to sexual relations. In almost all cases, the client's partner has not provided this approach and may be difficult to change. The dilemma of how to provide a successful sexual experience to a sexually distressed client is a real problem, but the answer is not found by including the therapist in his or her own bag of tricks. Such practice is most assuredly unethical, and not condoned by any professional organization. There is no guarantee that the therapist is a good player as well as coach, but more importantly, such unethical practice may be seriously harmful to a vulnerable client. If there is any suspicion that a therapist is suggesting sex with his or her clients, then that therapist should be avoided like the plague—or one of the social diseases.

In cases where sexual relations have occurred between a therapist and client, it has almost always been between male therapists and female clients. It is, of course, quite possible that relations could occur between a female therapist and a male client, although most likely such an arrangement would be suggested by the client.

In reputable centers for the treatment of sexual dysfunction the problem of how to deal with reorientation to sexual activity is solved in a number of ways. Certainly, if there is a sexual partner available, one should work very closely with that person. In cases where there is no sexual partner available, some centers have used surrogate sexual partners to help with the therapy process. The use of surrogates has raised a few eyebrows and is certainly of serious ethical concern, but it is, nonetheless, standard practice in several institutions. More definitive rulings on this practice may be in store in the near future.

SUMMARY

This chapter has presented a number of therapy approaches to various male sexual dysfunction complaints. Certainly there are common ingredients in the therapy treatment of both men and women. The procedures which have been discussed are largely applicable to problems which would fall into the category of primary, or essential, sexual problems. Problems of a secondary nature, which are part of more complex interpersonal difficulties, usually involve more long-term therapy solutions. Communication may have to be dealt with, basic respect or love for one's partner may be of concern, or even conflicts with homosexuality may be contributing to the observable symptoms. In these more complex cases, it is unlikely that efforts to treat the sexual difficulties will meet with success unless the underlying problems are dealt with as well. The experienced therapist must make a judgement concerning what problems interact with the sexual problem and what problems should be treated first.

6

Problems in Treatment, Female and Male

In every therapeutic endeavor problems will be encountered which will make therapy difficult, prolonged or in some cases impossible. But sexual dysfunctions pose their own peculiar difficulties, largely because they are an interaction of two people. And even though the therapist is dealing mainly with only one, the other, by virtue of his or her existence, intrudes in the therapeutic procedure. It is the object of this chapter to describe some of these problems and to attempt to demonstrate how they might be solved or mitigated. Some are peculiar to women, some to men, and some to both.

A basic problem, usually evidenced at the first interview, may be simply communicating with the client: talking in terms he or she understands. The therapist will make little progress (or sense) if he or she tries to discuss the clitoris, masturbation, foreplay, erection, vagina, coitus, intercourse, orgasm, climax, ejaculation, or genitals with a client who does not know what these terms refer to. One might just as well be speaking in a foreign language. So, one of the first things to do is to make sure that client and therapist are talking about the same thing and, where necessary, explain the meaning of these terms. Unfortunately, this is often easier said than done. To explain what masturbation or orgasm is, to a woman who has never experienced either of these, is no simple task. To discuss or describe coitus, penis, and vagina with a semi-literate man is to confound him beyond belief. Familiarity with a variety of synonyms for these terms and the ability to use them without embarrassment is a prerequisite to effective communication. An additional and valuable aid in explaining sex to the uninitiated or anatomically ignorant is a medical model of the male and female genitalia.

FEMALE DYSFUNCTIONS IN MARRIAGE

THE HUSBAND AS AN INTERFERING VARIABLE

In the treatment of women, a major source of trouble which interferes with or prevents effective therapy is, as one might suspect, the husband. The very one who stands to gain the most (apart from his spouse), from having his wife become an effective and gratifying sexual partner, is frequently the most serious impediment to achieving this goal. Unfortunately his nonadaptive behaviors, which can take many forms, are much simpler to catalogue and describe than to explain. But perhaps by describing the behaviors of some husbands, the reasons for their feelings, attitudes, and actions will become somewhat more explicable.

THE NONINVOLVED HUSBAND

First of all, too many husbands tend to view the problem solely as their wives'; she is the one who dislikes sex, who is nonorgasmic, who cringes when he approaches her, and so on, and therefore there is undoubtedly something wrong with her. One gains the impression from talking with some husbands that they view their wives' problems as they would were she suffering from a physical ailment. If his wife has appendicitis, why should he see the physician? Clearly it has nothing to do with him; he is not responsible for the ailment, nor is he equipped to deal with it. The extent to which they hold to this view largely determines the degree of cooperation the therapist can expect.

THE UNCOOPERATIVE HUSBAND: THE CHAUVINIST

Some husbands, for example, flatly refuse to be interviewed. This type completely absolves himself from his wife's sexual problem and says to her, in effect, "It's your problem, you do something about it. Don't involve me, but let me know when you're cured." His is a truly chauvinistic attitude and no amount of cajoling, either from the therapist or wife, will change his mind.

The effect of this attitude is first to deprive the therapist of a valuable source of information, and second, to prevent him from explaining to the husband the nature of the problem and what will be required of him if his wife's sexual behavior is to be altered for the better. More importantly, in the absence of knowing what his wife is attempting to achieve and how, the husband's behavior, sexual and otherwise, often remains unchanged—which either prevents or seriously impedes therapy. We have had more than one husband call us on the telephone, extremely aggressive and belligerent, wanting to know if we have told his wife that they are not to engage in intercourse for three or four weeks. And if so, by what right are we interfering with *his* sex life?

Attempts to have such men come in for an explanation, even at this point, is usually ineffective; they are simply unable to entertain the notion that they might, in some way, be involved and that they could possibly make a contribution to their wives' welfare. They recognize the problem only to the extent that it directly affects them. If all the husbands who behave in this way were stupid, then this attitude might be somewhat comprehensible. But not all are. In any event, stupid or brilliant, their actions are not designed to make therapy easier.

THE PATRONIZING HUSBAND

There are other husbands, nearly identical to the above, but with the difference that they make a pretense at cooperating. They will come for interviews and display a superficial interest in what is going on, but never become committed in any real sense. They, too, believe the problem resides in their wives, but are prepared to make a token effort in assisting them to overcome their difficulties. Very often this is an empty gesture, and they are no more understanding or helpful than the first group. Too often they are simply patronizing.

Case Report 25

An example of this type of husband was an engineer, intelligent and well educated. He overtly expressed appreciation of the nature of the problem and what was necessary to alleviate it, including coital abstinence. This he maintained for two weeks. However, his wife then appeared for a session distraught and in tears. It appeared that her husband had had intercourse with her the previous night while he was asleep! The following morning he denied that it had happened, but faced with irrefutable evidence to the contrary, he stoutly declared that he did not remember doing it and therefore must have carried out the act, in the absence of any cooperation from his wife (in fact, she fought him) while sound asleep. Nothing could shake him in this conviction.

THE INTELLECTUAL HUSBAND

A fourth group of husbands, just as troublesome, are the "intellectuals." They appreciate the nature and magnitude of the problem and are more than willing to discuss, in fine detail, their own and their wives' sexual difficulties and how these might be remedied. Frequently they have set ideas not only on why the problem exists, but on how it can be alleviated. Interviews with these men become extremely tedious, since every statement made by the therapist is challenged and alternative explanations offered. They have cherished opinions on all facets of psychology in general and therapy in particular, and go to great lengths to impress the therapist with their erudition.

The interview takes on unreal qualities, with the therapist being forced to justify every statement. It becomes more of a mental exercise than anything else. Furthermore, the irksome nature of these husbands does not end with the interview. They will meddle in the therapy, either by giving their wives contradictory advice, by phoning the therapist to discuss progress and engage in picayune arguments, and/or by accompanying their wives to therapy sessions where they initiate endless and fruitless dialogues on abstruse points of theory and procedure. Despite the continuous interjections of themselves and their ideas into therapy, they nevertheless remain skeptical of the entire process. This they do little to conceal, either from the therapist or from their wives. This subtle sabotage does no one any good.

THE IGNORANT AND INSENSITIVE HUSBAND

Opposite to the foregoing type are those husbands who are simply not intellectually or emotionally equipped to comprehend what is transpiring, what the problem is, and what is to be done about it. They are poorly educated, have a narrowly circumscribed vocabulary, and their behavior in general is governed by emotion rather than by rational thought. They are unsympathetic to their wives' problems because they cannot understand them. They view sex and intercourse as a right bestowed on them by virtue of being married, and are incapable of comprehending that their wives do not share this view. Sex, as they see it, is something you *do* and not something you *talk* about. (Consequently there is no communication between husband and wife.) Intercourse, and other sexual behaviors, are things you engage in when you feel like it, and the possibility that your wife may not desire this is never seriously entertained.

A most important wifely function is to be available at all times to gratify her husband's sexual needs. Furthermore, it is virtually impossible for these men to recognize that their wives find sex abhorrent: that they do not enjoy being grabbed by their breasts or having their husbands run their hands up under their skirts whenever they come within arm's reach. They do not believe, all evidence to the contrary, that their wives are less than ecstatic at the prospect of having intercourse on the living room floor at high noon. They are astonished that their wives should object to their telling their friends what a poor "screw" their wives are, and so on. In general, they are ignorant and insensitive, adopting the attitude that if their wives want to consult someone about their sex lives, then that's up to them—but it's all foolishness and don't expect any help from them! Obviously an atmosphere of this kind is not conducive to effective therapy.

These then, are some of the classes of husbands that we, and quite likely other therapists, encounter. This is not an exhaustive description, and it is probable that anyone dealing with sexual dysfunctions could add to it. Nevertheless, it is obvious that the husband can be a serious impediment in his wife's treatment. When husbands hold to notions of the kind mentioned, it is extremely unlikely that they will make any serious contribution to their wives' welfare. Too often the reverse is true; they do not modify their own behavior in ways consistent with therapeutic objectives, and continue to act as if there was nothing wrong; that the problem, if it exists at all, is in the wife's "head" and that if she would only stop acting so stupidly everything would be all right.

Unfortunately, too many wives acquiesce to their husband's sexual demands, although explicitly told not to, through fear, ridicule or an inappropriate and unwarranted sense of "duty." This, of course, only serves to exacerbate the problem and make it virtually impossible to treat. And when, after a number of therapeutic sessions, nothing has changed, this simply reinforces the husband's original views. Either there was no problem, or if there was, it is incurable. A good example of the self-fulfilling prophecy.

Fortunately the picture is not always as black as we have painted it. At least in those cases where it is possible to talk with the husband, some information, forcefully presented, and a measure of no nonsense persuasion can be effective in changing the destructive behaviors. Describing in graphic detail the possible outcomes of nontreatment is sometimes effective. The vision of divorce, estrangement, extramarital affairs (on their wives' part), constant and bitter strife and quarrels will frequently cause a husband to pause and ponder on the seriousness of the situation. With the wife's permission, presenting to the husband in no uncertain terms her feelings about some of their mutual sexual activities is sometimes cause for reflection. The knowledge, strongly presented by a third party, that it is not simply that his wife *dislikes* this or that sexual activity, but rather *detests* it and inwardly shudders when he does these things, sometimes has an impact on him.

In a more positive vein, and depending on the husband, it is frequently useful and beneficial to provide the couple with some written material pertaining to sex which can provide a basis for discussion. One strategy is to have each read an article dealing with sex problems and independently underline the parts they consider relevant to themselves. This will often come as a revelation to the husband (and frequently the wife as well), but it gives the husband some additional insight into the problem. Inasmuch as the material is written down in black and white, it appears to carry more weight than verbal advice and admonitions presented by the therapist. It also reinforces and lends a certain amount of credence to what his wife and the therapist have been telling him. The knowledge that his is not the only wife who has sexual problems may have a salutary effect. Perhaps she is not as queer as he had imagined!

These machinations do not always work and if the therapist cannot come up with a solution, the best he can do is to attempt to treat the woman and hope that his efforts will be successful in spite of the husband. Naturally, this imposes additional burdens on all concerned.

THE WIFE (CLIENT) AS AN INTERFERING VARIABLE: NONCOOPERATION

Not all problems encountered in sex therapy are a result of the husband's behavior and attitudes. Frequently the woman herself erects barriers which make therapy difficult or impossible. For the most part, these women fall into two groups: those who, for reasons not always obvious, do not wish to change, and those who use sex as a means of controlling their husband's behavior.

Some women in the first group might be termed asexual; they are simply not interested in sex even though they are capable of experiencing orgasms. Or they have a very limited interest in it; they can take sex or leave it, although they may on occasion initiate intercourse and become fairly highly aroused during the act. But by and large sex does not seriously intrude on their lives and the total absence of coitus would not be a matter of any great concern. Frequently they find it difficult to understand their husband's sexual behaviors and demands or why he should become so upset and annoyed over their indifference, an attitude often manifested by immobility and an absence of any emotional response. Their attitude seems to be that if he gets a kick out of it, what's he complaining about?

When they appear for treatment, it's because of their husband's insistence and not because they genuinely feel that there is anything wrong themselves. If anything, they believe that the trouble lies with him in that he is making a mountain out of a molehill. They themselves are content with the *status quo*. Not infrequently the impetus to seek treatment is provided by the husband's threats to leave if the situation is not remedied (although it's unlikely that this threat would ever be carried out). Not unnaturally, these women are not highly motivated to cooperate in the therapeutic procedures and this becomes obvious at the first interview.

During this interview we are concerned, as explained earlier, in securing as much information as we can. Getting relevant information from these women is like pulling teeth. They spontaneously offer nothing; everything must be dragged out of them. Their responses to questions are brief, and generally not illuminating. Everything you want to know must be elicited by a question. This is tedious, time consuming and frequently nonproductive.

This attitude pervades the entire course of treatment. Questionnaires which are typically completed and returned within a week, require three or four weeks. Learning to relax, which most women master in a week or two, is never satisfactorily achieved. Appointments are missed for no good reason; they forgot or did not feel well or the car would not start, and so on. The excuses are legion. It soon becomes obvious that nothing can be achieved with these women and they, of course, are not surprised when confronted with this fact.

However, the experience has served an extremely useful purpose so far as they are concerned. They can now face their husbands with the fact that they have *tried* to do something about the deficiency that he sees in them, but to no avail. *Ipso facto* they have an incurable problem which is not of their doing, and therefore they cannot be held responsible. Many women can present this to their husbands in such a way that he feels guilty about his behavior and ashamed that he forced her into seeking help in the first place. Their acting is ofttimes worthy of an Academy Award, and the secondary gains which result from the whole endeavour provide a certain amount of solace to their affected injured dignity and pride.

THE CONTROLLING WIFE (CLIENT)

The second group, those who use sex to control their husbands, are similar to those just discussed, but their approach is different. They seek therapy because both they and their husbands appreciate that their sex lives are something less than adequate and satisfying. Their problem may be aversion, disgust, absence of pleasure or orgasm, or some other deficiency. Whatever, it is cause for concern and sufficient reason for therapeutic intervention. There is little evidence that the women are not genuinely perturbed by the existing state of affairs, and they approach therapy in a realistic and well-motivated manner. Therapy itself progresses smoothly, and usually within a relatively short time the presenting problem no longer exists.

However, the story does not end here; the marriages do not suddenly become ones of nuptial bliss. Instead, the women conceal from their husbands their true state. That is, even though they now find sex enjoyable, they continue to express negative feelings about it—but only on occasion. Sometimes they are sexually aggressive, achieving heights of arousal which astonish their husbands and leave them gasping and convinced that Heaven on earth has been achieved. Knowing a good thing when they see it, the husbands of these hoydens can hardly wait until bedtime the following night for an encore of the best thing that's happened to them in years. Alas! it's not to be. The superamorous bed-mate of yesterday has vanished, replaced by a cold, curt, and unfeeling stranger who, when he makes a lunge for her, unceremoniously pushes him away with the acrimonius admonishment "for God's sake go to sleep." The bewildered husbands find this unpredictable change in behavior beyond comprehension.

Their sex lives then follow this same general pattern; sometimes the lady is loving and amorous but more often she is cold and forbidding. In psychological terms, the husband is now on an intermittent reinforcement schedule, which is notoriously difficult to extinguish. Behaviorally, this has the affect of making him appear a true "sex maniac," much to her surprise and often to her dismay. Her thoughts are that if you give him an inch he will want a mile. In any event, it may take the husband some considerable time to determine what behaviors of his are effective in determining the most desirable responses, and what will elicit a negative response. Eventually he becomes conditioned; he learns what is expected of him if he is to partake of the fruits of the marriage bed. With couples like this, marriage counselling may provide the best answer once the sexual problems have been dealt with.

THE CASTRATING WIFE (CLIENT)

There may be within this group women who can best be described as castrators. These are cases where the woman is clearly the dominant member of the pair. In some respects they resemble the women in the first group in that they are not particularly interested in sex, and women in the second group who use sex to control their husbands. An example of this is a young couple who were referred for treatment.

CASE REPORT 26

It was clear from the start who ran the household. The wife was aggressive and domineering, usually to the detriment of her husband. During the joint interview, whenever he began to speak she would take over and complete what he was trying to say, or what she thought he was going to say. She had him well conditioned, and he would stop talking as soon as she commenced.

It was not only that she spoke for him, it was also the way she went about it. When he started to talk, a pained expression came to her face and she would regard him with a look which suggested strongly that he was intellectually incompetent. This was soon followed by her breaking into the conversation, while conveying the feeling that *she* was the one who really knew what it was all about. To listen to what he had to say was obviously a waste of time. Strangely enough, he never once contradicted her or made any move to suggest that her behavior was discomforting or embarrassing. Her general attitude was that he was something of a simpleton (which he was not) and a man not to be taken seriously.

During the course of the interview it became clear that what the therapist was observing was a representative sample of her total behavior. She dominated her husband completely in all spheres. She made the decisions in the household and he offered only token resistance to her demands. For example, on one occasion they saw three paintings that they liked and wanted at an art show; there were two that she would like to buy, and one that he fancied. However, they felt that they could only afford two. The decision then became, which two? One might expect that in a situation like this they would buy one of the two that she wanted and the one that he liked. It did not work out this way; they bought the two of her choice. Her husband meekly acquiesced to this high-handed and selfish behavior, although he bitterly condemned his wife when alone with the therapist.

In any event, she completed the therapeutic program to no avail. She was inorgasmic when she started and inorgasmic when she finished. It seemed obvious that she used sex as a means of controlling and belittling her husband. He was as incompetent in bed as he was in everything else. For her to have an orgasm, to derive pleasure and satisfaction as a result of something he did, was unthinkable and would seriously mar her view of their relationship. She would sacrifice orgasmic pleasure for control and domination—which perhaps only demonstrates that there is no accounting for tastes.

As the foregoing indicates, the client can be as great an impediment to treatment as her husband. If therapy is to be successful, ways of dealing with her attitudes and behaviors need be devised. As with the husband, some straightforward talk is necessary. This can take the form used with husbands—emphasizing the dire consequences of failure to alter her behavior, mutual reading and discussion, and so on.

It is, of course, possible to conjure up a variety of dynamic explanations for both partners' noninvolved or destructive behavior. However, these would be untestable propositions and one can easily become sidetracked and led down many a blind alley, with little or nothing being accomplished. We have not found this a fruitful approach.

"MY SUGAR IS TOO REFINED . . ."*

There are women who have been so conditioned against sex that a complete restructuring of their sexual education is necessary before anything directed at the specific problem can be attempted. These are women who cannot talk about their problem; they talk around it, but are unable to discuss it in meaningful terms. Anatomical terms such as penis and vagina leave them blushing and speechless. Sexual words such as intercourse and masturbation are likely as not to elicit tears. Even completing the questionnaires is impossible. One such woman who appeared for treatment was given the questionnaires to take home and complete. Three days later we received a package through the mail containing all the questionnaires torn into hundreds of tiny pieces. She never returned for her next appointment. Another woman, strangely enough, could discuss sex without the slightest sign of embarrassment, but walked out of the second therapeutic session because she thought that the heterosexual behavior she was observing on the TV screen was filthy and disgusting. Her behavior was even more inexplicable since during the interviews she swore like a trooper and used the vernacular in describing anatomical and sexual behaviors.

*The song continues ". . . . she's one of them high-class kind . . ."

This exaggerated sense of propriety makes therapy difficult, first in eliciting information, and then in constructing the hierarchy and presenting this during the therapeutic sessions, either verbally or visually. It is necessary to desensitize these women, initially, simply to discuss their problems in terms which are both common and understandable.

We are fully aware that not all women are amenable to the type of therapy we employ; however, it's doubtful that *any* kind of treatment would be effective in certain cases. An educated guess would be that if there *is* an effective therapeutic procedure for these women, it will be found in a behavioral approach. There are a good many other parameters and modes of approach to be investigated; there are many procedures in the behavioral armetorium which have not been tried. Perhaps behavioral counselling would be effective.

DYSFUNCTIONS IN SINGLE WOMEN

Another type of problem which arises is concerned with single women who have no way of testing the efficacy of the treatment. (Actually this is not too common. Many women, although unmarried, have established a permanent or semi-permanent relationship with a man, so that to all intents and purposes they are married—but not quite.) Occasionally a woman, usually young, will present herself because of a sexual dysfunction but she has not formed a liaison with a man. In fact, it is her sexual problem which has prevented this. She has had a number of boyfriends, but these relationships have terminated when he has attempted, unsuccessfully, to seduce her. Not that she has been an unwilling partner, at least in the initial stages of the abortive seduction. She may have encouraged his advances and actually participated up to a point, but at some stage of the proceedings she has stopped and prevented him from going any further. A few sessions like this and the boyfriend permanently departs, seeking greener fields.

After a few of these experiences, the young woman becomes troubled and anxious, not only because of the immediate problem, but more because of her anticipation of what the future holds for her. If she is unable to respond sexually now, will she ever be able to effectively partake of sex when married, provided this comes to pass? The conclusion reached is that this is doubtful. A not altogether unrealistic conclusion.

As far as their sexual problems are concerned, these differ little if at all from those presented by a good many married women, and are therefore amenable to treatment. The difficulty arises post therapy, in attempting to determine the success or failure of the treatment. Some of these young ladies can be very cold-blooded about this and deliberately set out to test the effects of therapy. They find a presentable young man and use him as a willing guinea pig, albeit an unknowing one. If she is at all attractive, this presents no problem; most young men have few inhibitions regarding premarital sex. Even if she is something less than attractive, the same is true; she may have to lower her sights in terms of the winsomeness of her conquest, although not necessarily; many young men, where sex is concerned, are not particularly discriminating and hold to the view that in the dark all cats are grey.

However, some of these young women are more idealistic and are incapable of this straightforward, clinical approach. They view sex as something to be reserved for a man that they are able to fall in love with and whom they have the expectation, rightly or wrongly, of marrying. Testing the degree of change therefore becomes more difficult. But even if it becomes possible, there is no guarantee the experience will be fruitful or beneficial. Feelings of unease or guilt, the situation in which the act is carried out, concern for pregnancy, her notions of how the man will feel about her afterwards, and simply the effects of trying too hard can all work against her so that even if the basic problem no longer exists, secondary and transitory difficulties may interfere. She may conclude that she is no different now than prior to therapy. If this notion becomes entrenched, it can become a self-fulfilling prophecy.

What complicates the matter further, from the therapist's point of view, is that he or she does not have the benefit of a second opinion prior to therapy (from a husband, legal or common-law) and has no independent check, following therapy, from a third party as to the outcome of the treatment.

In addition to the women just described, who have had unsatisfactory sexual experiences, there are those who diagnose themselves as being frigid not because of unsuccessful coitus, but because they have attempted masturbation and have been unsuccessful. The conclusion may be based on the fact that they were unable because of guilt or anxiety to complete masturbation, or that they were unable to reach a climax after extended and prolonged stimulation. Problems similar to those described above exist with these women. In the absence of sexual experience or a sexual partner, all the therapist can really do is to attempt to overcome the orgasmic problem, as described in Chapter 4, and hope that this will generalize to heterosexual situations.

One of the enigmas surrounding some unmarried women who have experienced sexual problems is the degree of optimism they hold for their future sexual relations. We have seen young couples who have experimented with sex prior to marriage and on all counts found it unsatisfactory and anxiety provoking. Despite frequent experiences of this kind they have married, firm in the belief that the problem will disappear once the marriage ceremony is over. It may be true that in some cases this does happen, that the source of premarital failure was guilt, and once intercourse became legitimatized the problem ceased to exist. There is no way of ascertaining the occurrence of this phenomena since these people never appear for treatment. However, we have seen a sufficient number of young married couples of this type to convince us that marriage *per se* is not inherently therapeutic.

MALE DYSFUNCTIONS IN MARRIAGE

THE WIFE AS AN INTERFERING VARIABLE

As a general rule the treatment of male dysfunctions is somewhat easier than that of female dysfunctions. Many of the problems which arise in treating women, however, have their counterpart in men.

In a large percentage of cases of male sexual dysfunction the wife has proven to be, to some extent, an interfering variable. In fact, about 50% of couples seeking help for male sexual dysfunction in our clinic fall into this category. For some reason the problem of the interfering partner is more often found in couples seeking treatment for male sexual problems than for couples seeking treatment for female sexual problems. Perhaps it's because the male in our society is expected to be knowledgeable about all facets of sex, and capable of at least an adequate performance. Men who do not fill these expectations are often covertly scorned and emasculated by their wives. A scorned and emasculated man is a bitter and unhappy man, and this in turn leads to other problems in the relationship. Women, on the other hand, are not expected to be the knowledgeable partner is sexual matters, so a wife's sexual problem does not come as much of a shock to her husband or partner.

This is an incomplete explanation at best, but we are faced with the problem of the uncooperative wife over and over again and must search for an explanation. In seeking to understand this problem, it is important to survey the types of wives we have encountered who interfered with the therapeutic process.

THE UNINVOLVED WIFE

A large number of wives feel very strongly that their husband's sexual problems are just that; their husband's problem and not theirs. Some women manifest this by communicating with the therapist through their husbands; they refuse to confront the therapist in person. Some women will consent to talk to the therapist on the phone, but will not appear with their husbands for an interview. Some women are embarrassed, some cannot arrange coverage for their children, some feel that sex therapy cannot help, and undoubtedly some are frightened. Some women are very threatened by the therapist because they feel that the problem will be focused on them, or at least that they will come under scrutiny. In spite of what seem like compelling arguments, some women are still not convinced that they should participate with their husbands.

Case Report 27

Mrs. V refused to accompany her husband to the initial therapy session. A woman of some directness, she instructed her husband to tell the therapist that she wasn't coming in because it was not her problem. On reflection, and not trusting her husband to relate this information, she phoned the therapist to tell him herself. After discussing the matter with the therapist, Mrs. V finally agreed to be interviewed if the purpose were only to provide more information about her husband's problem. When she finally did come in, she made it clear right from the start that if there were any hint of blame being put on her, she would walk right out; she set the tone by flatly stating that she wanted sex all of the time, and if her husband couldn't give it to her there was no reason to stay married. After some cajoling she finally agreed that she would participate in the ongoing program.

Just prior to the first therapy session, she called the therapist again and stated that she had decided she was not going to accompany her husband. Furthermore, she said that she had told her doctor (a general practitioner) about the plan for sex therapy, and his response was to inform her that a woman her age (51 years old) should not have to put up with that "stupid stuff." He added that if Mr. V had not learned to do it properly by now he was hopeless, and hence there was no need for her to participate in her husband's therapy. She also stated her own observation that it was foolish to practice touching exercises, since the problem was "screwing."

This particular woman had, for 20 years of marriage, considered her husband a failure and an inadequate man, and nobody could convince her otherwise. Her husband was seeking therapy only because she had urged him to do so and only because she thought he could do it alone. What she apparently was seeking from the therapist was further confirmation of her husband's inadequacy.

This woman was extreme in her views, but by no means unusual. We have dealt with a number of similar wives and it is small wonder their husbands have sexual problems. When a therapist is faced with such rigidity and inflexible thinking coupled with a firm conviction that sex therapy is a foolish waste of time, the wife is omitted from the therapy plan or the couple is referred to another health professional, possibly a marriage counselor. A tremendous amount of valuable therapy time can be wasted dealing with clients in such situations.

Another case presents a similar example of female noninvolvement, but with a slightly different twist.

Case Report 28

Mr. H was a 38-year-old-laborer and had been married 10 years. On his first visit to the sexual clinic he described his problem as "coming too quick." When asked if his wife would accompany him in therapy, he stated that she had already decided that she would not. She had told him that it was his problem and not hers. The therapy procedure was explained to Mr. H and he was then asked if his wife could be called so that the therapist could explain the general approach to her and impress upon her the need for her cooperation. Mr. H said he would like that, but first he would like to explain it to her himself.

At the next appointment he stated that the squeeze technique worked and he did not require any further treatments. In spite of warnings of incomplete cure and doubts on the part of the therapist, Mr. H insisted that he would rather not continue in therapy, since he thought he was cured. The therapist tried carefully to extract from Mr. H the role which his wife had played in this decision, and initially Mr. H insisted it was his own. Finally he admitted that his wife felt that it was really stupid that she should have to participate, and that any therapist who would suggest such an approach wasn't worth going to. Mr. H was not seen again in therapy.

THE EMBARRASSED WIFE

We have treated more than one case in which the wife refused to be seen by the therapist because she was too embarrassed to discuss sex in general and her sexual life in particular. In all cases the wives were cooperative in their attitudes, but communicated only through their husbands or over the phone. One such case was that of Mr. and Mrs. N.

Case Report 29

Mr. N was a very successful businessman and both he and his wife (who were in their late twenties) were college-educated. In spite of her apparent liberal background, Mrs. N refused to participate directly in therapy interviews because she was too embarrassed. (Mr. N's problem was premature ejaculation without any loss of erection.) She consented to communicating with the therapist only through written notes, which were exchanged through the husband. After very detailed questioning of Mr. N, and after both partners had completed the questionnaires, the therapist decided to accept this arrangement and proceed with therapy, seeing only Mr. N and sending notes to Mrs. N. The reason for this decision was that there were no obvious secondary aspects to the problem of premature ejaculation and no other apparent complicating factors. Mr. N had experienced the problem with other women before marriage, and all indications were that while he and his wife were happily married, they would be happier in their sexual relationship if Mr. N did not ejaculate prematurely. The program was started and specific exercises were prescribed for both partners. After approximately 10 sessions they both reported success in controlling the problem. At this time, Mrs. N was again asked to see the therapist for further follow-up sessions, but despite the success and enthusiasm of her husband, she still refused to be seen. Mrs. N remains a mystery today, but in a recent note reports that her husband is still doing well and she is reaping the benefits of his improvement.

THE PATRONIZING WIFE

As do patronizing husbands, some women feign cooperation in sexual therapy. They will go along only if they can stay relatively uninvolved—and only if their husbands don't get better (they are fairly confident that the situation will not change). They attend the joint therapy sessions with apparent involvement, but at home find excuses not to cooperate. Often weeks go by and the couple reports that they were unable to practice their tasks for one reason or another. The unexpected guests that stayed, the busy holiday seasons, the prolonged menstrual period, the continued involvement in numerous conflicting activities, the repeated illnesses, and the unusual working schedule have all been used over and over again by wives as excuses for failing to practice therapeutic tasks. There are many legitamate excuses for missing therapy sessions or not following instructions. We become concerned only when excuse follows excuse, and weeks and weeks pass by without any progress. Very often throughout the period of little progress the wife's concern over the importance of the sexual problem begins to wane and the urgency for treatment is lost. She may finally say that she will call when she can get her schedule together. This is a sure statement that the wife has found that living with the problem is better than facing the type of treatment approach being offered, or facing the possibility that her husband will get better. It is surprising how many husbands are willing to go along with this behavior. They are apparently resigned to their dysfunctions, at least to the extent that they acquiesce in their wives' procrastinations.

We have tried to guard against this type of failure by specifically warning a couple that this may happen. Even though couples agree to have a very open, honest relationship with the therapist, there are repeated cases in which for one reason or another they have not abided by this pact. Lobitz and LoPiccolo (1972), in an effort to insure that clients do not drop out of experimental investigations for no good reason, have required clients to deposit a sum of money with the therapist at the beginning of treatment. As appointments are missed, the couple loses more and more of their deposit, until they are required to mend their ways or leave therapy altogether. Such a financial contract may be a helpful solution.

THE UNCOOPERATIVE MALE CLIENT

Most males who seek therapy for their own sexual problems are truly concerned and genuine in their quest for help. On some occasions, however, a therapist may see a male client who has entered therapy only because of his wife's urging. He may feign interest in the therapy program, but usually makes it clear from the start that he has serious reservations that his problem can be cured. He may have seen a dozen or so therapists before entering this therapy and has very low expectations. Such a client is difficult, because the only signs of improvement which he can accept are dramatic and sudden changes in his behavior.

If he is impotent, he expects to leave the first therapy session with his potency restored. If this does not occur, he will be discouraged and feel deep inside "I knew I couldn't change." So entrenched is his feeling of defeat and despair that even when positive signs of behavioral change appear, these are dismissed by the client as unimportant or insufficient. This type of client usually drops out after a few therapy sessions. A tell-tale sign of a poor prognosis is a client's remark, "O.K., I'll try anything." What the client is really saying is, "O.K., I'll go along with this therapy of yours, but if you don't cure me right away, without any effort on my part, then I'll drop out."

The clients we have seen who fit this pattern have all been men in their late 40s or 50s who have had a sexual problem for a good many years of marriage. They have lived with their problems for so long, and have experienced so much misery, that they are unwilling to invest any more hope in a cure. Another failure would be too painful to bear. Also, achievement of a cure in this late stage in the marriage is a depressing indication that years of past agony could have been avoided, had they experienced proper therapy in the first place. Related to this is simply the nature of the therapy offered. When a man has had a sexual problem for 10–15 years, and has consulted numerous professionals about it with no relief, it is only natural for him to conclude that his problem is one of some magnitude and complexity. When a behavioristic explanation for cause and cure is offered, he is frequently dumbfounded and highly skeptical. Such a simple procedure could not possibly work! Doubts of this kind are a serious impediment to therapy.

TREATING THE SINGLE MALE

Many men do not have current sexual partners. Many are single or divorced and have had a number of sexual experiences, but their current sexual experiences are intermittent, unpredictable and (usually) anxiety-ridden disasters. These men present a unique problem to the sex therapist. Since their sexual experiences are usually "one night stands," all of the instructions about graded sexual exposure and practice with an understanding partner are not immediately applicable.

The first step in dealing with single male clients is to impress upon them a need to approach sexual relationships more slowly and with more thought. They must avoid, at all costs, situations in which they are expected to perform sexually, i.e., the one-night stand bar pickup. Such clients are counselled to seek female companionship in which they can approach sexual matters gradually and with understanding. They are treated in therapy as if they had a considerate and understanding partner, and advised that the approach to sexual behavior which they learn in therapy can be applied at a later time. An example of the successful treatment of a single man is the case of Mr. K.

Case Report 30

Mr. K was a 25-year-old photographer who presented a three-year history of loss of erection. He first began having problems in sexual performance after dating a sexually aggressive woman. He reported that she "almost raped me on our first date," after he had picked her up at a party. He was inebriated at the time, and could not maintain an erection. His date was extremely annoyed and asked him if he were a homosexual. This upset him and he began worrying about his sexual prowess. His response following this incident was to have many "one night stands" to prove to himself that he could perform. Unfortunately, but predictably, he failed repeatedly and was driven deeper into despair. He totally lost confidence in his sexual ability. Treatment centered around careful explanation of the etiology of his problem, and video desensitization. He was also instructed not to attempt sexual relations with any females during the course of therapy, even if he felt he could perform on a given occasion. Toward the end of his participation in therapy, he met a woman of whom he was fond and he was advised to approach their sexual relationship cautiously. He followed these instructions. At a four-month follow-up he reported that he was having successful sexual relations with his new girlfriend and no longer felt that loss of erection was a problem.

The key to treating single male clients who do not have steady sexual partners is to break the cycle of "quick" and "pressured" sexual relationships. The case of Mr. K is typical in that he frantically went from one "one night stand" to another. Even more typically, this pattern may finally evolve to a pattern of avoidance of all sexual contacts, or, such troubled single men may seek the assistance of prostitutes to help them. Prostitutes have rarely proved helpful for the clients we have seen, and often clients complain of increased anxiety during such sexual contacts. (We, of course, have no way of judging the number of men who may have benefited from prostitutes, since we see only those men who still have sexual problems.)

A number of sex clinics offer surrogate partners for the treatment of male clients who have none. Some women who are employed as surrogates may be prostitutes by profession, but many are not and are often involved in other professions. Many, in fact, are willing housewives who view their participation as a form of "charitable work." Therapists who use surrogates prefer women who are not prostitutes by profession, since they are more likely to be sensitive to the necessary therapeutic subtleties.

One overriding problem with all clients seen without partners is the lack of an additional reference point from which to diagnose the problem and monitor therapy progress. The therapist must rely solely on the client's subjective impression of improvement, and run the risk of eliciting supposed therapist-pleasing information.

A single male client with a steady partner does not necessarily offer a better solution. In fact, such an arrangement may possess some hidden problems.

Case Report 31

Mr. R is a 45-year-old consulting engineer. He had been divorced three years prior to our seeing him, and had two grown children. Since his divorce he had established a close relationship with a 32-year-old woman. However, because he was a premature ejaculator, their sexual lives were highly unsatisfactory. He would ejaculate 15–20 seconds after intromission, and consequently his partner was constantly frustrated. This had led to arguments culminating with her threat to break off their relationship. However, during the initial interviews it was apparent that neither of them wished this to happen, since in general they were well-suited to each other.

The partners were seen together, the nature of the problem and the treatment procedure (using the squeeze technique) was explained to them. Both were highly enthusiastic, and following the preliminary assessment (teaching the client to relax) the treatment regime was begun. This involved the woman's stimulating the man to the point of ejaculation, at which time she squeezes the head of the penis until the ejaculatory sensation disappears and part of the erection is lost. They were instructed to repeat this as frequently as practical. It was pointed out to them that as this would likely result in frustration for the woman, since the procedure itself would be sexually arousing for her, the client could bring her to climax through digital stimulation.

Seen three days later, both reported that things were going well and that some control over ejaculation was being achieved. They were encouraged to continue. Because the man had to leave town, taking his friend with him, they were not seen again for two weeks. At this point the client returned alone for his appointment with the news that he and his girlfriend had separated. Apparently the procedure was simply too frustrating for her. In its performance she would become extremely aroused, and on occasion would not heed his instructions to stop and he would ejaculate. When she did follow instructions and he brought her to climax by manual stimulation, she was not satisfied. This did not release her tension as did intercourse, and initially she became annoyed. Annoyance soon turned to anger and bitter quarrels. She decided that despite her feelings for him she could not continue this practice, and therefore, separation was the only answer. She would not come in for an interview and so we never did hear her side of the story, but it might be reasonable to suspect that there was more to it than met the eye. But whatever, in this case the recommended procedure was not effective, and resulted in or contributed to the breakup of a fairly longstanding relationship.

DYSFUNCTION COMPLICATED BY MEDICAL PROBLEMS

While relatively rare, there are physical conditions which can hamper or prevent a man's normal sex relations. One such problem is kidney failure. There may be no direct physical linkage between the two, but in some instances there is a psychological one. The following case is an example.

Case Report 32

Mr. G is a 38-year-old man whose kidneys have been nonfunctional for two-and-a-half years. During this time he attended the renal clinic at a local hospital three nights a week, where he was put on a dialysis machine. In spite of this handicap he was able to hold down a full-time job as a bookkeeper.

Prior to the kidney problem Mr. G was sexually active, having intercourse with his 36-year-old wife two or three times a week. However, from the time he went on dialysis, the frequency of intercourse decreased to about once every two or three months. On these occasions he would ejaculate within one or two minutes, leaving his wife frustrated and angry. Her sources of dissatisfaction were the frequency (she would have preferred intercourse more often) and the fact that he ejaculated so rapidly.

Mr. G's answer to this was that too-frequent intercourse would only weaken him further, and that when he did have intercourse, he could not prevent himself from ejaculating prematurely.

The situation resulted in much friction between them. Although his wife recognized that the kidney problem had a debilitating effect and that he was much more tired than he had been in the past, she pointed out that he would use the excuse of tiredness for not having intercourse, and then 10 minutes later he would go out and cut the lawn or work in the garden for two hours. Her feeling, bitterly expressed, was that if he could do these things, then he could most certainly perform sexually for 10 minutes, a not altogether unrealistic appraisal of the situation.

After a good deal of enquiry with Mr. G it became apparent that the major reason for his relative lack of interest in sex was a result of his premature ejaculation. Half a dozen experiences and the concomitant expression of displeasure on his wife's part had convinced him that in some way the kidney problem and premature ejaculation were intimately related. To avoid the unpleasantness associated with intercourse he had decided to keep this to a minimum.

Over three sessions, together with his wife, the nature of the problem was explained to him and the strategy of ejaculatory control outlined. His wife was extremely enthusiastic and remarked that she had certainly nothing to lose by trying. Mr. G was somewhat skeptical, but agreed to cooperate. Over the following month they practiced the squeeze technique, including vaginal containment, 11 times. Mr. G's control increased from one or two minutes of penile thrusting to six minutes. Both he and his wife found this satisfactory, and at six-month followup were having intercourse at least once and sometimes twice a week with gratifying results. Mr. G's health did not suffer as a result.

There are a variety of other medical problems which may be directly or indirectly related to sexual dysfunction. Richard Green's book *Sexual Dysfunction: A health practitioners text* contains chapters on patients with spinal cord injury and heart problems which are relevant to medically related sexual problems.

UNSATISFACTORY EXPERIENCE DURING TREATMENT

On a number of occasions clients have left therapy sessions eager to try out the new ground rules, only to return upset or angry. Often their problems have been caused by not following instructions or by facing an unexpected situation. Unsatisfactory experiences arise whether the client with the sexual problem is a male or female.

One female client, for example, was making very good progress in therapy for treatment of her problem of sexual anxiety. Between therapy sessions one week she attended a party with her husband. At the party, a drunken male cornered her alone and asked her if she wanted to "ball." She misunderstood him and thought he was asking if she was "having a ball." When she repliied "yes," he proceeded to reach up her dress and grab her genitals. This proved to be an extremely upsetting experience for her, and confirmed her original impression that all men were unpredictable animals. Following this incident, therapy proceeded very slowly for a long time, and eventually terminated in only partial improvement in her condition. She was eventually much more comfortable with her husband, but continued to harbour fears of men in general.

Often the upsetting experience is caused by more subtle factors. Men and women may judge the outcome of therapy by asking themselves how they subjectively feel about their problems. In some cases, the feeling is dependent on the objective evidence of being able to do something one was unable to do previously. For men, the measure of improvement is judged almost entirely on whether or not functioning has been restored, i.e., achievement of an erection or ability to ejaculate when desired. If these functions are not restored, then therapy has failed. Because of the importance of these signs to dysfunctional men, they often are the focus of attention even if the therapist has attempted to redirect the client's attention. If a man has not experienced the agony of sexual dysfunction or has not dealt with men who have, it is difficult to appreciate the extent to which a client's attention is turned toward looking for signs of improvement. This attention is often difficult to distract, and at times can result in unsatisfactory experiences during therapy.

One client we dealt with presented a complaint of failure to achieve an erection. Mr. B (age 35) had experienced this problem for five years prior to entering our program. His wife was extremely upset with his problem and had been separated from him for over a year.

Case report 33

Mr. B was a construction worker who reported normal sexual desires prior to marriage, although he had only a few sexual contacts. After marriage, for some inexplicable reason, he began to experience loss of erection, to which both he and his wife reacted with great concern. As one disappointing experience followed another, the problem intensified and Mr. B noted a lack of desire for sexual contacts. This seemed to generalize to a lack of arousal (but not interest) toward females. In spite of the therapist's careful warnings during the initial therapy sessions to not look for immediate progress, Mr. B could not refrain. It was as if he had forgotten how a man with normal erections reacts to everyday situations. During video desensitization sessions he expected to achieve erections, even though he was explicitly instructed by the therapist to attend to his feelings of anxiety and not arousal. This instruction was like asking him not to think of a pink elephant crossing a stream. He could not get the thought out of his mind and he still appeared disappointed, and reported during the first two video sessions that he had not experienced an erection.

His attention toward achieving an erection was not distracted outside of sessions either. Upon returning for his third therapy session, Mr. B appeared especially upset. He had seen a beautiful woman with a tight sweater walking near his construction site. Other men on the site reacted to the woman with cat calls and much joking. Mr. B assumed that a normal man should achieve an erection when looking at a sexy woman. Since this did not happen to him, he interpreted his experience as failure, and he was as devastated as if he had attempted intercourse and had failed. Therapy sessions finally were terminated without success. Mr. B never learned to stop putting pressure on himself to achieve erections.

With other clients unsatisfactory, interfering experiences have included a wide range of problems, such as children suddenly appearing in the parents' bedroom during practice sessions, or couples disagreeing and fighting about the extent to which they should follow the therapist's instructions. As a therapist gains in experience, he or she can better anticipate many such problems, help clients deal with them, and ideally, prepare for them before they come up.

PROBLEMS EXPOSED AS A RESULT OF THERAPY

It is not unusual for couples involved in sexual dysfunction therapy to discover hidden secrets in a partner or even in themselves. Sometimes revelations can prove to be unburdening and fulfilling and contribute to a successful therapeutic process. Kaplan (1974) discusses the concept that rapid treatment of sexual problems can provide experiences of previously avoided issues. In spite of setbacks and slowing in the psychotherapeutic process, facing of previously avoided issues most often leads to resolution and success if handled properly by a skilled therapist. Most commonly, the therapist may be given information by one partner that the other partner is unaware of. For example, a partner may have had extramarital sexual experiences, or even unusual experiences such as incest or homosexuality, that the other partner is unaware of. Whether or not the secret information should be revealed to the unknowing partner is a decision which the client must make, and *under no circumstances should a therapist violate a client's confidentiality.* If, however, it is clear to the therapist that the secret information is likely to stand in the way of therapeutic progress, then the therapist can suggest to the client that the information should be shared. The therapist can often guide a couple in presenting the information in its proper perspective, and help the couple to deal with adverse reactions to the information.

In cases where it has been decided that confidential information should be shared with a client's partner, the first move by the therapist is to explain to the client the reasons for this step. The client must fully accept and be in agreement with the therapist before proceeding. The next step is to decide how the information should be presented, whether in therapy sessions by the therapist, or at home by the client. In either case, the competency and feelings of the client should be taken into consideration in making a decision.

It is important in these situations for the therapist to have a very clear idea of the client's motivation in unburdening him or herself. Too frequently this is done solely to salve the conscience of the partner concerned. Divulging various transgressions does not typically improve or hasten the therapeutic process, and can frequently lead to more serious problems—at the time or in the future. If in the therapist's opinion this is likely to be the case, the client, after detailed explanation, is advised to remain silent. As a general rule, our practice is to work with the here and now. The past cannot be altered.

In addition to exposing secrets during sex therapy, many couples often uncover new sexual problems. The treatment of male sexual problems, for example, often reveals a female partner who hates sex or is inorgasmic. In one couple we treated, for example, the wife tearfully revealed that she could not achieve orgasm once her husband was successfully treated for premature ejaculation. Through therapy, her residual feelings of her own sexual inadequacy were revealed, and this depressed her very much. The rapid successful treatment of the husband upset her, and forced her to face problems which had lain dormant and forgotten for many years because of the focus of attention on her husband's premature ejaculation. Kaplan and Kohl (1972) discuss a similar case, and there is reason to believe that this may be an infrequent problem but not an unusual one. In the case we dealt with, the woman was so disturbed by her realization that she too had a hangup, that it was decided to refer her to a psychotherapy program before dealing with her sexual problem.

CULTURAL EFFECTS

Many problems can be traced back directly to either an absence of knowledge of things sexual, or too-rigid notions of what normal heterosexual behavior consist of. Learning about sex and the environmental context in which this learning has taken place are important. These elementary facts have been well and thoroughly documented by Kinsey and colleagues (Kinsey et al., 1948, 1953).

For example, something as simple as position during coitus can cause no end of trouble. Many couples believe that there is only one normal way to effect sexual union. This is the missionary position with the man on top and the woman below on her back—a position one might add, not assumed by any other primate or other class of mammal (Ford & Beach, 1951). As pointed out by Kinsey, education and social class are two factors which determine coital position, the better-educated from upper social classes displaying more variety than the poorer-educated from lower social classes. That is, the latter group is much more likely than the former to adhere rigidly to the missionary position and to consider any variation to be either abnormal at best or perversion at worst. Unfortunately, this position is not conducive to maximum pleasurable stimulation as far as the woman is concerned.

From an anatomical point of view, the female above, face to face with the man, provides the surest way of effective female stimulation. Some women, in fact, can achieve orgasm only by this means. It allows them much more freedom of movement than when lying beneath the man. However, many husbands will not tolerate this afront to their manhood; they feel threatened. Anyway, if God did not intend the man to be on top, why did He make him stronger? In any event, it can be extremely difficult to change some men's views on this, to convince them that by simple experimentation they may hit upon a position which is satisfying and gratifying to both themselves and their wives. And that not only will this improve their sex lives, it will also add immeasurably to the general quality of their marriage. The obvious conclusion to be drawn from this elementary fact is that in therapy, the attitudes, prejudices and biases of the couple need to be considered. Too often therapists, who themselves have middle or upper middle class backgrounds, automatically assume that their notions and values *viz a viz* sex are the same or very similar to their clients'. This is a fundamental error.

INDIVIDUAL DIFFERENCES

A second problem has to do with the female climax. The assumption is often made that the orgasmic capabilities of all women are identical; that both quantity and quality are the same from woman to woman. This notion, of course, is fostered by movies, books and magazines where the heroine or anti-heroine is depicted as losing all contact with reality while in the throes of violent and ecstatic orgasm. What is true for these fictional characters is assumed true for all women. And when a woman does not attain these heights of frenzied rapture, she may begin to think that something is amiss, she does not measure up as a woman. Too often her husband shares and reinforces these notions, since he uses his own climax as a yardstick by which to gauge his wife's responses.

The truth of the matter is that there are wide individual differences in the orgasmic capabilities of women. These probably arise from variations in the autonomic and central nervous systems, the musculature, and other systems involved in the sexual response. Kinsey (1953) has pointed out that ". . . the exceedingly rapid response of certain females who are able to reach orgasm within a matter of seconds from the time they are first stimulated and the remarkable ability of some females to reach orgasm repeatedly within a short period of time, are capacities which most other individuals could not conceivably acquire through training, childhood experience or any sort of psychiatric therapy. Similarly, it seems reasonable to believe that at least some of the females who are slower in their responses are not equipped anatomically or physiologically in the same way as those who respond more rapidly."

Unfortunately, these individual differences go unrecognized, and rather than accept the fact that there are both inter- and intraindividual variations in orgasmic capabilities, many women (and their husbands) become distressed when these differences become apparent. Husbands can be unrealistic in that they expect their wives to behave in ways which they themselves do not. The majority of men, if they are at all sensitive to their own sexual responses, recognize that the quality or intensity of their own sexual climax is not static; it varies from time to time. The most obvious example of this is relative deprivation; the intensity and pleasure of the male ejaculation is greater if the man has not had this experience for a week or two than it is if he is having intercourse every day. However, it should be recognized that, as in the female, there are individual differences here too.

FOREPLAY AND STIMULATION

A third problem is concerned with the preliminaries to intercourse: foreplay. Both men and women are victims of erroneous beliefs in this area of sexual expression. Many women, for example, believe that men, by their very nature and sexual aggressiveness, do not require any stimulation prior to coitus and that they are ready to proceed at a moment's notice. They do not, therefore, participate in foreplay but leave it up to the man to make all the advances until he, in some magical way, decides that his wife is ready to proceed with the business at hand. Not only does the woman refrain from stimulating her husband prior to intercourse, she continues this passive behavior during the act and remains immobile during intercourse. Thus sex becomes a mechanical, one-sided affair, and it is not surprising that at its conclusion the man rolls over and falls asleep without considering his wife's enjoyment or whether she has reached a climax.

These female attitudes and behaviors are much less common among the young than the middle-aged. Young women of today are not satisfied with things that their mothers found, if not enjoyable, at least acceptable.

Related to this problem are situations where couples are encouraged by marriage counsellors, sex therapists, and sex manuals to continue foreplay for extended periods of time, sometimes an hour or more, in the belief that this will increase the probability of the woman reaching orgasm. What these advisors fail to take into account is that many women, even though they have no serious problems, do not derive any great amount of satisfaction from this extended foreplay. Many, in fact, find it offensive and disturbing. If, as is frequently found, women have particular hang-ups about having their genitals and breasts manually stimulated, this continuous and seemingly endless foreplay only serves to heighten their already high levels of anxiety and thus increases the probability that their aversion to sex will increase. In essence, the assumption is made by the therapist that individual differences do not exist, or if they do, they are minor and of little practical consequence. So, regardless of the couple's age, education, socioeconomic background, sexual sophistication and equally important, the nature of the problem, all are given the same or similar advice and instruction on how to cope with their sexual difficulties.

MYTHS AND MISCELLANEOUS PROBLEMS

There are a host of other difficulties that arise to exacerbate an already difficult situation. Their source is ignorance on the part of the husband or wife, and/or bad advice from counsellors and sex therapists. These problems include the ingrained notion that all wives derive erotic pleasure from seeing their husbands naked; that showing a woman erotic films will predictably and/or consistently increase her sexual arousal and responsiveness; that women naturally enjoy sex with an aggressive and domineering man; that the couple should reach orgasm simultaneously; that the size of a man's penis is positively correlated with a woman's pleasure; that if a couple engage in intercourse often enough, her problems will disappear; that if a woman cannot achieve orgasm from penile stimulation, she can and will enjoy this through digital stimulation or from oral sex; that male and female sexual responsiveness remain consistent throughout their life span; that men do not like to be seduced, and so on. These myths, and for the most part that is all they are, are not likely to improve the situation or alter a couple's basic views on sex. Too often the reverse is true. They simply make matters worse. What goes unnoticed is the part played by learning in both male and female sexual responsiveness and behavior. From birth, men and women possess the anatomical and physiological capacities and potential for sexual behavior, the ability to respond to various psychological and physiological stimuli. But this is all they have. All other aspects of sexual expression are learned in the process of growth and development. The environment in which this learning takes place varies, and this elementary fact imposes powerful effects on future sexual behavior— particularly for women.

RELATIONSHIP PROBLEMS

In addition to the specific and obvious problems there are occasionally less conspicuous ones of which the therapist need be aware. The sexual problem presented may be neither the only problem nor the major one that the woman and/or her husband is experiencing. Nor is it true that once this is remedied, marital harmony will be restored and both will live happily ever after.

In some men and women sexual difficulties are only a part of a more general conflict which will also have to be dealt with. Or, a woman or husband, may find they are unable to cope with their new-found sexuality. On the other hand, they may discover, together or independently, that while their sex lives are more satisfactory, they now find that they do not really like their spouses, and that orgasms do not compensate for this. Or the problem may be even more complicated. For example, we successfully treated a man for premature ejaculation and assumed that since he was now functioning well, we would not see him again. However, as it turned out, this was not the case; his wife was sexually dysfunctional. This possibility had never been considered, since she never mentioned it while her husband was in trouble. Closer investigation showed that she was not unhappy with her own problem, and in subtle ways conveyed the idea that she preferred her husband as he had been—a premature ejaculator—to what he was now—an effective lover.

More seriously, the therapist may be faced with a client who is psychotic (or borderline psychotic), and unless the clinician is astute, his ministrations may exacerbate matters. The very fact that problems like these arise argue that sex therapy is not within the realm of amateurs, well-meaning or otherwise. It is an endeavor that requires professional training. To say that all that is required is "common sense" is to pointedly demonstrate the ignorance of the proponents of this naive notion. It's almost tantamount to saying that because one eats meat, he is qualified to practice surgery.

THE THERAPIST AND PROCEDURAL PROBLEMS

There are two additional sources of difficulty. These are concerned with therapist and procedural variables. The first is usually not serious, in that it occurs infrequently— although when it does, it can make treatment impossible. The problem, in psychiatric terminology, is described as *counter-transference.* This means simply that occasionally a patient will appear for whom the therapist has no sympathy or empathy. The therapist takes a dislike to the client right from the start, and there appears to be no way to alter his feelings. For some inexplicable reason, the client grates on the therapists's nerves and, try as he or she may, the clinician cannot establish a productive therapeutic relationship.

It's often assumed that the therapist, because of his or her experience and training, should be able to overcome such negative feelings and successfully work at developing a liking for the client—perhaps by "analyzing" one's own feelings and behaviors and seeking the underlying cause for this unprofessional behavior. We find it more practical and utilitarian simply to turn the client over to another member of the team who can perhaps establish better rapport. To continue therapy with someone with whom a therapist has no affinity almost certainly guarantees failure.

The reverse can be true: the client may have no affinity for the therapist. He may be too young or too old, too fat or too thin, too authoritarian or too nondirective. Or it may simply be that for some unspecifiable reason the client does not "take" to the therapist. Lazarus (1971) has detailed this problem. In any event, when this happens, our solution is to allow another therapist to deal with the case.

The procedural variables which can cause problems have to do with the actual presentation of the hierarchial items. These are of two kinds: the client is unable to imagine or visualize the scene described with any degree of clarity, or even if this is possible, the visualization does not result in anxiety. The first situation can usually be solved by using TV or slides as visual aids. The vast majority of clients respond well to this. The second difficulty, where no anxiety is manifested, is tougher. The mere watching or imagining of a couple engaging in fairly intimate sexual behavior may not, in some clients engender anxiety, although if they themselves were performing, they would be extremely anxious.

Most people can easily experience and report anxiety in terms understandable to the therapist. They can recognize bodily and visually concomitant cognitive feelings which they interpret as signs of anxiety. If you enquire as to what they are experiencing, they will say that they get these "funny" (unpleasant) feelings in their stomach and they are breathing more rapidly but shallower. However, some clients report that they do not feel anxious, and since desensitization is designed to remove anxiety, on the face of it one might conclude that desensitization is therefore inappropriate.

It may be better to consider that even though a client does not report anxiety, anxiety is present but being experienced in ways not readily identifiable to the client or to the therapist. This rationale is based on the work by Malmo and Shagass (1949, a, b) and Lacey and his colleagues (Lacey & Lacey, 1958; Lacey, Bateman and Van Lehn, 1953) on autonomic response specificity. These investigators demonstrated that there are individual differences in the ways in which anxiety is expressed. Autonomic arousal is idiosyncratic and differs from person to person, although it is consistent for any particular individual, regardless of the source or kind of stress. In practical terms, this means that stress and anxiety may be expressed by increased heart rate only, or by changes in respiration only, or by changes in muscle tension only, and so on. Or it may be expressed in more than one of these systems. In terms of the people we are discussing, monitoring a number of their autonomic responses would make it apparent that stress existed, although not overly manifested.

While the foregoing notion is a hypothesis that requires testing, a clue to its possibility came from the treatment, by one of the authors, of a man with a public-speaking phobia. In the course of desensitization it seemed, from observation, that none of the items made him anxious or nervous. In an attempt to validate this, the highest item on the hierarchy —proposing a toast at a large, formal gathering—was presented, and the client was instructed to imagine this situation for an extended period of time. After about one minute of this the man began to perspire, his face became flushed, and he spontaneously remarked that he was going to be sick. He was immediately instructed to stop thinking about the anxiety situation but it took about fifteen minutes for the feeling to pass and for him to regain his composure. Questioned about this experience, the man said that while he did not experience anxiety as he did in a real life situation, he felt himself growing hot, beginning to perspire, and gradually getting a queasy feeling in his stomach which he recognized as a prelude to vomiting.

Acting on the assumption that these responses were in fact anxiety responses, the therapist resumed desensitization in the usual way with the result that when this high-anxiety item was finally encountered, it failed to produce flushing, perspiring and nausea. Furthermore, the man no longer dreaded the prospect of speaking in public and demonstrated this by giving a 15-minute speech to a group of 60 people. While he did not do this in the complete absence of anxiety, what anxiety he experienced was easily managed. A six-month follow-up not only showed no relapse, but in fact an almost complete absence of anxiety in public speaking situations. (Prior to treatment he could not speak to more than three people without becoming anxious, flustered and incoherent.)

CLIENTS AS INDIVIDUALS

To be successful in treating sexually dysfunctional men and women, the therapist must recognize that he is dealing with individuals; individuals whose histories, learning and environment vary, whose problems, while apparently identical, are not necessarily the same; who come from a variety of educational and socioeconomic backgrounds; who have husbands or wives who also possess distinct and idosyncratic characteristics, and so on. In essence, the general class of behavior may be the same or similar, but the people exhibiting the behavior are not homogeneous. Each is unique. Not to recognize these differences—and more important, failing to take them into account when attempting therapeutic intervention—is a cardinal error.

It might seem that we are laboring the obvious and that no sensible therapist would ignore these impornt variables. That they do, in too many cases may be a holdover from medicine. When someone presents himself to a physician with a broken leg or appendicitis, the personal characteristics of the patient are not of serious import. He can be illiterate or he can be a Nobel prize winner, his response to having his leg set or his appendix removed will be the same. (Although, as physicians recognize, there are factors here too that can affect outcome, e.g. economic status. If, because of financial pressure, a patient is forced to return to work before his fractured leg or appendectomy is properly healed, complications can result.) Nevertheless, in general, the variables that are important when dealing with physical ailments are of less consequence than those pertaining to sexual dysfunctions and this is the nub of the problem. There is a strong tendency to view psychosexual problems as being simply another class of medical problems.

When clients appear for treatment of a sexual problem it matters very much if they are illiterate or have a graduate degree from a university. It is of some importance if they come from a low or high or middle class background. It's useful to know if husband and wife come from the same or different economic and educational classes and to what extent they have similar values and common intersts, and so on. To ignore these differences when planning treatment is to almost guarantee a high and unnecessary rate of failure.

SUMMARY

In this chapter we have attempted to describe and illustrate some of the many problems encountered in dealing with sexual dysfunctions. Clearly there are many more, but these are major ones which frequently arise.

Husbands can in no way be absolved from their wives' sexual problems, any more than wives can claim no measure of responsibility for their husbands' difficulties. Both are involved in one way or another and disclaimers to the contrary, the fact remains that sex and marriage involve two people. Husbands may be chauvinistic, patronizing or attempt to wish their wives' problems away by intellectualization, but these are not modes of behavior conducive to helping their spouses. They may be ignorant in ways more than sexual, and completely insensitive to the feelings of others, which only adds to the general misery.

In attempting to solve their problems, women too often act in ways not consistent with their own best interests. They may be noncooperative and thus defeat their own purposes. Or they may use sex to control their husbands to a greater or lesser degree. The same situation is frequently encountered in dealing with male problems.

Of course a client need not be married to experience sexual dysfunction, and in our permissive society the number of single men and women seeking treatment is increasing. These cases pose special problems, particularly if there is not a lasting and stable relationship with a member of the opposite sex.

Most of our failures have been with couples married 15 years or longer. In older couples who have been exposed to each other for many years, there are generally too many other problems associated with the sexual problem for brief sexual therapy to be effective. Very often basic respect has all but disappeared and the sexual problem is lost in a quagmire of communication problems. In older couples, it is extremely difficult to dissociate the sexual problem from other interpersonal problems which have evolved in the marriage. On the other hand, younger couples more often present very uncomplicated and uncontaminated (from the therapist's point of view) sexual problems which are much more amenable and responsive to brief sexual therapy.

The culture and society in which people live create their own special difficulties, since behavior is determined and affected by these. And similarly with individual differences and individual responses to sexual acts and sexual behaviors. A cardinal error is to assume that because there exists a certain communality in observable behavior, the determinants of this behavior are the same. It is also a mistake to blithely assume that when a couple appears for treatment of a sexual problem that this is the only area of difficulty. It may or may not be, but the possibility should be seriously entertained that this is only the tip of the iceberg.

Therapist, client, and procedural variables which interfere with or affect successful treatment have been discussed. These are important, and the degree to which the therapist is sensitive to them and is able to cope with them without losing sight of the fact that he is dealing with unique individuals will, in the final analysis, determine his effectiveness.

7

Masturbation: Its History and Role in Sexual Dysfunction

Most people have had the experience of masturbating. According to Kinsey (1953) 58% of women have masturbated to orgasm at some point in their lives and 47% have experienced guilt, anxiety or fear because of it. This compares with 92% of men, with the "majority" feeling guilty or anxious. Quite apart from the accuracy of these figures today, a major question is simply what, if any, are the effects of masturbation, physically and psychologically? This is an important question since masturbation is an integral part of human sexual behavior. To fully understand it and its ramifications it is necessary to consider the question in the context of the history of masturbation, as this is related to human behavior and welfare.

For about 200 years (1700 to 1900) it was medical dogma that masturbation was a major and frequent cause of a wide variety of physical disorders and of "insanity." From about the beginning of the twentieth century, this notion had pretty well fallen into disrepute—not entirely, but at least to the extent that only a minority, albeit a large minority, of the medical profession believed it. However, the notion of the evils of masturbation did not vanish; rather than resulting in these very serious physical and psychological problems, masturbation was discovered to be the source of neurotic disorders. Freud (1938) was perhaps the major proponent of this view. This notion too has undergone changes over the past 30–40 years, and current thinking has it that it is not masturbation *per se* which causes psychological problems, but feelings of guilt and anxiety attendant upon or engendered by masturbation. However, even in the darkest days there were exceptions, and Kinsey and his colleagues (Kinsey *et al.*, 1953) have noted that despite the predominant attitude, there were professional views published as early as 1786 which contradicted contemporary thinking, pointing out that little or no physical or mental harm resulted from masturbation. But these were in the minority and were voices crying out in the sexual wilderness for all the effect they had on either professional or popular thinking.

THE EARLY PERIOD: PHYSICAL AND MENTAL EFFECTS

For our purposes, the most important aspects of the history of the evils of masturbation can be traced back to the beginning of the eighteenth century and the publication in England of a book with the tongue twisting title: *Onania, or the Heinous Sin of Self-pollution and All Its Frightful Consequences, in Both Sexes, Considered with Spiritual and Physical Advice to Those Who Have Already Injur'd Themselves by This Abominable Practice, to Which is Subjoin'd A Letter from a Lady to the Author, Concerning the Use and Abuse of the Marriage Bed, with the Author's Answer.* The anonymous author of this treatise is thought to be a clergyman who abandoned the cloth for the more lucrative practice of medicine (he offered, at half a sovereign a box, a secret remedy for not only masturbation but sterility and impotenence as well). By 1764 this book had reputedly gone through 80 editions. According to the author, a multitude of physical and mental problems were the lot of masturbators and the only cure was abstinence from this repulsive activity. This could readily be achieved through liberal use of his secret remedy.

Despite the fairly widespread dissemination of this book, its impact would not have been so great had not its thesis been taken up by reputable physicians. In 1758, Tissot, a well-known Swiss physician, published a book entitled *Onania, or a Treatise Upon the Disorders Produced by Masturbation*. This book, coming as it did from a reputable physician, had a tremendous impact upon both the public and the medical profession. Tissot corroborated the English author and reinforced the notion that sexual excess, particularly masturbation, lay at the roots of a wide variety of disorders, both physical and mental. In general, the problem was seen as a loss of semen and this resulted in not only a general debility but also failing eyesight, consumption, gonorrhea, hemorrhoids, digestive disorders, melancholy, catalepsy, imbecility, loss of sensation, pervasive weakness of the nervous system, impotence and insanity. Tissot provided documentation in the form of case studies and describes one man, a chronic masturbator, who ". . . dried out his brain so prodigiously that it could be heard rattling in his skull" (in Spitz, 1952). Strong and heady stuff indeed.

Like the earlier writers on onania, Tissot was as much concerned with the moral aspects of masturbation as with the physical. He regarded the practice as a "flagrant crime" which entitled the victim only to contempt rather than pity, his legacy of disease for his contemptible acts in this world, only a forerunner to eternal damnation in the next. Following the publication of Tissot's book, the general notion of the debilitating effects of masturbation gained widespread acceptance both in Europe and somewhat later in America. This was true of the medical profession and through this body, the public in general. Furthermore, what the Church had always maintained and taught was now buttressed by medical opinion. If anything was required to lend credence to the proscription against masturbation, this was it.

If one cannot be sympathetic towards the early physicians for their preoccupation with masturbation and its attendant ills, one can at least attempt to understand it. There appear to be at least three major elements involved: 1) Masturbation was considered morally wrong, a sin, although this concept resulted from a misreading or misunderstanding of the Biblical story of Onan; 2) It had long been recognized that too frequent sexual intercourse was followed by a feeling of weakness and lethargy; 3) Medicine was in its infancy, and while it was possible to describe symptoms, it was not so easy to explain the cause of these symptoms. Taken together, these three facts were largely responsible for the hysteria over masturbation. Once these notions were accepted in isolation, it was a short step to discover causual relationships among them. If inmates in madhouses were observed or known to be chronic masturbators, which many in fact were, it was an easy task to attribute their madness to this heinous behavior. (In fact, in 18th Century madhouses, masturbation was probably the only source of fun and pleasure.) If the village blacksmith appeared lethargic at the end of a day and was known, or suspected, to masturbate, then the reason for his lethargy was quite clear. If an adolescent developed pimples and complained of difficulty in seeing, then obviously he was practising self-abuse, and so on. It required little imagination to make the leap from seeing masturbation as a concomitant of some "illnesses" to hypothesizing masturbation as the cause of the illness.

However, these fanciful notions could not be sustained forever in the absence of more concrete evidence, and with the increase in knowledge of anatomy and physiology the conviction that masturbation was the source of a whole host of physical disorders began to weaken. By the end of the eighteenth century only the moralistic diehards of the medical profession continued to put much credence in it. Nevertheless, if masturbation did not result in physical disorders, the same could not be said of mental disorders. To the degree that masturbation as a cause of physical disabilities decreased, the notion that it was intimately involved in insanity increased so that the French physician Esquirol in 1816 was able to declare: "Masturbation is recognized in all countries as a common cause of insanity." He elaborated on this in 1822 when he said, "Onanism is a grave symptom in mania; unless it stops at once, it is an unsurmountable obstacle to cure. By lowering the powers of resistance it reduces the patient to a state of stupidity, to phtisis, marasmus and death." In 1838 he was to write "[masturbation] may be a forerunner of mania, of dementia and even of senile dementia; it leads to melancholy and suicide; its consequences are more severe in men than in women; it is a grave obstacle to cure in those of the insane who frequently resort to it during their illness," (in Hare, 1962). Strong words indeed, and coming from a man of Esquirol's stature and reputation, they carried weight not only in France, but in England, Germany and finally America, where it came to full flower. What had begun as an obscure and whimsical idea now had the full weight of medical authority behind it. The position was unambiguous: masturbation resulted in madness.

In America, Benjamin Rush, the "father" of American Psychiatry, was to declaim in his *Medical Enquirees upon Diseases of the Mind,* published in 1812, that "four cases of madness occurred, in my practice, from this cause [masturbation] between the years 1804 and 1807. It is induced more frequently by this cause in young men than is commonly supposed by parents and physicians. The morbid effects of intemperance in a sexual intercourse with women are feeble, and of a transient nature, compared with the strain of physical and moral evils which this solitary vice fixes upon the body and mind." Rush added to the list of disabilities attendant upon this wretched practice: seminal weakness, impotence, dysury, tabes dorsalis, pulmonary consumption, dyspepsia, dimness of sight, vertigo, epilepsy, hypochondriasis, loss of memory, manalgia, fatuity and death. Rush was obviously not convinced that mental disorders were the only legacy of masturbation. Furthermore, this would appear to be a gross example of generalizing from a small sample. Allowing that masturbation does result in lunacy, four cases in four years hardly suggests an epidemic. But then Rush, like many of his European (and American) colleagues, was carried away in the heat of his own enthusiasm. In the absence of any known cause of mental disorders, masturbation provided as good a scapegoat as anything currently available. And this was not Rush's first expedition into murky and uncharted waters (Szasz, 1970).

THE MIDDLE PERIOD

The idea that masturbation was a prime cause of insanity underwent a transition during the nineteenth century, from certainty at the start of the century, to doubt during the middle years, to disbelief at the close. Nevertheless, in the English speaking world its demise was somewhat later than in Europe in general. While by the 1850s and 1860s some German physicians were less dogmatic in their pronouncements on this problem, the Scottish physician Skae in 1863 came up with the notion that mental disorders should be classified according to their natural history rather than by their symptoms. Masturbation was included in his system, and he wrote: "The third natural family, I would assign to the masturbators (idiocy and epilepsy were the first two). Yet I think it cannot be denied that the vice produces a group of symptoms which are quite characteristic and easily recognized, and give to the cases a special natural history: the peculiar imbecility and shy habits of the very youthful victim; the suspicion and fear and dread and suicidal impulses and scared look and feeble body of the older offenders, passing gradually into Dementia or Fatuity" (in Hare, 1962).

By 1874 Skae conceded that the prognosis was not as gloomy as originally predicted and wrote: "If these cases are put under proper care and treatment before the mind has become too impaired to exert self-control when reasoned with, they generally recover. But when dementia has begun to show itself in impaired memory and energy, silly vanity and self-satisfaction, the cases assume a very hopeless aspect with a tendency to gradually increasing dementia if the vice is persevered in."

Skae's writings were not particularly influential in Continental Europe, but this was not true in England and America where the most emminent physicians accepted them wholeheartedly and uncritically. In America as late as 1887, Spitzka, Professor of Medical Jurisprudence in New York, continued to expound on masturbatory insanity, that the most common age of onset was between 13 and 20 years, that it occurs in men and women and in a ratio of 5:1, that in the majority of cases there was a rapid decline into agitated dementia; however, where deterioration progresses more slowly ". . . the obtrusive selfishness, cunning, deception, maliciousness and cruelty of such patients: is such that . . . the most kind hearted and philosophical alienist may find it impossible to reconcile himself to regarding them as anything else than repulsive eyesores and a source of contamination to other patients, physically and morally" (in Hare, 1962).

If masturbators could conceal their solitary practices from their families, they could not so easily fool an expert. Over the years there were developed diagnostic signs which enabled medical practictioners unerringly to distinguish the masturbators from the non-masturbators. Some of these signs in males were a downcast or vacant appearance, pallor, easy blushing, solitariness, vacuity, loss of attention, inability to love anyone, lack of emotion, absence of generiosity or loyalty, timidity and suspicion. It was not so easy to diagnose female masturbators. However, if a girl or woman displayed an unsteady or peevish disposition tending towards anger, an exaggerated timidity in the presence of parents and a surly attitude towards strangers, profound idleness and a tendency to lying, then one could be almost certain, denials to the contrary, that one was faced with a masturbator. In general, the principle used in diagnosis was simple: those who confessed to masturbation were believed, those who denied it were not believed. A clear case of heads I win, tails you lose and a procedure not radically different from that used in earlier times to distinguish witches from nonwitches. Those suspected of being witches were bound and thrown into a pool of water. If the victim floated she was a witch and promptly burned at the stake. If she sank she was not a witch. However, since she drowned, the question became academic.

Moving into the twentieth century, there were still believers in the older notions and an exaggerated degree of watchfulness was necessary to ensure that the practice did not take root. Writing in 1904, Dr. Emma Drake cautioned that: "Mothers need to be Argus-eyed, to guard their babies from all the evils that beset them . . . While yet very young, they can be taught that the organs are to be used by them only for throwing off the waste water of the system, but that they are so closely related to other parts of the body that handling them at all will hurt them and make them sick. Tell them that little children, sometimes when they do not know this, form the habit of handling themselves, and as a result they become listless and sick, and many times idiotic and insane, or develop epileptic fits. This will so impress them that they will not, properly guarded, fall easily into the bad way . . . Should you discover your child listless, and preferring solitude rather than companionship, averse to exercise, averted look, hypochondriacal, restless in sleep, constipated, pain in the back and lower extremities in the morning, appetite vacillating, hands cold and clammy; if you have not already been suspicious, watch carefully now, even though not half these symptoms are present. Another diagnostic symptom is this: The body emits a peculiar, disagreeable smell, and there is emaciation. Some of the terrible results are epilepsy, idiocy, catalepsy and insanity."

TREATMENT AND PREVENTION

A logical extension of this preoccupation with masturbation was the development of procedures to prevent the practice. Since the effects of self-abuse were in a sense cumulative, it was important that it be nipped in the bud if dire consequences were to be avoided. There was little point in exhorting the culprits to abstain from masturbation, since the majority appeared to be quite incapable of giving it up despite their knowledge that the road they were travelling led initially to the madhouse and eventually to Hell. Therefore, if they would not voluntarily abandon their evil ways, steps would have to be taken to alter their behavior. As in a good many instances in the history of medicine, the cure was worse than the disease, with the physician justifying his actions by claiming that his treatment, no matter how horrendous it might be, was for the benefit of the patient.

In the early nineteenth century the treatment of choice was chemical. One physician suggested that the local application of camphor was the most effective antiaphrodisiac. Another thought that tincture of cantharades as the most efficacious means of a cure. A third suggested potassium bromide, but this soon fell into disrepute because it led to weakness and emaciation. Later, two American physicians, Bucknill and Tuke (1874), were forced to the gloomy conclusion that none of the existing medical procedures were satisfactory in preventing masturbation and they doubted that more radical measures were appropriate. They remarked: ". . . if it could be supposed that any great mind likely to be of use to the human race was in danger of being destroyed and lost through this habit, the question might fairly arise whether an effectual operation was justifiable; but those miserable helots of sensation who are the usual victims of this despicable vice are not worth the responsibility even of such a thought." What these authors are really implying is that the urge to masturbate is inborn; that there are two mutually exclusive classes of people, those who masturbate and those who do not. The former have the potential for being masturbators at birth and nothing can be done about it. They are predestined for the madhouse, or at the very least, being the derelicts of society. They do not possess the potential for contributing to society. The latter, on the other hand, are born clean and pure and not tainted with this malady, and it is from this group that all great men are drawn. That educated men should hold to such utter nonsense is, only 100 years later, difficult to comprehend.

As the century progressed, however, more radical procedures than chemical were in fact in vogue. These involved a variety of surgical procedures. For the treatment of masturbation in girls and women, clitoridectomy (the surgical removal of the clitoris) was recommended (Brown, 1866). Dr. Brown, a president of the Medical Society of London, was the innovator of this procedure and although he was expelled from the Obstetric Society, not so much because of the clitoridectomies *per se*, but because he was suspected of advertising, blackmail, and performing the operation without the patient's consent, including women 70 years of age. Nevertheless, the operation was not abandoned, and as late as 1894 an American surgeon, Block, referred to female masturbation as a form of "moral leprosy" and suggested an even more radical surgical procedure in treatment of women, i.e. ovariotomy (the removal of the ovaries). Dr. Block gained a measure of fame as an ovariotomist, and in 1895 Spratling, an English surgeon, was so impressed by this kind of mutilation that he concluded that "nothing short of ovariotomy will be found to deserve even the term palliative" (Spratling, 1895).

If the treatment of masturbation in women was an abomination, that recommended

for men was no better. These ran the gamut from physical restraints to surgical intervention. The English physician Milton (1887) favored locked chastity belts by day, and spiked
or toothed rings by night. Spratling recommended the "complete section of the dorsal
nerves of the penis" while others cut the pudendal nerves. Where the dorsal nerve was
sectioned, thus anesthetizing the penis, it was observed that the patient "was much
depressed for sometime after" (Spratling, 1895). The unkindest cut of all, castration, was
also carried out, and in 1891 it was Hutchinson, president of the Royal College of
Surgeons, who not only advocated circumcision but avowed "that measures more radical
than circumcision would, if public opinion permitted their adoption, be a true kindness
to many patients of both sexes." Comfort (1967) notes that this "true kindness" was not
neglected. He remarks that: "It is still with us today in some civilized countries in the
castration of sexual offenders—albeit not by penile amputation. Our medical ancestors
were less generous when scared. An unfortunate Texan actually was *castrated in this way*
for masturbation" (italics added). A less permanent solution to the problem, albeit strange
and discomforting and designed to discourage genital manipulation, was infibulation. This
novel treatment consisted of placing silver wires through the prepuce (foreskin) so as to
prevent its retraction behind the glans penis. As late as 1892 the Scottish physician
Yellowleess considered this method to be the best method of prevention. He had been
performing this operation for a number of years and reported in 1876 that: "The sensation
among the patients themselves was extraordinary. I was struck by the conscience-stricken
way in which they submitted to the operation on their penises. I mean to try it on a large
scale, and go on wiring all masturbators . . ." This observation must be among the classics
of understatement.

An authoritative textbook on epilepsy by Gowers, appeared in 1885. While not completely convinced that masturbation could result in epilepsy, Gowers nevertheless notes
that a thirteen-year-old boy, who admitted to masturbation, was cured of epilepsy by
circumcision. ". . . a blister on the prepuce reduced the fits (from 12–14 a day) to from
two to seven daily. He was then circumcised, and the attacks ceased at once, and did
not recur."

In a critique of the masturbation myth, and in reference to the therapeutic procedures
designed to eliminate masturbation, Comfort notes: "Over this period (1850–1890) there
was a truly remarkable upsurge of what can be only termed comic-book sadism. The
advocacy of these bizarre therapies was not confined to eccentrics. By about 1880 the
individual who might wish for unconscious reasons to tie, chain or infibulate sexually
active children or mental patients—the two most readily abailable captive audiences—
to adorn them with grotesque appliances, encase them in plaster of paris, leather or
rubber, to frighten or even castrate them, to cauterize or denervate their genitalia, could
find humane and respectable medical authority for doing so in good conscience. Masturbation insanity was real enough—it was affecting the medical profession. The fetishistic
antics which some of its members seriously recommended would have been thought a
little exorbitant in a brothel—and few of them, even including clitoridectomy, were really
capable of preventing the practice at which they were nominally directed."

MASTURBATION AND NEUROSIS

No one was more involved than Freud in formulating and enunciating the view that
masturbation provoked neurotic disorders. Thanks to him, the legacy still exists to bedevil
boys and girls. The amount of psychic damage that this notion has done, and continues
to do, is beyond measure. Among the women interviewed by Kinsey (1953), some firmly
believed that masturbation caused among other things pimples, poor posture, ovarian
pains and cysts, cancer, appendicitis, weak eyes, sterility, headache, kidney trouble,

weak hearts, lack of hormones, and mental dullness. Kinsey notes that: "It is significant that those who had most often found moral objections to masturbation were the ones who most often insisted that physical and mental damages had resulted from their activity." More recently, in a study conducted in 1961 in five medical schools in the Philadelphia area, it was found that half of the graduating medical students believed that masturbation caused mental illness. Furthermore, but not surprising, one in five faculty members also held to this view (Greenbank, 1961).

Freud's preoccupation with masturbation came about as a result of his notions of the etiology of neurotic disorders; these were concerned with infantile sexuality. An early reference to this occurred in 1894, in relation to a girl suffering from "obsessions of self reproaches." Freud wrote: "Close questioning then revealed the source from which her sense of guilt arose. Stimulated by chance voluptuous sensation, she had allowed herself to be led astray by a woman friend into masturbating, and had practiced it for years, fully conscious of her wrong-doing and to the accompaniment of most violent, but, as usual, ineffective self-reproaches. An excessive indulgence after going to a ball had produced the intensification that led to the psychosis. After a few months of treatment and the strictest surveillance, the girl recovered."

He was later to write (1912) "We are all agreed, (a): on the importance of the phantasies which accompany or represent the act of masturbation, (b) on the importance on the sense of guilt, whatever its source may be, which is attached to masturbation and (c) on the impossibility of assigning a qualitative determinant for the injurious effects of masturbation." Freud never abandoned the idea that masturbation was harmful and a source of mental problems such as neurasthenia, hypochondriasis and anxiety neuroses. However, some of his disciples were less convinced of this than he was, and in the early part of this century Stekel disagreed with Freud and regarded the relationship between mental illness and masturbation as a "senseless prejudice."

More recently, Fenichel (1945) has written: ". . . it is clear that masturbation in adults in some circumstances operates as a *symptom* of a neurosis; but it does not *create* a neurosis. However, it may be part of a vicious circle: if neurotic shyness induces a person to masturbate rather than to approach an object sexually, he never learns that an object actually is capable of giving a higher pleasure; the way to the masturbatory "substitute" is an easy one, and this *ease* may bring a kind of "spoiling," that is, make the subject more unwilling to sustain the difficulties of attaining an object, and thus increase the shyness that was the first cause of his masturbation."

Having said this, his next statement is: "Masturbation as such does not produce neuroses. It has been proven clinically, however, that unsuccessful masturbation, that is, masturbation that increases sexual tension but is not capable of discharging it adequately, results in actual neurotic symptoms." Apparently there are two kinds of masturbation, the successful and the unsuccessful. The two are differentiated in terms of whether or not they discharge sexual tension. Unfortunately this kind of statement explains nothing, and the only way in which success in discharging sexual tension can be defined or determined is by the outcome of masturbation; if one develops a neurosis from masturbation, then one has been unsuccessful; if one does not become neurotic from masturbating, then the sexual tension has been adequately discharged. In any event, Fenichel's is perhaps the definitive psychoanalytic statement of the problem, although it must be conceded that not all psychoanalysts share his optimistic views (e.g. Hammerman, 1961).

While this may be the last word as far as psychoanalysis is concerned, the issue did not die in the 1920s. In the 1938 edition of Griffith and Mitchell's *Diseases of Infants and Children,* the authors, while noting that even extreme degrees of masturbation apparently cause little damage, nevertheless devote three pages to treatment and suggest that: "In bad cases, and especially if the act occurs during sleep, some appliance must be employed that will mechanically make friction impossible. A small pillow may be placed between the thighs and a bandage applied around them; or the knees kept separate by a rod terminating at each end in a leather collar fastened around the thigh just above the knees . . . where the hands are employed, it may be necessary to confine these, as by elbow splints or in other ways . . . Circumcision is . . . sometimes curative in older children through the soreness produced by the operation . . . if necessary, circumcision of the clitoris [must be] performed." From this it is obvious that the clock has been turned back and the remedies recommended do not differ in any real way from those advocated and practiced in the nineteenth century.

As late as 1940 it was a regulation of the U. S. Naval Academy at Annapolis that candidates be rejected if evidence of masturbation was found (Kinsey et al., 1953). As in the English public schools of the nineteenth century, masturbation was recognized as a potential menace and those suspected of this heinous practice need be sought out and severely dealt with.

THE EFFECTS OF THE MASTURBATION MYTHS

This resumé of its history provides a background from which to view contemporary notions about masturbation and the effects of these views *viz a viz* current problems in sexual conduct. As is evident, notions of the evil effects have undergone radical changes over the past 200 years, at least within medical circles, and a logical question at this point might be: Why, in the complete absence of any credible evidence, and despite the fact it has been scientifically discredited, do otherwise reasonable people continue to believe that masturbation has deleterious effects on one's physical and psychic health? Many persons presenting sexual problems firmly believe that masturbation is dirty, sinful, abnormal, or a combination of these. Those who have engaged in it feel guilty about the practice; those who have not, have thought about it but rejected it because they consider it either abnormal or not the sort of thing a nice person does—even though some of them have petted to orgasm.

There is no simple answer. Indeed, there are a host of reasons for this irrational attitude toward masturbation. The prime reason appears to be the fact that attitudes toward sex, including masturbation, are shaped by one's environment: by what has been learned through observation and by more formal instruction received in the formative years when one is extremely receptive to new ideas, accepting uncritically virtually everything that parents and other authority figures proclaim. This is understandable; young children have no basis for rendering judgments on the truth or falsity, appropriateness or inappropriateness, of statements made by adults. They accept as true pronouncements made by those they look up to. It is only after they mature intellectually and begin to acquire knowledge and information from other sources that they become capable of assessing the validity of what they have been taught. Unfortunately, by the time they reach this stage, their notions about a variety of issues have become pretty firmly fixed and it is no easy task to alter their ways of thinking. (This, of course, is a truth not restricted to masturbation, and one has only to look at attitudes towards minority groups, for example, to see the effects of early learning; prejudices are not genetically inherited.)

Albert Ellis has probably done more than any other single individual in debunking the myths of the evils of masturbation and related problems (Ellis, 1962, 1965). His response is that they are complete and utter nonsense and have no basis in fact. One can only echo his statement that they ". . . constitute a modern carryover of old antisexual moralizing."

MYTHS AND LEARNING

The kinds of experiences which lead to rejection of masturbation as a form of sexual expression need not be overt and blatant; these can be subtle and nonspecific. Mothers frequently become distressed when they see their young children playing with their genitals, although the mothers, if questioned about their feelings, are extremely vague about why they are distressed. They are very nonspecific and will only say that children should not play with themselves, other people might see them doing this, it just is not right, and so on. They do not, as a general rule, come right out and say that it is bad for the child's physical or mental health, that it will cause one to become simple or insane. The chances are that they do not believe this anyway. The reasons for their distress at the child's behavior are as nebulous to them as they are to the child. Nevertheless, the seeds are being sown in the child for future feelings of disquiet about handling his genitals. And children learn very quickly; not many learning trials are required before, for instance, a little boy will stop playing with himself, at least when his mother might observe him. Instead, he will do it in the privacy of his bedroom or bathroom. Then this can engender guilt feelings because here he is doing something secretly which he knows, because of his mother's frequent admonitions, is not quite right.

This kind of situation can become exaggerated, and instead of showing gentle disapproval, mother can become extremely upset, screaming and slapping the child when she sees him engaging in self-manipulation. In general, her behavior is spontaneous and irrational, and its effect is to frighten the child and impress upon him that touching his genitals is an horrendous crime.

Case Report 34

One woman who came for treatment behaved in just this way. She found her four-year-old daughter and a male companion of like age comparing their respective sexual equipment. She became hysterical, beat the little girl, and threatened both of them with a fate worse than death if they ever did such a thing again. It was only after it was pointed out to her that she had behaved exactly as *her* mother had behaved that she realized she was well on the way to creating the same problem in her daughter that she herself had. It came as a revelation to her. Furthermore, she began to attend to her daughter's behavior and noticed that the little girl already had the notion that to be seen naked was bad and took care not to be seen naked by her father and older brother if this could be avoided. (One of the mother's problems was an exaggerated sense of modesty.)

This is not an isolated case; many women, and some men too, pursue the same irrational goal—teaching their children that playing with their genitals and masturbation is dirty, bad, and nice children do not do it. Furthermore, they maintain this attitude in the face of overwhelming evidence to the contrary; they continue to hold to this archaic view despite the fact that virtually every authority on human sexual behavior condemns it. Almost without exception, every sex manual or text on human sexuality published in the last 15–20 years goes to great lengths to debunk this myth, and these books are readily and freely available. The time is past when books on sexuality came wrapped in plain brown paper. (Check any book shop or library—or drugstore!)

Furthermore, if parents paused to think seriously about masturbation, it is difficult to imagine that they would fail to see the irrationality of their views. If masturbation were as serious as it has been made out to be, there would not be enough mental hospitals in the world to accommodate its victims. Without exception, where the sexes are segregated for extended periods of time, masturbation provides the major outlet, in both men and women, for sexual expression. And this is true of prisons, the armed services, and indeed in any situation where normal heterosexual behavior is impossible because of absence of the opposite sex or by sanctions, i.e., monasteries and nunneries. To believe otherwise is to fly in the face of human nature and human conduct. Fathers in particular have a short memories, and will admonish their children for committing acts that they themselves once did—or, perhaps, continue to engage in. But this is only additional evidence of human irrationality.

CURRENT THINKING

Not only has the myth of masturbation's evils officially fallen into disrepute, the pendulum has swung the other way: it has been clearly demonstrated that rather than being bad for the individual, masturbation is in fact beneficial not only for its own sake in relieving sexual tension and frustrations, but as a method of enhancing sexual arousal and responsiveness. As mentioned earlier, Kinsey and his colleagues alluded to this elementary fact more than twenty years ago, and Ellis has been beating the pro-masturbation drum in numerous publications for an equally long period of time. Unfortunately, this information appears to have met with something less than universal acceptance, and in fact public abuse and condemnation has been the major legacy of Ellis's attempts at education in this field. However, the degree to which the attitudes have changed is exemplified by Kaplan (1974). She states: "In contrast to men, where the *absence* of adolescent masturbation raises a question of psychiatric disturbance, women who never have masturbated are *not necessarily* pathological" (italics added). This is reversal on a grand scale. Originally masturbation *caused* physical and mental problems or was a symptom of neurosis. Now the absence of masturbation in men is a sign of mental disturbance, while in women it may be.

Within the last five years or so there have been a spate of articles in various popular publications, and a great many books on sexual problems published, where masturbation has been discussed (often accompanied by line drawings and explicit instructions about procedures), with the result that it has become a topic more freely discussed. Most of this advice, as one might expect, has been directed towards women. In general, these publications are of three types.

One has taken advantage of the relaxation and changes in the laws regarding censorship and this has resulted in a number of "confessional" books which can best be described as salacious, although their stated purpose is to educate through example. These books have in common an absence of literary merit and a pedagogical value which is nil so far as people with sexual problems are concerned. They likely do more harm than good since they convey the impression that all sexual hangups are a result of poor technique, lack of experience and a puritan reluctance to engage, if only ineptly, in any sexual activity other than "standard intercourse" in the missionary position. Their main thesis appears to be that everyone can become a sexual athlete if only one mimics the antics of the characters (supposedly autobiographical) in the story.

Unfortunately their major thesis is in error, and furthermore, they impose impossible tasks on the reader. Women who feel that masturbation is dirty or sinful are unlikely to be swayed by the argument that masturbating to orgasm ten to twenty times a day will solve their problems. It seems quite likely that the majority of women who read these books are in fact the very ones who require no instruction. In this case the information (or some of it) may give them some novel ideas of sexual practices (intercourse in the broom closet or under the bed or hanging from the chandelier) which they find titilating and which will astonish and confound their husbands. However, apart from increasing their sexual repertoire, little is derived from such readings.

The second type of publication dealing with sexual problems is of semiscientific nature in that it is usually written by a medical doctor, psychologist, or some other "authority" on the matter. Frequently the word "love" is incorporated in the title, the implication being that sex and love, if not equated, do, in some divine way, go hand in hand. The world is portrayed as idylic where two (but not necessarily only two) people join in romantic and loving embrace, with satisfaction guaranteed to all.

These are essentially sex manuals; how-to-do-it books. If you follow the instructions, avoid the many pitfalls to trap the insensitive, the unwary, the hurried and the harried, then you too can reach sexual nirvana and be a better person for it. The major object of these books appears to be to "bring sex out into the open," and as vividly as possible, in the misguided hope that by doing so sexual problems will cease to exist or will at least be mitigated.

When one views the drawings depicting various positions recommended for intercourse (and other sexual behaviors), the feeling is that they were designed for olympic caliber gymnasts. The average, run-of-the-mill sexual athlete would likely end up with a slipped disc or a charley-horse, if he were to attempt to assume the coital positions depicted. But perhaps this is part of the strategy. Certainly both the man and the woman would have to put their whole minds into what they were doing, which would tend to reduce performance anxiety. Or, perhaps by the time they assumed the position, both would fall asleep from sheer exhaustion.

These books are generally better written than the first group mentioned, and they are salted with scientific or medical terminology whose function is to lend a certain amount of credence to an otherwise mundane or untenable thesis. Here, too, the emphasis is on technique; with respect to masturbation, various procedures, stratagems and aids are discussed and espoused. The goal to be achieved is orgasm, the minimum being one, and the maximum only determined by stamina and available time. The hope or expectation is that if a woman can reliably reach orgasm through self-stimulation, chances are she will be able to repeat this feat during intercourse. Believing this, the women valiantly try, and in too many cases the result is failure, frustration, anxiety and exaggerated guilt feelings and, more important, an overwhelming feeling of inadequacy and despair. This is carried over in their sexual relations with their husbands and it should come as no surprise that the problem is exacerbated as failure follows failure.

The general philosophy which governs these books appears to be that sexual dysfunction does not exist in any real sense. The problem is seen as a lack of knowledge and an inability to communicate effectively with one's partner. If these two hurdles are overcome, a satisfactory and satisfying sex life will naturally follow. Problems such as vaginismus, aversion to sex, anxiety about sex and so on are summarily dismissed as being of little consequence. The fact that many women will not or cannot masturbate without intense feeling of guilt, shame or anxiety is ignored. To a woman who feels this way, the very idea of suggesting to her husband that he masturbate her, with his finger or his tongue or even his toes, is unthinkable. Nevertheless, this is the kind of program advocated by these publications; in reading them one can only conclude that, like the publications mentioned earlier, they are primarily designed to excite, provoke and whet the sexual appetite of those whose only problem is a lack of imagination. They may enhance pleasure; they do little or nothing to overcome sexual problems.

The third and final type of publication comprises those genuinely concerned with sexual dysfunctions. The authors are specialists in their field, and recognize the severity and magnitude of the problems; they are concerned with bona fide attempts at alleviation. Their discussion of sexual dysfunctions are rational and realistic, and the treatment procedure they advocate are rooted in sound experimental ground. No attempt is made to gloss over the fact that a large proportion of women have sexual problems which will not vanish as a result of reading a how-to-do-it manual, and they include the most effective and efficient ways to masturbate without guilt. These publications are directed towards other workers in the field, either therapists or researchers, although they too often catch the public eye and become "best sellers." Masters and Johnson's *Human*

Sexual Inadequacy (1970) would be an example. The fact that texts of this type are widely disseminated may have a salutory effect; they tend to counteract the how-to-do-it manuals, and clearly demonstrate to men and women who find sex troublesome that sexual dysfunctions really do exist and will not be magically removed. (Unfortunately these books, too, have serious shortcomings which have been mentioned in Chapter 4.)

Masturbation is an integral part of human sexual behavior and it is unlikely that a women will reach her full sexual potential unless she is able to stimulate herself to orgasm without feeling sinful or guilty. But, conversely, because a women can reliably masturbate to orgasm is no guarantee that she will enjoy sexual intercourse and achieve orgasm in the process. Nevertheless, removing the myths and anxieties surrounding masturbation is important in treating sexual dysfunctions. Methods of achieving this end are incorporated, as part of a general therapeutic procedure, in valid texts dealing with sexual dysfunctions.

On the face of it, introducing anxiety-free masturbation to women with lifetimes of negative learning experiences would appear a virtually impossible task. How can one overcome long ingrained habits of thinking and acting? Can, in fact, strongly held attitudes and beliefs be altered through argument and persuasion? Unfortunately, the answer to the second question is a qualified no. Argument and persuasion are, in most instances, ineffectual. There are effective procedures which can be used which do not presuppose that people behave in rational ways. They do not assume that explaining to a woman that part of her problem lies in her attitudes toward masturbation will make her see the logic of this and alter her behavior accordingly. Neither do they assume that learning and acquiring the habit of masturbation is something which can be accomplished by simple instruction and practice.

What they do assume is that for many women even the thought of masturbation is anxiety provoking, laden with associations of guilt, sin, or immorality. Teaching or exhorting them to acquire a new behavior will not be enough: they also have to *un*learn the habit of *not* masturbating.

Recognizing that masturbation is more than friction, and cognizant of the role that it plays in many cases of sexual dysfunction, attempts have been made to delineate and specify the problem and to devise rational procedures in dealing with it. No one who has had the experience of treating sexual problems is naive enough to believe that convincing women to masturbate and teaching them how will, in and of itself, solve their problems. But it is a step in that direction. So, let us rid ourselves of the notion that masturbation is evil and bad for you, and accept instead that it does no harm and is in fact beneficial.

The next chapter is concerned with attempts to initiate masturbation, their rationale and procedures. Some of them appear to make sense in terms of what is known about the learning of sexual roles and sexual behavior, and some of them are buttressed by experimental demonstration. No claim can be made that they are totally rational or completely effective. They are not a panacea but they indicate what can be done to alleviate a distressing problem.

SUMMARY

We have, in this chapter, traced the relevant aspects of the history of masturbation as this is related to an understanding of human sexual functioning and dysfunctioning. Over the course of 200 years, masturbation has evolved from being a source of physical and mental disturbances to some present day thinking where the absence of masturbation is viewed as a possible source of psychological trouble.

It is difficult to comprehend the earlier notions about masturbation and its attendant ills. From this vantage point they are bizarre and nonsensical. The peculiar notions of the effects of this activity are only exceeded by the strange and often inhuman procedures and devices designed to prevent and eliminate the habit. By and large these were ineffectual; they were bound to fail.

And despite the gloomy prophesies of the early, and not so early, anti-sexualizers and anti-masturbators, the fabric of society was not torn asunder. The human order has survived despite its almost universal practice of masturbating.

8
Masturbation as Therapy

The purpose of this chapter is to examine current attitudes and changed thinking, and to consider the influences in the twentieth century which are responsible for this change. We will attempt to explain why masturbation is now an approved therapeutic tool, describing in some detail specific applications of masturbation in the treatment of sexual problems.

In the late 1940s and early 1950s, widespread support was gained for the position that masturbation is not harmful. The monumental work of Kinsey and his colleagues (1948, 1953) gave the scientific world for the first time reasonable, accurate information concerning the occurrences of masturbation in human males and females. The effect was to seriously challenge the irrational and condemning attitudes toward what was now shown to be an almost universal phenomenon. Once these beliefs were challenged, it was only a matter of time before masturbation was looked upon as a therapeutic device.

As therapy, masturbation has been utilized in somewhat different ways for the treatment of male and female sexual problems, and it is very likely that these divergent applications were given impetus by Kinsey's work. In men, masturbation has been used in two ways: 1) as a method of changing sexual orientation through conditioning, and 2) as a treatment for premature ejaculation. Masturbation therapy for women has been applied exclusively for treating primary orgasmic dysfunction. The development and application of masturbation-based therapy will be discussed separately for males and females.

The first part of this discussion is concerned with the treatment of homosexuality. While this topic is somewhat removed from the general thesis of this book, it is important in that it is in this context that masturbation as a therapeutic procedure received much of its early support.

TREATMENT FOR MALES

CHANGING SEXUAL ORIENTATION

Within recent history attempts have been made to change the sexual orientation of homosexual males. For the most part the legal and therapeutic efforts have been punitive ones. Aversion therapy, for example, has come under a great deal of attack because of its punative and dehumanizing aspect. Humanitarian and Gay Liberation groups have organized well-run attacks against aversion therapy which have resulted in demonstrations at and disruptions of Behavior Therapy conventions, concerned articles in newspapers and magazines, anti-behavior therapy books and movies (e.g., A Clockwork Orange), governmental investigations, and legislation making aversion therapy illegal in some States. A good deal of the controversy is aimed at behavior modification in general (usually by misinformed people), but the criticism is almost always aimed at the use of aversion therapy. Because of the ethical and public concern surrounding and permeating such therapy, therapists and clinical researchers have increased the search for alternative strategies for dealing with traditional problems. One of the most popular resultant developments has been increased focus on building-in new behaviors in troubled individuals rather than simply eliminating undesirable behaviors. The use of masturbation therapy is one result of this tide of interest.

Aversion therapy has also been criticized for being an incomplete treatment approach. If it is effective when applied, it could leave an individual sexually neutered. He would no longer be a homosexual, but would not have the skills to function heterosexually. Although this position is a theoretical one, it does make some sense since a majority of homosexuals have inadequately developed heterosocial and heterosexual behaviors. Even in the very early applications of behavior therapy to male homosexuals there was a recognition of the need to develop heterosocial and heterosexual behavior concomitant with the removal of homosexual tendencies. Initially the attempts to increase these behaviors were based on hormonal injection therapy. This proved something less than satisfactory. Subsequently, attempts and hopes have been based on orgasmic reconditioning (ORC).

ORGASMIC RECONDITIONING

ORC is a conditioning therapy in which a male is asked to masturbate in the presence of whatever stimuli sexually arouse him and then, at the time of orgasm, to switch his focus of attention to heterosexually appropriate stimuli.

It is interesting how such a conditioning-based procedure evolved both theoretically and empirically. Theoretically, its evolution is well-supported and seems sound, while empirically there is the age-old problem of uncontrolled enthusiastic evidence versus controlled but not so compelling evidence.

Dollard and Miller (1950) provided the theoretic basis in which masturbation could be potentially viewed as a classical conditioning experience. In this major work, Dollard and Miller translated the observations made by psychoanalysts (or more accurately, psychoanalytic theory) into a learning theory framework. Psychoanalysts have traditionally stressed the importance of masturbatory fantasy as a means of looking into the structure of pathological behavior. While Dollard and Miller were impressed by this observation, they suggested that associating the strong sexual reward of orgasm with fantasy cues may represent a classical conditioning situation. That is, the individual will learn or become conditioned to the appropriate sex object—the pleasure of ejaculating will be associated with women.

There are two important papers in the literature which apply the theory and emphasize the importance of associating positive feelings of sexual arousal with heterosexual stimuli. A review paper by Freund (1960), and a case study by James (1962), described treatment techniques for homosexuality which consisted of injecting the client with testosterone propionate to induce sexual arousal and exposing him to erotic heterosexual stimuli. This procedure was described as useful when employed in conjunction with aversion therapy procedures. Thorpe, Schmidt and Castell (1964) were the first, however, to use masturbation as a means of inducing a state of sexual arousal which could be associated via a classical conditioning procedure with heterosexual stimuli. Subjects exhibiting homosexual behavior were asked to masturbate using whatever fantasy they found arousing and then switch to fantasies or pictures of heterosexual encounters a few seconds before orgasm. Presumably, after a number of such classical conditioning trials the person would develop an attraction toward heterosexual stimuli. The evidence for the efficacy of this procedure unfortunately was presented entirely in case studies.

The next important development in the field was the publication of a theoretical article by McGuire, Carlisle and Young (1965), entitled "Sexual deviations as conditioned behavior: A hypothesis." In this article, the authors drawing upon their clinical experience presented the following theory:

It is in accordance with conditioning theory that any stimulus which regularly precedes ejaculation by the correct time interval should become more and more sexually exciting. The stimulus may be circumstantiated (for example, the particular time or place in which masturbation or intercourse is commonly practiced) or it may be deliberated (for example, any sexual situation or a fantasy of it, be it normal intercourse or wearing female apparel). It is hypothesized that the latter process is the mechanism by which most sexual deviations are acquired and developed.

It is quite possible that this paper was responsible in promoting the use of masturbatory conditioning for the treatment of male sexual deviancy. The theory suggests that heterosexual arousal can be *instrumentally* conditioned by repeated efforts to fantasize heterosexual stimuli just prior to orgasm.

Staats, on the other hand (1968; 1970) has argued that this procedure produces its effect predominantly through *classical conditioning* rather than instrumental conditioning, with conditioning occurring throughout the entire masturbatory session. Regardless of the theoretical basis underlying the procedure, the end results should be an increased arousal to heterosexual stimuli. Marquis (1970) termed this procedure orgasmic reconditioning and, with others (Davison, 1968; Jackson, 1969), reported impressive changes in the sexual orientation of their clients undergoing ORC. As Barlow (1973) has noted, however, this evidence has not gone beyond the case study level. Furthermore, investigations of the efficacy of ORC have been characterized by one or more of the following shortcomings, and thereby present evidence of limited value: 1) inadequate designs which employ more than one treatment intervention, preventing the isolation of treatment effects; 2) a lack of objective measurement of arousal patterns; 3) an exclusive reliance upon subjects' self-reports to evaluate the outcome of therapy (Conrad and Wincze, 1976).

In an attempt to provide a controlled evaluation of the conditioning effects of ORC, Conrad and Wincze (1976) assessed changes in homosexual arousal patterns and heterosexual arousal patterns in four males undergoing ORC, all of whom wished to increase their level of heterosexual arousal. Assessment of sexual arousal patterns occurred on three levels: 1) attitudinal (client's self-report of improvement); 2) behavioral (client's self-record of *all* sexual urges, fantasies and contacts); 3) physiologic (penile circumference changes as measured by a strain gauge during exposure to homosexual stimuli and heterosexual stimuli).

The basic design of the study allowed for assessment of change during baseline, ORC to fantasy stimuli, and ORC to visual stimuli phases. Each subject was exposed to approximately 40 ORC sessions, and each subject was able to achieve 100% arousal to heterosexual stimuli during ORC sessions by the end of the study. All subjects at the conclusion of the study reported feelings of increased awareness of females and improvement in sexual adjustment. Notably absent, however, were reports of any changes in actual sexual behavior. None of the subjects *decreased* the amount of homosexual urges, fantasies, or contacts, and none of the subjects *increased* the amount of heterosexual urges, fantasies, or contacts. Similarly, there were no changes at the conclusion of the study in physiologically measured arousal patterns to homosexual or heterosexual fantasy or visual stimuli.

The results of this study point to the importance of using multilevel analysis in evaluation of therapy outcome research. It is quite possible that the previous reports of success with ORC presented in case studies were examples of subject-inflated data to please the therapist. Certainly, the results of the above investigation do not support ORC as a viable and efficient procedure for producing heterosexual reorientation. In addition, we have treated one client who reported feeling completely humiliated by his participation in ORC therapy and elected to terminate therapy after a few sessions. Careful questioning of a client's feelings about the type of therapy he is undergoing is a necessary requirement for ORC therapy and other potentially humiliating approaches.

Other procedures for increasing heterosexual arousal, such as the fading technique described by Barlow and Agras (1973), may be more promising. In the fading procedure, male homosexuals are first exposed to a slide of a nude male in order to induce sexual arousal. While in a state of arousal (full erection) a second slide of a nude female is superimposed at a low light intensity over the male slide. If arousal is maintained, subsequent trials are aimed at slowly and progressively fading-in the female slide (increase light intensity) while fading-out the male slide (decrease light intensity). Barlow and Agras report success in increasing heterosexual arousal in three male homosexuals following the fading procedure. The results were made more impressive by the authors' solid use of single-case design methodology in which it was demonstrated that positive changes in heterosexual arousal were associated only with the fading procedure.

In spite of these encouraging results, widespread support of fading has not as yet appeared in the literature. As of this writing, there is little available to the clinician in the way of reliable and effective procedures for increasing heterosexual arousal.

There are no reports in the literature of ORC therapy applied in the treatment of lesbianism. The simple facts are that homosexuality among women is much less frequent than homosexuality among men and lesbianism has traditionally been more widely accepted than homosexuality among men. Kinsey postulates a number of reasons for the more tolerant attitudes of society toward lesbianism but the important fact, regardless of the reasons, is that lesbians are far less likely to seek treatment concerning their sexual activities. Certainly they are not under as much legal or moral pressure to change their sexual behavior. Kinsey reports that in New York City from 1930 to 1939 there were over 10,000 cases of male homosexuality brought before the courts, while during the same period of time only three cases of female homosexuality so appeared and all three cases were dismissed.

Davison and Neale (1974) point to current changing attitudes and laws regarding homosexuality in the direction of more tolerance and acceptance. Therapists' attitudes are changing too, and Davison has raised the question whether homosexuals should be treated even when they voluntarily seek therapy. His argument is, briefly, that therapists and clinincians should focus their attention on the quality of human relationships, on the way people deal with each other, rather than on the particular gender of the adult's partners. Homosexuals do not have any more interpersonal and personal problems than heterosexuals do. The fact that many homosexuals seek treatment Davison sees as a symptom of the pressures of our North American society. Homosexuals should first be treated for their guilt associated with their homosexuality and then, and only then, will they be free to choose one sexual life style over another.

One of the results of the changing attitudes toward homosexuality has been that fewer and fewer homosexuals are seeking treatment. This has certainly been our experience over the past five years so far as men are concerned. The probability of a woman seeking therapy to redirect her orientation from homosexual to heterosexual is most likely extremely slight.

TREATMENT OF PREMATURE EJACULATION

Publication of Masters and Johnson's classic tome *Human Sexual Inadequacy* (1970) sparked a sudden and enormous interest from clinicians and researchers in the area of human sexual problems. Prior to the advent of this book, scientific analysis and treatment of sexual dysfunction was present but not widespread. Growth in terms of new therapy approaches, including masturbation, and research aimed at sexual dysfunction is continuing and is certainly one of the important areas of the future.

But masturbation as a treatment of sexual dysfunction was presented much earlier, in 1956, by James Semans. Semans, a urologist, published an article in the *Southern Medical Journal* entitled "Premature ejaculation: A new approach." Premature ejaculation is a condition experienced by males in which there is loss of ejaculatory control before satisfaction of the female partner is reached. Clincians usually consider ejaculation premature if less than 50% of sexual experiences are unsatisfactory. Another criterion of premature ejaculation is the unexpected occurence of ejaculation before intromission, or shortly after intromission. Semans' treatment focuses on repeated masturbatory practice by the patient to the point where the warning sensations of ejaculation are experienced. At this point the patient stops masturbating and waits until the sensation has disappeared. Semans reported successful treatment of eight patients by this method. In every case, the premature ejaculation was successfully treated within one month, with a minimum of 3 ⅓ hours spent with each patient and his wife. The exact parameters of the procedure were not described, and it is not known how many sessions of training on the average a patient had to participate in before he felt he could endure prolonged stimulation without ejaculation.

Kaplan (1974) using Semans' procedure with her patients reports that men are instructed to stimulate themselves, or have their wives stimulate them, to the point where they feel the "premonitory orgastic sensation." Once this point is reached the patient is instructed to stop, or tell his wife to stop, until the sensation is lost and then begin stimulation once again. Ejaculation is allowed to occur on the fourth trial. Kaplan reports that some control of the ejaculatory response usually occurs within three to six practice sessions.

Masters and Johnson (1970) employ a variation of this in their treatment of premature ejaculation by instructing their patients to "squeeze" the penis on the frenulum and coronal ridge when stimulation reaches the point where orgasm is close. This "squeeze" procedure is otherwise similar to the Semans procedure and it is not known if the squeeze adds to its effectiveness. Practicing either of the ejaculatory control procedures demands a relaxed, guilt-free environment and usually a willing and accepting female partner. Given these prerequisites, the procedures seem to be highly effective, although no hard data are available which would substantiate Kaplan's or Master and Johnson's claims of success.

As previously mentioned, both Kaplan and Masters and Johnson have dealt mostly with educated middle and upper middle class people. In our own clinical experience in dealing with lower class, uneducated clients the outcome is less impressive with use of the squeeze technique. Although our experience tends to be limited to this area, we have found a large number of these clients unable to profit from this rather simple procedure in spite of repeated instructions and video tape demonstration programs. One problem seems to be making the client aware of the "warning" signs of ejaculation. Clients report squeezing too soon or too late, and feeling embarrassed by the whole idea of squeezing the head of their penis after masturbating, or having their wives do this. Some of our clients have lived with the idea that masturbation is something that "queers" or "weirdos" do when they do not have a female partner. Such attitudes have been corroborated by Kinsey et al. (1948), who observed that definite taboos against masturbation are more commonly associated with lower levels of education in adults.

In our experience, we have found the male from lower socioeconomic levels to be particularly resistant to learning theory explanations of premature ejaculation. These individuals interpret as a definite threat to their masculinity the suggestion that by going through certain different behaviors their sexual problem could be remedied. After all, males are supposed to know everything there is to know about sexual technique, and premature ejaculation must be a medical problem curable with pills.

Trying to explain the concept of premature ejaculation to an individual who can neither read nor write, and who does not understand the words *orgasm, climax* or *masturbation*, presents a challenge to the most creative therapist. One often has to use "street" language in order to discuss the problem and its remedy. Consider the following interview with Mr. R.

Therapist (T): How long have you been married Mr. R.?

Mr. R: Seven years.

T: And this problem is something that has existed from the start of the marriage?

Mr. R: Right from the start.

T: Exactly what, in your own words, is the problem?

Mr. R: She don't get no satisfaction out of me. The problem is I can't help myself stop.

T: Does this mean that you come too quickly? Do you come even before you have intercourse?

Mr. R: I come inside her but before she gets satisfaction.

T: How long do you last before you come?

Mr. R: About 4 or 5 minutes.

T: How long does your wife think you should be able to control yourself?

Mr. R: I should control myself much longer than this . . . ten minutes or so. She can last longer because she is a woman and is stronger than I am. It isn't only her, it's other women, too.

T: Are you talking about sexual experiences before marriage?

Mr. R: Before marriage and in marriage.

T: Have you had other women other than your wife while you have been married?

Mr. R: Right. This was one of the ways I tried to get over my problem . . . but she don't know about this.

T: And you had the same problem with other women too?

Mr. R: Yes.

T: Have you ever had the problem of losing your hard on?

Mr. R: Yeh. I lose my hard on when I drink too much.

A continuation of this interview revealed that Mr. R's wife probably had sexual problems too. It was very difficult to determine from the interview if the premature ejaculation was a true problem or if it was a result of unrealistic expectations combined with an inorgasmic wife. Unfortunately, Mrs. R refused to be interviewed and it was impossible to conduct therapy without her cooperation. This interview points to some of the difficulties a therapist may be faced with in dealing with the less-educated and less-articulate client. It is possible that a great deal could be lost in the translation unless the therapist is skillful. Printed monographs and available films are of little help for the uneducated client. For example, a film entitled "The Squeeze Technique"* is available, but is aimed

*For information on ordering, See Appendix A.

mainly at the well-educated. Consider the following quotes from the movie from the point of view of a man with a 5th-grade education.

The female partner brings the male to the point of ejaculatory inevitability through manual or oral means, at which time the male communicates this to his partner.

or

The technique should be repeated several times in one session, once a day, for 2 or 3 days before the second stage of intravaginal containment of the penis.

With uneducated individuals, the film is actually more useful if the therapist turns off the soundtrack and explains the behavior of the actors to the client.

Naturally, our treatment approach does not simply ask clients to go forth and masturbate–squeeze, etc. Since many clients have misinformation and negative feelings about masturbation, a great deal of therapy time is spent on correcting misinformation and assuring clients that masturbation is natural and not harmful. It is surprising to us that in spite of careful explanation and attempts at dispelling myths and negative feelings there is still considerable resistance to masturbation in a number of clients. A procedure of therapist self-disclosure may be an additional strategy which a therapist could consider for clients who are troubled by the concept of masturbation. Under this procedure the therapist unashamedly discusses his or her own masturbation after the client has had time to develop some regard and respect for the therapist. But again, this may be effective only with educated clients. Self-disclosure to many lower class clients might only serve to reinforce the common notion that psychologists are a bit weird.

INVOLVING THE SEXUAL PARTNER

Most therapists agree that in order to treat a sexual dysfunction problem it is crucial to enlist the assistance and support of the client's sexual partner. This seems to be especially true for treatment of premature ejaculation by the squeeze or Semans procedure. When using either technique the female partner is encouraged to take an active part in the therapy procedure. Very often a therapist will encourage the male initially to practice the procedure on his own and then practice it with the cooperation of his partner. By directly including the female partner in the procedure she learns to be more sensitive to her husband's arousal and assist in the delay of orgasm. As in the example of Mr. R, it is sometimes the case that a man's sexual partner will refuse to cooperate and refuse to become involved in the therapy program. This is a discouraging prognostic indicator and therapeutic efforts will usually have to be abandoned. Relaying therapeutic instructions through one partner to another is undesirable and usually does not work. Stunned amazement is a typical response on the part of a poorly educated woman when her less than articulate husband attempts to describe how she is to "squeeze the end of my pecker."

TREATMENT FOR FEMALES

ACHIEVING ORGASM

As in the development of therapeutic procedures for males, Masters and Johnson have been influential in their development of treatment techniques for sexual dysfuction in females. Although they did not specifically employ masturbation as part of their treatment package for orgasmic dysfunction, their observations certainly encouraged others to do so. Through observation of thousands of female orgasms in their laboratories, these researchers concluded that masturbation is the most probable means of producing orgasm, and results in the most intense orgasm. In addition, intense orgasm leads to increased vascularity in the vagina, labia and clitoris—which may in turn enhance the potential for future orgasm (Bardwick, 1971).

Acting on this information, LoPiccolo and Lobitz (1972) developed a masturbation program for treatment of primary orgasmic dysfunction in women. This is similar in a number of ways to the masturbation programs for premature ejaculation in men. In both programs it is extremely important to dispel any myths and negative feelings associated with masturbation before starting. Here again, LoPiccolo and Lobitz suggest therapist self-disclosure as an aid to those who are especially unfavorable toward masturbation. These authors insist that the women should be made to feel that masturbation is perfectly normal. Husbands are encouraged to discuss their own masturbation with their wives and to participate in their own masturbation sessions in order to help their wives feel more comfortable.

As in the procedure developed for male sexual dysfunction, women are encouraged to begin therapy sessions alone. LoPiccolo and Lobitz (1972) suggest that genital touch and self-exploration should be primary in their step-by-step program. Almost all men are familiar with the appearance and feel of their own genitals, but it is not unusual for a woman to state that she has never carefully looked at or explored her own genitals. Neither is it unusual for a woman who has never masturbated to say that she has never touched her genitals except for hygienic purposes.

The steps leading to orgasm begin with asking a client to increase self-awareness by means of visual and tactual exploration of her own genitals. There is an emphasis on exploring and touching during the initial steps to avoid putting the client under any pressure by demanding arousal. During the next few steps the client is encouraged to experience arousal sensations, and is instructed by a female therapist on specific masturbatory technique. If orgasm does not occur at this point, then clients are encouraged to use a vibrator, lubricant jelly and pornographic reading material or pictures to enhance arousal. Should orgasm still not occur, systematic desensitization (described in Chapter 4) may be used as an adjunct procedure for clients who are afraid to have orgasm.

Leslie LoPiccolo and Julie Heiman have produced a series of three films for women who have never experienced an orgasm and for women who have difficulty experiencing orgasm with a partner*. The movies are based on the step-by-step program developed by Joseph LoPiccolo and are designed for single and married women. A book entitled *Becoming Orgasmic: A Sexual Growth Program for Women* has been written by Leslie LoPiccolo and Julie Heiman to complement the films.

In our own experience we have dealt with clients who have expressed fear of orgasm for a variety of reasons, ranging from fear of fainting to fear of losing control of oneself. Systematic desensitization has been helpful in all cases. The following is part of an interview with a client who had a fear of having a climax.

Therapist (T): Mrs. P, would you please describe for me what your problem is?

Mrs. P: My husband asked me to go and see what was wrong with me. He thought maybe I was repressing my sexual arousal. I explained to him that, well, before we were married—I wouldn't say we had actual intercourse, but—we got close to it a couple of times. It would get to the point where I knew I was going to reach a climax and it scared me cause I thought I was going to black out, I thought I was going to lose complete control of all my rational senses. So I stopped myself and that was it, so I kept stopping myself.

*See Appendix A for information on ordering.

Two weeks before we were married, I went on the pill and I thought this was great. I've got no fears of getting pregnant now, so what difference could it make? But I couldn't reach a climax at all, and it just got worse as things went on.

T: Tell me more about your feelings when you are approaching climax.

Mrs. P: I feel that I'm getting there but I haven't quite reached the peak, but then I feel that I'm going to die or pass out and then I'll be laying there unconscious and I won't know what's going on and it bothers me. I really feel that I'll pass out, though. The feeling that I have, whether painful or pleasurable, it's kind of both. Sometimes the pain part gets to be worse than the pleasure part and it scares me.

T: Why do you think that you may pass out during orgasm? Have you ever heard of anyone passing out, or have you ever read about this?

Mrs. P: My husband was describing to me one time when he was masturbating when he was a kid and he said he passed out, he thought he had done something really horrible to himself cause he passed out and he woke up and this semen was all over his body. He was really scared and he promised himself never to do it again.

The remainder of the interview focused on Mrs. P's sexual history and a discussion of the physiology of sexual response. It was further learned that the description of female orgasm in D. H. Lawrence's *Lady Chatterly's Lover* also frightened her. Therapy focused on dispelling myths surrounding sexual behavior and desensitizing Mrs. P to feelings of fainting during sexual intercourse.

Once a client has experienced orgasm through masturbation, the last steps of the program involve the introduction of the male sexual partner and transfer of sexual arousal from masturbatory stimulation to a combination of masturbatory and coital stimulation, to coital stimulation alone. LoPiccolo and Lobitz report success in eight out of eight casses using their nine step masturbation program.

Kaplan (1974) reports a similar program of masturbation for orgasmic dysfunction in women. Her program does not appear to be as thorough as the LoPiccolo and Lobitz program, but is nonetheless reported to be successful. Kaplan also discusses the use of a vibrator as an adjunct to orgasmic training but warns of some potential pitfalls. Since the vibrator method of stimulation can produce a very intense orgasm, Kaplan feels that it is possible for a woman to get "hooked" on it. However, with an impotent husband, this may be a point in its favor! It is suggested that the vibrator be used only during the initial steps of orgasmic training when manual stimulation had initially failed. Kaplan's advice concerning the use of the vibrator has good common sense appeal but is lacking empirical evidence.

DIRECTED PROGRAMS OF MASTURBATION

There is at least one study in the literature which supports the directed masturbation procedures as an effective treatment of primary orgasmic dysfunction in women. Kohlenberg (1974) presents evidence which points to the efficacy of directed masturbation following the failure of a treatment program modelled after that of Masters and Johnson. Kohlenberg treated three couples, all of whom were reporting orgasmic dysfunction of the female partner. Throughout the study the female partners recorded four types of data: 1) the occurrence of orgasmic experiences during masturbation; 2) the occurrence of orgasmic experiences during coitus; 3) self-ratings of sexual arousal experienced during the husband–wife sexual encounter; 4) self-ratings during the self-stimulation sessions. The data from the Kohlenberg study are presented in Figure 8–1.

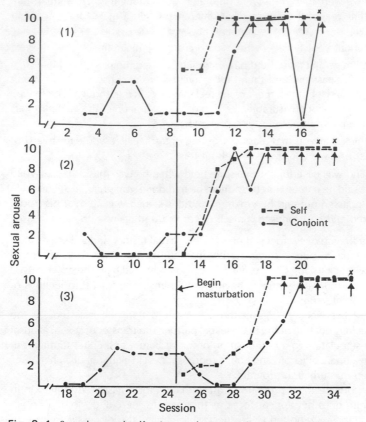

Fig. 8–1. Sexual arousal self-ratings and orgasms for female member of each couple. Orgasms elicited during masturbation are indicated by arrow, orgasms occurring during intromission by an X. (Kohlenberg RJ: Directed masturbation and the treatment of primary orgasmic dysfunction. Archives of Sexual Behavior, Vol 3, No 4: 349–356. New York, Plenum, 1974)

This study is unique because it demonstrates changes in cognitive levels of arousal following directed masturbation training. There are few studies in the literature which have presented evidence of arousal changes as a result of therapy intervention. Our own research was initially aimed entirely at measuring changes in sexual anxiety. With the development of the SAI (see Chapter 3) and valid physiologic measures of female sexual arousal, there will be substantial interest in the future in recording accurate changes in arousal as a result of therapy.

The measures used by Kohlenberg are subjectively biased, but presumably would have shown changes during the Masters and Johnson therapy procedure if they were primarily influenced by a therapist-pleasing variable. As shown in Figure 8–1, changes did not occur in arousal in any of the three female partners until directed masturbation training was introduced. Since this procedure was introduced at different points in time, and changes only occurred after its introduction, it is unlikely that arousal changes resulted from the passage of time or therapist attention. Assuming that the arousal changes recorded in this study were valid, it is interesting that increases in cognitive levels of arousal were noted in all three subjects before orgasm was achieved. Following experience with orgasm, all three subjects maintained high cognitive levels of arousal throughout the experiment.

It would now be interesting to extend the Kohlenberg findings by looking at a generalization of arousal following masturbation. Such instruments as the SAI and photoplethysmography could be used for evaluating the effects of directed masturbation for women complaining of little or no arousal, as well as inorgasmic women. Physiologic measures could be taken while exposing a client to a variety of potentially sexually arousing material. This procedure could be conducted before directed masturbation therapy, after therapy, and at a followup. Similarly, the SAI could be administered before therapy, after therapy, and at followup. Such measurement procedure would allow an objective evaluation of both physiologic and cognitive arousal changes.

SOCIAL LEVEL AS A FACTOR

The clinical and experimental evidence is encouraging and seems to support directed masturbation as a viable therapeutic approach for treating primary orgasmic dysfunction in women. Our own clinical experience with sexually dysfunctional women suggests that class differences again may play an important role this time in the type of therapeutic goal a women presents. Women from lower socioeconomic status more often maintain as their goal satisfaction for their sexual partner, while women from upper socioeconomic status very often have as their goal their own sexual satisfaction. In the former case, women would more likely be treated for anxiety reduction, while in the latter case, arousal enhancement—including orgasmic achievement—would be the treatment goal. Indeed, a number of well-educated women we have counseled sought treatment following the reading of such material as *The Sensuous Woman.*

If our observations are correct, most female clients seeking treatment for primary orgasmic dysfunction would come from middle and upper socioeconomic status. Empirical evidence to support this observation is needed, of course, but it is logical to assume that the upper socioeconomic status woman is more likely to have been exposed to current feminist influence. This group may also be more compelled by logical argument in favor of directed masturbation.

It is surprising, however, that in spite of compelling challenges to a woman's beliefs about masturbation, among our clients there is still considerable resistance to this mode of therapy. Typical of our experience is the following response: "I kow that everything you are saying about masturbation is right. I know that my feelings are not logical, but I am just not able to even try doing it. The whole idea turns me right off."

SUMMARY

We have seen a changing perspective on masturbation. No longer should masturbation be considered neurotic or physically damaging, for it is a universally common activity. It is also an activity which may be predictive of successful sexual adjustment and may be used as therapy for some sexual problems.

As a therapy procedure masturbation has been employed in three different ways:

1. Masturbation leading to orgasm has been used as a conditioning procedure for changing sexual orientation in homosexual men. The pleasure associated with orgasm is paired with heterosexual stimuli in an attempt to strengthen the value of heterosexual stimuli. Research suggests that this procedure may be important for changing one's cognitive appraisal of heterosexual stimuli in a positive direction, but there is little or no evidence that changes also occur on a behavioral or physiological level.

2. Masturbation has also been used for the treatment of premature ejaculation in males. The technique in this case is one of repeated practice with masturbation to the point where warning signs of orgasm can be experienced, and then stopping masturbation and waiting till these signs pass, or squeezing the head of the penis to force the signs to pass. There seems to be widespread clinical support attesting to the effectiveness of this approach, although there may be some difficulty in convincing some clients to undergo the procedure. Participation of the female partner seems to be mandatory.

3. Finally, masturbation has been used for treatment of orgasmic dysfunction in women. Under this procedure, inorgasmic women are encouraged and instructed through a number of steps from self-genital exploration to mutual heterosexual masturbation and coitus. Clinical and experimental evidence seems to support this approach as an effective intervention strategy.

Therapists must expect to spend time prior to masturbation therapy in talk session, dispelling guilt and myths surrounding masturbation. Our own experience has been, however, that in spite of logical argument and revelation of facts, the resistance to masturbation is so deeply ingrained in many clients that this approach to therapy is ill-advised. Clients would rather drop out of therapy and live with their problems than engage in masturbation therapy. Clients should not be pressured into this form of therapy in any way. The conditions of therapy should be clear from the onset: it is always the client's choice whether or not to participate. Clients should not feel guilty about their reservations, and should be able to openly express any doubts without feeling that they are uncooperative in therapy. This is a very delicate situation which a therapist must appreciate, because most clients will go along with anything the therapist suggests. If clients are pressured into a therapy to which they deeply object, it is highly probable that the program will be unsuccessful and may even cause undue stress or harm.

9
Communication in Sexual Dysfunction

THE IMPORTANCE OF COMMUNICATION

Sex is intimate sharing. Acceptance of this fundamental fact is basic to a satisfying and satisfactory sexual relationship. And sharing does not mean simply joint tenancy in a home or dual occupancy of a bed. It is much more complex than this. It encompasses a communality of interests and experiences, a genuine desire and an ability to share one's innermost thoughts and feelings with another in a frank, honest and straightforward way, and to feel comfortable while doing so. It means reciprocal love and respect and a desire to become involved with another person without reservations, without holding back, without hiding part of oneself from the other. It means recognizing that marriages are not made in Heaven and that two people cannot live together in a state of perpetual bliss. In recognizing this, being free enough to attempt to resolve difficulties that arise in a constructive and satisfactory manner.

Unfortunately, too many couples do not or cannot respond to each other. They are two people who happen to be living together, but with separate existences. There is nothing deliberate in their isolation; they have just never learned to share. And they have never learned this because they have never learned to communicate; to talk to each other in an open and unrestricted way. It has been noted that, of a group who sought marriage counseling, communication and sex were the two major problem areas, (Azrin, Naster & Jones, 1973). However, these two cannot be divorced; poor communication and sexual problems go hand in hand. In some cases, absence of meaningful communication is directly responsible for the sexual problem. In other instances, absence of communication may exacerbate an already poor sexual relationship. It is possible that a therapist may have to devise different strategies in dealing with each type, but in general this would be more a matter of emphasis and detail. The primary objective would be to increase and enhance communication in a broad sense.

There is little doubt that the common thread running through the fabric of sexual problems is an absence of meaningful communication. Each member of the pair is unaware of what the other is thinking and feeling, and both find it impossible to inquire. Or, if they do inquire, it is at a superficial level. There is no dialogue, no exchange of information, no expression of true feeling. Instead, there is a suppression of thoughts and feelings, with the result that rather than airing and resolving grievances, these become bottled up and allowed to fester and become magnified out of all proportion. Problems which initially were superficial and of little consequence become exaggerated and assume an importance completely unwarranted. The woman who received roses from her husband on her every birthday when she hated roses and would have preferred a bottle of sherry, is a case in point. Surely it would have been better to communicate this to her husband rather than meekly acquiesce for more than twenty years, while boiling inside? Her view of the situation was that her husband was an insensitive beast. However, in the absence of any feedback, verbal or nonverbal, how could he possibly know her true feelings? The explanation that she did not want to hurt his feelings is not adequate to explain her behavior. Perhaps a better explanation would be that she did not possess the communication skills necessary to convey her message. She saw any attempt to alter the situation as a confrontation, and it never occurred to her that it was possible to change his behavior without alienating him or "hurting his feelings." It is possible to be assertive without being aggressive.

The inability to communicate does not appear full blown when two people get married. The man and woman are not communicators who have been suddenly struck dumb at the conclusion of the wedding ceremony. In reality the problem has always been present but has never had occasion to become manifest. Young people in love are notorious for the superficiality of their premarital conversation. Their concern is the here and now and the feeling they have for each other. If the future is considered, it is usually viewed as a blissful extension of the present. When one is young and in love the world and the future hold no terrors. There are no problems that cannot be overcome, no adversity that cannot be met and bested. And this is as it should be: youth and love should conquer all.

But, sad to say, this idyllic state is rarely realized because too many people enter marriage with an unrecognized gap in their communication skills, particularly in the area of things emotional and sexual.

EARLY LEARNING

It is no accident that a great many people have difficulty discussing and expressing sexual urges and sexual behaviors, i.e. in communicating. A study reported by Mann (1970) showed that in a sample of couples married an average of 17.5 years, many had never discussed sex with each other.

It has been pointed out by Hulse (1952) that: "In our culture probably no other important basic human need is so encrusted with prejudices and misconceptions, no other activity is so distorted from early infancy onward by proscriptions, taboos and frustrations as is the sexual life of the average person. At every phase of psychosexual development, the repressions and inhibiting social forces, both parental and extra-familial (such as church, school, legal and local standards) tend to increase the pressures that compel conformance to frustrating and emotionally disturbing standards of sexual behavior. Frustration and inhibition are part and parcel of the socialization process, and restriction of the social urges of the child is therefore essential."

And so from childhood, the individual is discouraged from sexual expression, both verbally and through action, and encouraged to muffle and hide his sexuality. Not only do some mothers become distressed when little Johnny or Jane "play" with themselves, they frequently express concern when their infant of six months gets an erection when being bathed. Neither of these is unnatural, and all children certainly go through a phase of self-exploration. Children are naturally curious, and this curiosity encompasses their own body, the body and sexual equipment of their siblings and playmates, as well as things in the world around them. What could be more natural than for a small boy or girl to ponder on the difference between the sexes? There are things here which obviously require investigation. But this is not to be. Parental sanctions are enforced to prevent this visual or tactile exploration, and the child is punished or threatened or otherwise admonished when discovered in such actions. And children learn very quickly. It does not take them very long to discover the relationship between their sex organs and punishment, no matter how mild this may be.

This direct kind of learning is not the only way children acquire knowledge. Much of what they learn comes from modeling other people's behavior. They see what their mothers or fathers do or say and they copy this behavior; it becomes part of their behavioral repertoire. If a little girl consistently sees her mother express annoyance when father puts his arm around her, it would be surprising if the girl did not learn this same response. If a girl hears her mother discussing with a girlfriend the vicissitudes of married life and the sexual burdens that women bear, it would be surprising if the girl grew up with the notion that sex was wonderful and something to be eagerly anticipated. And these are the kinds of situations that too many children are exposed to. Unfortunately, parents do not realize what long-term effects their actions can have. A child may not understand all the implications of her mother scowling and slapping her father's hand when he touches her breast, but she is learning a type of response which she may not forget—and which may not be the most adaptive in later life.

Many people, when they reach adolescence, already carry with them a legacy of negative learning about sexual matters. But whether they do or not, the period between ten–eleven and fourteen–fifteen is a singular time of stress, and adolescents fall prey to a barrage of well-intentioned but often misguided advice and information on sex and sexuality. This is particularly true of girls, since they are the ones likely to get into "trouble." Mothers tend to be averse to the unexpected announcement that their fifteen year old daughter is pregnant. Fathers, on the other hand, overtly or covertly, frequently encourage their sons to "sow their wild oats," ignoring the fact that these will be sown with the cooperation of some other father's fifteen-year-old daughter.

Children, depending on the wisdom or ignorance of their parents, will acquire information, modes of action and communication skills which they will likely carry with them for the rest of their lives. These will come through direct instruction and discussion, from modeling, from reading, from movies and television, and from interacting with their peers. Perhaps the most important is what they learn from their parents, both from instruction and observation. What they learn may be useful and adaptive and herald a healthy and realistic attitude towards sex. Furthermore, if this is the case, then they are better able to realistically assess the information they get from other sources, and they are better able to cope with their newfound sexuality. They are better able to understand what is happening to their bodies, to recognize the stirring of their sexual impulses and feelings, and accept them for what they are. Too, they are able to understand and allow for these same feelings in others and not get upset or alarmed if they are exposed to the sudden, ineffectual groping of a like-age companion. They can understand the situation and deal with it.

Too often, though, this is not the pattern and adolescents find themselves in both an emotional and intellectual bind; they frequently receive conflicting messages from the same source and are unable to decide, in a rational way, which to believe. (And no matter what the choice, there is always the doubt that they may have made the wrong one.) This situation is exemplified when what mother says is at variance with the way she behaves. Girls find it extremely difficult, if not impossible, to reconcile the message from their mothers that married sex is wonderful and fulfilling, while at the same time observing their mothers doing everything in their power to discourage even the mildest sexual overtures from their husbands. When a girl sees her mother retreat when her husband approaches, the girl may begin to wonder how frank her mother has been. And in a situation like this, most girls are likely to believe their eyes rather than their ears. Communication need not be verbal or explicit.

Probably the most destructive situation, and the one which has serious long-term effects, is where the child has a history of negative learning of sex which is continued through adolescence. (Examples of this have been provided in Chapter 1.) When children have been on a constant diet of antisexual fare, beginning when they are toddlers and continuing until they marry, it is unlikely that their sexual adjustment after marriage will be smooth. When a child has been slapped for playing with his or her genitals or severely scolded and told that nice children do not do such things; when a mother continuously harangues her daughter for imaginary sexual transgressions; when sex is explained as something dirty and evil and sinful and something a poor woman is forced to bear; when men are described as filthy beasts who want only one thing from a girl and having got it tell all their friends about it; when sex is described as something a woman has to do but nice women do not enjoy; when girls are told that sex is something one just does not talk about, then it is not surprising that so many people have sexual hang-ups. It should not be wondered at that a couple will have difficulty in establishing a good sexual relationship, and equally important, that they should feel free to discuss sex in an open and straightforward way.

Too many couples, when asked if they have attempted to resolve their sexual problems by discussion, shamefacedly admit that they have not; it's something they cannot talk about. Furthermore, when seen alone, a wife will frequently bemoan the fact that her husband never talks to her. Her husband will echo this statement when he is interviewed. Both convey the impression that they would be more than willing to talk things over if only the other would reciprocate. Experience has taught us that this is just not so. A man or woman who can speak freely with a psychologist or psychiatrist, discussing the most intimate details of his or her sexual life with no hesitation or restraint, becomes an incoherent nincompoop when attempting the same thing with a spouse. It is this deficiency that needs to be remedied.

COMMON PROBLEMS

It might be worthwhile at this point to consider the source and the nature of some of the specific problems which bedevil couples. Some of these are common, and originate in cultural myths which are accepted uncritically. Others are more idiosyncratic, while still others have their basis in sheer ignorance. Some are peculiar to women, some to men, and some are shared jointly. All could be dispelled by some judicious instruction and communication.

A common problem, evidenced mainly in husbands, is a complete failure to appreciate the nature and extent of their wives' problems. Too often they view her reluctance to have intercourse, or her obvious lack of enthusiasm and pleasure during intercourse, as malingering. There is, in their view, nothing wrong (in a psychological sense), and if the wives would only pull themselves together the problem could be cleared up in short order. Or, they take a lack of interest in sex as a sign that their wives have fallen out of love with them, or, in more extreme cases, that they find them sexually repulsive. A third alternative is acceptance, at least on the surface, that a problem exists, but that it resides solely within their wives and that, as benevolent husbands, they should do something about it—while at the same time refusing to cooperate with either wife or therapist in this endeavour. This kind of thinking often goes something like this: "When we were first married you enjoyed sex (which may be a misconception) and now you don't. I haven't changed but you have, so obviously it is you that has the problem." As ridiculous as this sounds, it is frequently implied by husbands. A more destructive alternative is where the husband pays lip service to his wife's plea that she is experiencing a problem, but at the same time uses a variety of strategies to coerce her into sex. For example, "If you really loved me you wouldn't mind," or more insidious, "After all I've done for you, you should be happy to have sex," or "If two people don't have something physical, then they don't have anything."

It is doubtful if anything could be more destructive to a relationship than these sorts of ploys. Furthermore, they are often self-fulfilling prophesies. Coercion in a sexual relationship, where one partner finds sex repugnant, is guaranteed to engender uncharitable thoughts, feelings and actions in that partner. Love can rapidly turn to disgust and revulsion. When a woman begins to see her husband as an insensitive and selfish brute whose only thoughts are self-gratification, she will soon begin to reassess her husband and her relationship with him; she will begin to scrutinize his behavior in general. Not too many husbands can undergo this intense scrutiny and emerge unscathed.

In cases where the husband refuses to recognize his wife's problem it is virtually mandatory that a third party intervene, usually the therapist, to impress upon him the genuineness of the problem. Husbands are more prone to believe a stranger than they are their own wives. This is not to say that they accept the verdict with good grace. Childish and often churlish exasperation is a frequent response. Nevertheless, they may be cajoled into accepting that the wife is not just fabricating a story or being bloody minded, and will make a commitment to stop pressuring her while therapy is going on. This is a victory in itself. Had this couple been able to talk to each other their problem may not have arisen, or at least not achieved the magnitude it did. Furthermore, there would have been more reason for optimism as to the outcome of therapy and their future relationship.

Not infrequently wives have good cause to be unhappy with their husbands' sexual behavior. Perhaps his techniques are not good; perhaps his staying power is not great; perhaps his sexual demands are too frequent and/or inappropriate. Women have to be loved in the full meaning of the word; they are not simply receptacles for holding a penis. Too many husbands forget, if they ever knew, this elementary fact. Women need be made to feel that what is happening is for their benefit as well as their husbands', and that he has her pleasure in the forefront of his mind. They have to be confident that sex is exciting and fun and mutual. Hence when a woman suddenly finds herself beneath a gasping and groaning husband two minutes after she is in bed, she is justified in being something less than enthusiastic about his amorous overtures. This frustrating state may be exacerbated if her husband ejaculates 30 or 60 seconds after entry. These problems could be eliminated if she were able to verbally convey to her husband that she needs to be sexually aroused to derive any of the benefits of intercourse.

If she could teach him how to do this, then so much the better. She could tell him that she liked her back or arms or thighs or stomach or breasts gently stroked. That touching and stroking these should precede touching her genitals, including her clitoris. She could tell him, or indicate in other ways, when and where to proceed. She could signal to him that now she was ready for his penis. These suggestions or instructions need not be blatant and overpowering; many need not even be verbal. A little appropriate guidance of her husband's hands would do the trick. And she does not have to scream in his ear that she is ready. A little gentle body manipulation would convince him of this. Too many husbands immediately zero in on the clitoris because they believe that this is what women really enjoy and the sooner you get down to business the better. The same in reverse is true with respect to early or late ejaculation. If the woman has overcome the notion that men do not enjoy or require manual stimulation, her husband can indicate to her just how far this should go before ejaculation is inevitable. If he has a tendency to premature ejaculation, then clearly a minimum of manual stimulation is indicated. If, on the other hand, he requires a good deal of stimulation, the opposite may be true. But whatever the case, this is something which can be unambiguously communicated with harm to neither and benefit to both.

It is not unusual for husbands to imagine that their wives' sexual desires are a mirror image of their own. That their wives are ready for sex at all times just as they themselves are. It frequently requires a good deal of persuasion to disabuse them of this idea. It is here that some straightforward talk is needed, with perhaps the intervention of a third party. Women, because of their emotional involvement, cannot turn on at a moment's notice. Outside, and, to men, often extraneous influences, govern their sexual receptivity. Many husbands have to learn this and behave accordingly.

By the same token though, there are times—just before, during or just after their period —when a woman does want to have intercourse, and wants it badly. However, because of cultural influences, where women have been taught to be passive and to wait for the man to make the first move, she is frequently at a loss as to what to do. After all, nice girls don't ask men for sex! If a communication problem exists, how then can she make her needs known? If she has her wits about her she will solve the problem by nonverbal means. Most men are ludicrously easy to seduce and most women are acquainted with strategies to achieve this. And there is, of course, no reason why a woman should feel embarrassed or uncomfortable about using her natural endowments to their full potential. What most women do not appreciate is that many men would thoroughly enjoy being seduced, particularly if this were done in subtle and tantalizing ways. Men, by and large, are not so delicate that they would be destroyed by the subtle sexual manipulations of their wives. However, again it should be kept in mind that there are educational and socioeconomic factors at play here. The poorer educated and those in the lower socio-economic brackets have, in general, different views on the masculine–feminine role in sex from the better educated and higher economic groups. The latter are much more flexible and open-minded in this area.

In the same vein, problems arise as a result of differences in what is considered the appropriate time for sex. There is a great deal of variability here; sexual desires appear to be distributed throughout the twenty-four hours of a day. Some men and women are at their peak in the morning, some in the early evening, some in the late evening, and so on. The difficulty arises when two people differ radically in when they are most receptive. A woman may only want sex in the late evening when the children are in bed asleep and she feels that she can now relax. Her husband, on the other hand may be simply too tired at this point to be interested. All he wants is to go to sleep. Consequently, they may rarely get together, and when they do someone is dissatisfied. When this problem is not discussed and when the woman is rebuffed in the evening and the man is rejected in the morning, each may misconstrue the nature of the problem. Too frequently each will assume that the other has no interest in sex, and if this continues, the frequency of intercourse decreases with a concomitant increase of stress and tension both in bed and in the household in general. Obviously this could be avoided if the couple were able to discuss their mutual problem and arrive at a solution satisfactory to both.

A related problem, and one found in older couples, is the change in sexual desires with age. Kinsey (1953) notes that men are extremely interested in sex in the early years of their marriage. Women, however, are frequently not, largely because of old inhibitions. With the passing of years, many women are successful in ridding themselves of these inhibitions and may develop a strong and abiding interest in sex. Unfortunately, by this time the husband has begun to lose interest and may have little desire to have intercourse with a woman who for years rejected him. Communication as a therapeutic strategy at this stage is not too likely to be useful. The damage done over the years may be too severe to repair in the absence of professional assistance.

MYTHS AND FALLACIES

There are a number of destructive fallacies associated with sex, particularly orgasm, that cause no end of unnecessary problems which could be avoided by communication. That is, if the couple were to discuss their feelings and responses, these would not arise. Some of these have been briefly mentioned or alluded to in Chapter 1. The most common that we have encountered are: 1) the notion that for sex to be really good the couple must reach orgasm simultaneously; 2) that a woman cannot enjoy sex in the absence of an orgasm, and that it is absolutely necessary for both people to reach orgasm on every occasion; 3) that sex will be good and satisfying right from the start; 4) that a woman should maintain a strict sense of decorum while having intercourse and not allow herself to express her feelings either physically or vocally; 5) that it is up to the man to "give" his wife an orgasm. These notions can be examined in the light of what people actually say and do.

SIMULTANEOUS ORGASM

The fable that simultaneous orgasm is the hallmark of sexual satisfaction has no basis in fact, but is a strongly held belief. One does not have to look far for the reasons for the perpetuation of this myth. Books and magazines have for years portrayed intercourse as a violently active exercise where the couple thrash around—in a bed, among the daisies, or wherever until, with one tremendous explosion climaxes are achieved leaving both partners gasping. More recently, these sexual thunderbolts have been graphically displayed on the movie screen. Unfortunately, people who should know better, whose total sexual experience has been to the contrary, accept this sexual misconception as a model of sexual behavior in general. This striving for the seldom-attainable is only one more testimony pointing up human irrationality.

This is not to say that simultaneous orgasms do not occur, for quite obviously they do. However this is not the natural or usual course of events. When they do happen it is more by chance than good management. Women, by and large, are much slower to reach climax through penile stimulation than are men by vaginal friction. This is why so many women are left sexually frustrated. The average man will reach orgasm within two or three minutes of intromission. Few women, unless they have been adequately stimulated prior to intromission, can match this. After the man has ejaculated there is a refractory period, lasting perhaps 15–20 minutes but depending on age, when initially, further stimulation of the penis is painful, and later, when a full erection is not possible (this is nature's way of insuring that men do not do themselves to death). If a woman has not reached orgasm first (or at the same time), there is little chance that she will unless extra-penile stimulation is employed. But the very fact that there is this difference in speed of response mitigates against both partners reaching climax at the same time. Most men and women recognize this, but men in particular continue to believe that they in some way are being cheated or that they are missing out on a fabulous sexual experience if this does not happen. Fortunately most women are firmly rooted in sexual reality and are willing or more than willing to accept an orgasm no matter where it comes in the sequence. The fact that they do not explode in synchrony with their partner is seldom a matter of concern, not something they will lose much sleep over.

If a man feels that he must achieve what his fictional models achieve or die, then he can attempt this, but it means communicating with his partner. Too often both men and women operate in the dark, literally and figuratively, and never know where or at what stage the partner is. Communication here involves the conveyance of appropriate information as to what is happening. It also implies that the woman will be the one who controls the situation. She knows when she is ready to receive the penis, where she should be stimulated to help her achieve orgasm, and when orgasm is imminent. This basic information is what she should communicate to her husband and he should help her in this, if necessary by asking questions. With practice, a couple may well achieve simultaneous orgasms, at least part of the time. If this has any value, it lies in the fact that the overall probability of the woman reaching climax will be increased. It may also make sex a little more exciting and titilating for the man, and increase his self esteem.

ORGASM VS. SATISFACTION

The fiction that only through orgasm can a woman achieve sexual satisfaction is another strongly held belief on the part of men. To some extent this is fostered by women themselves, but at the same time it represents a basic male misconception as to the nature of female sexuality, female gratification, and female pleasure. Many women do not require an orgasm on every occasion in order to derive enjoyment from sex. There can be a certain romanticism about sex that gives them pleasure. Women will readily admit this to a therapist. However, because their husbands have opposing views (which basically derive from the notion that if his wife does not reach climax he in some way is deficient as a man) a woman will fake an orgasm. As mentioned earlier, she does not have to be a very good actress to convince her husband.

Similarly, it is not imperative that a man reach climax or ejaculate every time he has intercourse. There may well be that, for one reason or another, a man does not ejaculate and there is nothing peculiar in this. Unfortunately, men are tremendously success or performance oriented with respect to sex. They may be lackadaisical to the point of absurdity in all other areas, but when it comes to sex they see themselves as studs and undisputed masters of the bedroom. The possibility that they may fail seldom enters their heads, and when it does they are frequently reduced to a quivering mass of overwhelming shame and self-doubt. Rather than accept failure as a temporary phenomenon, they begin to question their virility, speculate on the cause of failure and torment themselves with gloomy prophecies. If by chance this is repeated on a second occasion, their despair is magnified tenfold and they may well be preparing themselves for a bout of impotence. In men, more so than women, failure breeds failure. Anxiety reduces the probability of successful sex and as anxiety mounts performance declines. And men being such fragile creatures, not many failures are required before they begin to view the situation with frantic alarm.

To a lesser extent women, too, are success oriented, with this attitude intimately involved in and determined by stereotyped sex roles and expectations. So long as people view a periodic failure for what it is and not exaggerate it out of all proportion, there is very little to worry about. When a woman seeks treatment (and this is a measure of her view of the seriousness of the situation) because she is experiencing orgasm only 70–80% of the time when previously it had been 90%, the chances are that her and/or her husband's concern is unwarranted. In the same way, episodic failure on the part of a man is not a matter of concern unless he makes it so. Nevertheless, these failures or reduction in frequency of orgasm do pose problems for couples, and the best therapy is an understanding that failures do occur in the absence of any pathology, and discussing them as they arise. But above all, love and sex are not occasions for keeping tally sheets—so many orgasms for you and so many orgasms for me. This basic fact needs to be acknowledged and accepted and the only satisfactory way to achieve this is through discussion.

INSTANT SEXUAL SATISFACTION

Another fanciful notion is that when people get married they will lead a life of sexual bliss which will commence on the wedding night. Perhaps this happens but if it does it's a rarity. Most couples require time and practice to perfect their coital skills. Many wedding nights are occasions for trauma and disappointment. The things that brides and grooms have independently read in books, magazines and marriage manuals somehow have not told the whole story; something is missing. Nevertheless, each has preconceived notions of what to expect, and when these are not realized there are bound to be tears, frustration and unspoken but gloomy predictions for the future.

It takes time for two people to get to know each other sexually, and if a marriage is to progress relatively smoothly it is absolutely necessary that the couple, right from the start, admit to each other that there are many things they do not know about sex; there are wide gaps in their knowledge of love making. If they can do this, they will be paving the way for a more harmonious and satisfactory relationship. But the key is communication. Old ghosts have to be laid; old inhibitions cast aside. New ways of responding have to be learned and it takes time to accomplish these. If a couple has had the good fortune to be brought up in an atmosphere of healthy sexual discussion and freedom then they have the basis for a good sexual relationship. If, on the other hand, they have grown up in an antisexualizing environment where sex was never discussed, or only discussed in negative and pernicious ways, then it will not be easy to eradicate past learning or to dispel cherished beliefs. It will be difficult but not impossible.

For example, to the sexual novice it is axiomatic that a man achieves ejaculation through penile stimulation while the penis is contained by the vagina. Similarly, a woman reaches orgasm by the thrusting action of the penis in the vagina. What could be simpler than this? Acting on this self-evident truth, a newly married couple proceed on the basis of their book learning—only to discover that the book was only partially correct. Sure enough, the man ejaculates—but his wife does not even approach orgasm. In the absence of communication (learning by trial and error) it will likely take a long time to rectify the problem. On the other hand, if the wife can successfully tutor her husband and indicate to him that she requires much more stimulation than he does, then a great deal of frustration can be avoided. If she can convey to him the stimulating and arousing properties of a little more appropriate foreplay, if she can convince him that there is nothing sacrosanct in the man being on top and that the reverse position is much better for her, if she is able to persuade him to engage in a modicum of delicate digital stimulation of the clitoris during intercourse, then the road is open to a more satisfying sexual relationship, not only for her but for him as well. But this goal can only be achieved if the couple feel free enough and secure enough to discuss the problem in an open and forthright manner, not expecting instant success.

DECOROUS SEX

A Victorian attitude still prevalent today is that women should smother their sexual feelings during intercourse and inhibit any display of sexual excitement during orgasmic release. If they are not to lie as mute mannequins they should at the very least maintain control, behaving in a prim and proper way and certainly not signifying in a rude manner that they are doing anything more than passively accommodating their husband. In Victorian England the generally accepted notion was that a woman who enjoyed sex was a little better than a prostitute. While the rules of sexual conduct have changed somewhat since that time, it is still frequently considered indelicate if a woman lets her enjoyment be known—at least aloud.

This archaic view is not only untenable, it is nonsensical as well. If a woman is enjoying sex and is highly aroused, then there is no reason in the world why she should not express her feelings, no reason why she should not act and say the things she feels. Nothing she does is intrinsically wrong; nothing she says is something her husband has not heard before. For some women strong and active physical movement is an important and necessary component of sex. They cannot achieve orgasm without it. To attempt to stifle this is to inhibit or eliminate a major source of stimulation and gratification. For a husband to try to control his wife's sometimes violent physical movements is to indicate that his knowledge of sexuality and lovemaking is sadly deficient. Nevertheless, many women on many occasions will, during intercourse, behave as a mute paralytic, when the seizure of a grand mal epileptic would be more appropriate.

If a woman can overcome her ingrained inhibitions about expressing herself, and if her husband is wise enough to encourage her in this endeavour, then there is little doubt that sex will become infinitely more exciting and satisfying for both. Prostitutes are well acquainted with this basic truth and the fact that they are simulating arousal and faking orgasms does little to detract from the client's pleasure. The notion (erroneous) that he can rouse a woman to such ecstatic heights is tremendously gratifying to him. Furthermore, this is what he expects and when the prostitute, in breathless passion, whispers exotic and erotic suggestions in his ear and accompanies this with controlled but energetic body movements, nothing on earth will convince him that he is not one of the world's great lovers. It is this kind of sexual response that wives should consider and husbands should encourage and foster. Wives could take a page, figuratively speaking, from the prostitute's book. Many would do so spontaneously if given the least encouragement, but unfortunately inhibitions from internal or external sources prevent this.

The presence of children and other people in the house will clearly have a dampening effect, and for this reason it is a worthwhile expenditure for a couple to get away from home periodically and stay in a hotel for a night or two where they can behave in more spontaneous ways. Or, at least in the case of children, there are ways of getting them out of the house for a couple of hours on Saturday or Sunday afternoons when the couple can engage in uninhibited lovemaking. One man, only half-facetiously, suggested scattering a double handfull of green jelly beans on the front lawn whenever he wanted the children occupied for an hour or so! But none of these things can happen if the couple does not communicate, and communicate in ways more than verbal.

THE "GIFT"

Among men (and to some extent women) the conventional wisdom is that men "give" women orgasms. Medieval as it is, many people firmly believe in this sexual gift concept. This notion is part and parcel of outdated sex role stereotypes where men are seen as dominant and sexually aggressive and deliverers of a service, if only as a not too important by-product of self-gratification. Many women have had instilled in them the idea that they are in no way responsible for their own sexual gratification. This has been abrogated to men and thus they are at the mercy of men's idiosyncratic and often eccentric behavior. Nothing could be more fallacious, and in a real sense degrading, than this kind of thinking.

If a woman is to derive pleasure and satisfaction from sex, then it is imperative that she accept the fact that what she gets out of sex is in large measure dependent on what she puts into it. She has to learn to accept the responsibility for her own enjoyment and gratification, for if she doesn't, who will? This does not imply that sex is a selfish endeavour where two people engage in a common exercise while independent of each other so far as outcome is concerned. It does mean though that during intercourse a woman should not be excessively concerned about satisfying her husband, particularly if this interferes with or sacrifices her own pleasure. Men, in this situation, are more than capable of looking after themselves. And if a woman is to consider her own interests, then it is incumbent on her that she manipulate the situation to her own advantage and not worry that her demands or actions will castrate her husband. Most men want their wives to reach orgasm, although frequently for selfish reasons: it allows them to feel more competent as lovers and husbands and it quite clearly improves their wives' dispositions. But a woman should not rely on her husband's charity to satisfy her. She should do everything in her power to insure that pleasure comes about, and to do this successfully requires communication.

MASTURBATION

Failure of a woman to derive sexual satisfaction breeds a host of problems, many of which have been discussed. However, there is one which has proven to be particularly distressing and threatening to some husbands, particularly those in middle-age and beyond: female masturbation. Apparently nothing shakes a man's faith in his sexual prowess as much as the discovery that his wife masturbates. (It should be noted, though, that younger husbands are much less concerned about this—and many of the more knowledgeable ones will in fact encourage their wives in this after reading that masturbation may improve sexual responsiveness and performance.) The fact that he may masturbate and finds nothing wrong with it is ignored. That his wife, the mother of his children, would do such a thing is beyond his comprehension! As mentioned in Chapter 7, masturbation among women is a common practice and this does not necessarily cease at marriage. When a woman is sexually frustrated because of inability to reach orgasm through intercourse, what could be more logical or natural that she do something about it? Furthermore, even when women do derive satisfaction from sex, there are times when she will feel like having an orgasm in isolation and, as Arafat and Cotton (1974) point out, more than 50% of women achieve orgasm as intense or more intense through masturbation than they do through intercourse. There is nothing unnatural or peculiar about this behavior, and for husbands to condemn their wives for self-stimulation is to display an irrationality almost beyond belief. Solving this problem, rectifying misconceptions and erroneous beliefs, and convincing husbands that they are not married to nymphomaniacs is a matter for enlightened discussion. This, of course, is not always easy because many women feel guilty about this practice. Nevertheless, with effort it can be discussed and wise husbands will simply accept it for what it is—a natural and beneficial phenomenon.

The reverse is equally true. Women will, in anguished tones, recount the shattering discovery that their husbands masturbate. Their response to this knowledge is frequently disgust or dismay. They tend to view this as an unmistakable sign that they have failed as wives and lovers. It is because they are sexually deficient that their husbands have had to resort to this strange behavior. Clearly the road is open to the divorce court, or it is a signal that an extramarital relationship is in the offing. What they fail to appreciate, and in the absence of communication this is reasonable, is that masturbation among men is a common practice and is not necessarily a sign that a marriage breakdown is inevitable. Nevertheless, it *may* mean that the man is dissatisfied with the quality or quantity of his sexual relationship and that something need be done. If the problem can be viewed rationally and maturely and discussed in a nonhysterical manner, it is on the way to solution.

CULTIVATING COMMUNICATION

There are many other aspects of sexual and nonsexual behavior where communication is vitally important. It is probably no exaggeration to say that effective communication between two people is the single most necessary ingredient for a harmonious and successful marriage relationship. There are two guiding principles which can assist people in improving their communication skills in general. These are: to begin with simple problems and progress to complex ones; to start with general problems and advance to specific ones.

A major difficulty is in recognizing and acknowledging that a communication problem exists. Once this hurdle has been overcome, the above two principles can be applied. In practice, this may mean setting aside fifteen minutes every evening when the couple can sit down and talk. This can be about anything—the children, what the husband did at work, and whether the boss is or is not a son-of-a-bitch. Husbands may learn that looking after a home is more than making beds and cooking meals, and that his brief happy encounter with the children does not represent a true sample of their day-to-day behavior. In this process the couple begin by *talking* to each other. In the end they are *communicating* with each other.

Once a couple can establish this kind of a relationship they may well discover that fifteen minutes has stretched into half an hour or more, and that the kinds of things they are discussing are becoming less mundane and more personal. For the first time they are learning how and about what the other thinks, and furthermore their level of discomfort has radically decreased. When communication is possible in the living room, it is a short and not too difficult step to transfer this to the bedroom. There are a variety of strategies to assist in this. Some of these are outlined in *Homework on Counseling and Psychotherapy* (Shelton & Ackerman, 1974), and *When I Say No I Feel Guilty* (Smith, 1975).

In general, these books are concerned with assertiveness training, which in a broad sense is learning to communicate and express one's feelings in adaptive and significant ways. An excellent strategy to improve communication in sexual relations is detailed by Shelton & Ackerman, Chapter 9. This strategy and variations of it are used in conjunction with treatment of specific male and female sexual dysfunctions. Essentially the procedure consists of planned homework assignments for couples and for individual members of the pair. For couples there are six of these and they involve: 1) Reading sexually informative books and discussing these in detail in order to become familiar and comfortable in using sexual terminology and becoming acquainted with their own bodies. 2) Identifying their own and their partners' genitals and to feel comfortable in naming these aloud and displaying them to their partner. 3) Showing and naming their sexual equipment to each other and discussing sensations each have experienced in their breasts and/or genitals. 4) Engaging in nonsexual pleasuring in a variety of situations with the receiver providing verbal and nonverbal feedback to the giver as to the pleasure this evokes. The roles of giver and receiver are interchangeable. 5) Preparing lists, conjointly, of the things which each find enjoyable and what displeases or annoys them. These are derived from pleasuring, fantasy and previous knowledge. 6) Mutual reading and discussing erotic literature such as *The Joy of Sex* (Comfort, 1972) and sexually explicit novels. These homework assignments form only part of the therapeutic package. The couple meets with the therapist and the assignments, progress, and problems are discussed and problems resolved. As can be seen from these brief descriptions, a couple who conscientiously follows the program is going to be communicating, and communicating with increasing ease and facility. Since all of these are carried out in an anxiety-free atmosphere, desensitization should rapidly occur.

This does not mean however, that all couples will be able to carry out these assignments with equal ease and in the absence of anxiety. There will be individual differences to consider. Here again it may be necessary to initiate communication at a simple and rather general level, and as mentioned earlier, some of this can be done by nonverbal means. As this progresses, it becomes easier and easier to discuss in meaningful ways sex in general and their own sexual desires, needs and proclivities in particular.

We do not mean to imply that this entire process of learning to communicate is easy, free from tension or anxiety, and something which can be accomplished overnight. When two people have a long history of verbal isolation it would be unrealistic to expect sudden and dramatic changes. But changes are possible provided the people concerned are motivated and tenacious and are not prepared to settle down for a lifetime maintaining the *status quo*. It means work and often hard work, but the benefits which will accrue will far outweigh the temporary discomfort and disquietude.

SUMMARY

We have pointed out the importance of communication in a sexual relationship. This is a skill in which too many couples are sadly deficient. Because of proscriptions of one sort or another, people are discouraged from discussing sexual matters or verbally expressing sexual desires and needs. This begins early in life and carries through into adulthood. Often what children learn about sex is negative, and this comes from both overt and covert training. Children are frequently the victims of their parents' sexual hangups. By the time they marry many people do not possess the ability to communicate with a partner and this can create or exacerbate problems. Obviously, if two people do not communicate there are going to be areas of conflict never touched upon; there are going to be difficulties which are never satisfactorily resolved.

A major difficulty is a failure of one partner to recognize the nature and the validity of the other partner's problem. Frequently, the problem is misinterpreted, and this results in maladaptive behavior on the part of one or both. Effective communication could mitigate or prevent this kind of misunderstanding.

There is a host of myths associated with sex, which, if allowed to persist, cause no end of trouble. Expecting simultaneous orgasms is one such myth. The idea that sex is good only if both partners reach orgasm at exactly the same time is prevalent and firmly entrenched in the minds of a good many men. This, of course, is fallacious and a state seldom achieved in real life.

Another mythical notion is that only through orgasms can a woman or a man obtain sexual satisfaction. If either fails in this respect, the whole exercise becomes a write-off. A third fallacy is that a couple will lead a life of sexual bliss commencing on their wedding night. If this expectation is met it is a rarity. Most people require time to learn coital skills which will lead to mutual satisfaction.

Many couples believe that a woman should be restrained and modest while engaging in sex, and not behave in unseemly ways. The major effect of this attitude is to stifle the woman and interfere and/or prevent her from realizing her full sexual potential. Related to this is the notion that men "give" women orgasms; that, in effect, she is a sexual charity case. That a woman is responsible for her own pleasure is a concept not too frequently entertained.

These and other myths can be destructive if they are allowed to govern the sexual lives of men and women. Unfortunately, too many people do not possess the communicative skills to discuss and, by doing so, dispel them. Part of the problem here is simply recognizing that a communication problem exists. However, if this recognition can be achieved there are ways to foster and improve communication. In general, this consists of practice in talking to each other, reading informative books, and in the final analysis, desensitizing themselves to discussing sexual matters.

10

Prescription for Prevention of Sexual Dysfunction

THE OUTLOOK

We have attempted in this volume to describe in meaningful terms some strategies for the treatment of both male and female sexual dysfunctions. Problems experienced by women have been emphasized simply because, like it or not, women are psychologically different than men. They are, by the very nature of their womanhood or femininity, much more susceptible to the vagaries of sexual misinformation and misunderstanding which lead to sexual disorders. Inappropriate early learning experiences have much more impact on women than on men.

The therapeutic approaches described are obviously not the only ones possible. Individual differences preclude standard, routine approaches which will guarantee universal success. Nevertheless, with the problems described, the procedures we have advocated can be extremely helpful, supportive empirical evidence shows.

If one were now forced to make a prediction for the future of sexual dysfunctions, the only rational one would be that they will be with us for a long time to come. Professionals who devote their time to assisting men and women to overcome their sexual hang-ups will be overburdened for as far as one can see into the future. Furthermore, the dramatic increase in the number of "sex therapists" will do little to stem the tide. The problem could be drastically reduced or mitigated—but not in this generation.

But therapy or intervention are holding strategies at best. They make minor inroads into serious and widespread problems. Therapy, no matter what its guise, will not solve the problem. Intervention only provides a relief for those already afflicted. Of itself it does little to prevent the occurrence of sexual problems. The possible exception to this statement is in the treatment of young people, where changes in attitudes and behaviors may be reflected in a more enlightened sex education for their children. But no one should be deluded (or delude themselves) that the sexual millenium is at hand.

THE PUBLIC ATTITUDE

Why should this state of affairs exist? What is it that hinders the acquisition of more healthy and adaptive attitudes toward sex and sexual behavior? A partial answer to these questions lies in the irrationality of current public attitudes toward sex; the difference in public response to sex information, depending on the source of the information. For example, one frequently encounters the term "sexual revolution" used to describe contemporary sexual practices and mores and the widespread dissemination of sex-oriented material via the various media. The message seems to be that we live in a sexually liberated age, and that basic sexual patterns have radically changed—which in turn heralds a new understanding and a better way of dealing with human sexual problems. In our view this is erroneous. The visibility of sex cannot be equated with changes in significant sexual attitudes as these are related to the day-to-day sexual interactions between men and women. It seems more likely that what passes for a sexual revolution is in fact a clear indication that many people are deeply troubled about sex and sexual expression. They manifest this by an attitude or expression of braggadocio.

There is no question that sex is much more freely discussed than in the past and that people will honestly and frankly discuss their sexual attitudes and behaviors, not only to scientific researchers, but among themselves. Many women have little hesitation in discussing their pre-or post marital sexual adventures, comparing the relative merits of their nebulous lovers. And only the most staid and stuffy individual thinks anything of it. Sex is no longer confined to the bedroom; it has invaded the livingroom with a vengeance. Similarly, twenty years ago for a woman to use so-called "four letter words" in a social conversation would have been unthinkable. Today, these are integral parts of many women's vocabularies and they feel as free to use these terms as do men at a stag party. Applause, not censure, should be the typical response to these honest expressions of feeling.

This change in verbal behavior results, in large part, from the exploitation and commercialization of sex which has taken place over the past ten years. When one is constantly barraged with things sexual, sexual expression and sexual meaning cease to have validity. The words become divorced from the act. The term fuck, and its derivations, is used as a verb, an adverb, an adjective or a noun, all in a variety of ways to convey different thoughts and meanings, most of which have nothing to do with intercourse. Synonyms for this term are used even more freely.

One does not have to look far for evidence of the commercialization of sex. Movies, books, magazines, stage shows, topless and bottomless bars, massage parlours, all attest to the availability of sexual titillation of one sort or another. None of these is presented surreptitiously. Their advertisements blaze forth boldly before the public eye. *Last Tango in Paris* and *Deep Throat* adorn the marquees of theatres for all to see. Local, conservative newspapers, carry advertisements for topless–bottomless shows and massage parlours. The corner drug store abounds with erotic magazines, and book sellers have no hesitation or compunction in displaying The Joy of Sex and similar works of art-cum-sex. Pimps and hookers (a word thought to be more genteel than whore or prostitute) are displayed daily on T.V.

The proliferation of sexually connotated material is sound business practice; there is a large and increasing market. There is virtually nothing concerned with sex that one cannot see, do, or buy. The mind boggles at some of the offerings. For example, massage parlours offering "reduced rates for senior citizens." (The mental picture of geriatric old men tottering up the stairs to take advantage of this munificent offer can only cause one to laugh—or weep.) Love shops, where the variety of goods defies description but includes electro-mechanical penises and vaginas which can be plugged into a car's cigarette lighter, love potions to solve a myriad of physiologic problems or deficiencies, life-sized inflatable dolls designed to provide sexual substitutes for men and women. And so on.

The relevance of this adult preoccupation with things sexual to current sexual dysfunctions is that it brings sharply into focus the irrationality of contemporary sexual attitudes.

SEX EDUCATION

There is a widespread discrepancy in public attitudes and behaviors between what is tacitly acceptable in the commercial sphere, and what is acceptable in the realm of education *vis-a-vis* sex. On the one hand, children and adolescents are constantly and repetitiously exposed to the most blatant forms of the wholesaling of sex and there seems to be little public or official concern about it; it is accepted as a normal part of twentieth century life. On the other hand, let anyone suggest a rational approach to sex education in the public schools and see what happens! The howls of outrage, the screams of protest will be deafening. Those foolhardy enough to even broach the subject will be accused of attempting to corrupt the morals of the nations, to undermine the commonwealth, to destroy the very basis of civilization. And it makes no never mind that these hysterical utterances and shrieks of anguish are nonsensical and derive from a relatively small but powerful segment of the community. This is irrationality on a grand scale. This is casuistry carried to the ultimate.

This is not to say that all people are opposed to education in sex. A majority would welcome it (C.O.P., 1970). However, they are easily shouted down by a highly visible and extremely vocal few. A situation analogous to this might be prohibition in the United States. The proscriptions against alcohol continued long after public support for it had vanished, and this was achieved by well-entrenched and powerful pressure groups whose influence was out of all proportion to their numbers. Politicians are always one step back of public opinion.

If significant inroads are to be made in preventing sexual dysfunctions and alleviating the accompanying misery, serious attempts will have to be made to recognize, understand and devise strategies to overcome this schizophrenic view of sex. It would be gratifying if some all-embracing panacea could be offered, but unfortunately there is no ready answer to this complex problem. There are no known strategies for miraculously altering public and private opinion overnight.

It has been aptly pointed out that: "Ignorance is the lack of useful sexual learning due to unavailability of factual information, misinformation such as stereotypes and myths, and distorted information including faulty learning and inability to integrate factual information when it is available" (Chernick and Chernick, 1971).

It is not too difficult to pinpoint the sources of this lack of information and proliferation of misinformation. Home and school are the culprits. As mentioned earlier, children's attitudes and feelings are formed very early. They become conditioned to behave in particular ways and to express their feelings in predictable fashions. This conditioning comes about, in large measure, from modeling the behavior of others and through a process of positive and negative rewards or reinforcements. Children are rewarded for behavior their parents consider appropriate, and punished for behaviors considered inappropriate. Unfortunately, what parents consider to be appropriate or inappropriate is determined by their own attitudes and feelings. Genital exploration may pass unnoticed (or disregarded) by some parents, while others view it with alarm and disgust—and behave accordingly. This can carry over to other aspects of sexual behavior as well. Children raised in such divergent households are going to have quite conflicting views of sexual conduct. Each will probably mirror the actions of their parents.

What children learn is effective in determining their future sexual behavior, which sexual stimuli they will find aversive and which they will seek out, and what sexual actions they will feel comfortable employing. The kinds of parental and societal sexual approval or disapproval they have been subjected to, the attitudes and feelings acquired over the years, will either enhance or interfere with their adult sexual responses and will determine, in large measure, the kind of sex education they provide their children.

It would seem a formidable task to alter the behavior of all parents in the direction of sexual adjustment, to remove their misconceptions, to eradicate their cherished mythical beliefs, to reshape their attitudes. Nevertheless, at least in some it might be possible to alter their behavior (even if they themselves have sexual problems) in such a way that they do not pass on their sexual hang-ups to their children. It is conceivable that some parents can recognize that their own attitudes towards sex are not all that might be desired and in recognizing this, try to ensure that their children do not end up the same way.

Unfortunately, many parents do not fulfill their role as sexual educators. The responsibility for this is left to someone else. In a study by Athanasiou (1970) it was found that about 49% of a large sample of adults polled indicated that they believed their parents to be the best source of sex education information. However, only 12% received it from this source. On the other hand, 4.5% thought peers and friends to be the best source, but nearly 54% actually got their sex education here. Twenty-three percent named school as the best source, but in fact only 3% received their sex education in the schools. Data from Abelson, Cohen, Heaton and Suder (C.O.P., 1970) confirmed these findings. It would appear from these figures that both home and school are deficient so far as sex education is concerned. And the story of 13-year-olds providing sex education for 11 and 12-year-olds at the corner candy store may not be too far off the mark.

It will be a difficult task to introduce rational sex education either in the home or in the school system. In the former case many parents are not equipped to do it. They do not feel comfortable enough with their own sexuality to impart information that is both realistic and healthy. Too often their concept of sex is based on what they would like it to be and not how it actually is. Their notions of sex simply do not conform to contemporary sexual mores. Being the victims themselves of an unsatisfactory sexual education, and heir to all the popular myths of sex and sexuality, their attempts at sex education are bound to be less than adequate. What they too often succeed in doing is to perpetuate the myths and create unnecessary and debilitating anxieties in their children. Their attempts at sex education frequently reflect the conventional wisdom which attempts to divorce sex from normal everyday human behavior.

The problems of sex education in the schools are even more complex and pervasive. One difficulty in attempting to introduce rational sex education in the schools is the covert message that parents are incapable of doing this themselves. Many parents react negatively to this despite the truth of the message. Another problem is the notion that if you teach children what to do then they will attempt to do it. A third is the feeling among some parents and some educators that this is not the proper function of the school. A fourth problem is the belief that exposure to sex education will destroy the innocence of youth and that this is inherently bad. An example of this, contained in the report of the C.O.P. (1970), goes as follows: people advocating sex education . . . "are doing something which has been regarded for countless generations as one of the most revolting crimes. They are setting out, with their benevolent voices, their paternal manner, their beautiful arty pictures, even with musical accompaniment, to destroy the innocence of a whole generation of young children."

Nevertheless, despite this kind of thinking, there are many school programs where sex education is being provided. While these vary in detail and emphasis, unfortunately most of them miss the point entirely. Because this is an emotionally charged topic, sex education is presented as "family living," "home adjustment," "guidance" or some equally euphemistic term. The content is primarily concerned with the physiology and biology of sex, under the guise that this will be useful, instill a wholesome attitude towards sex, and prepare the adolescent for sexual expression. That there is in fact little or no *sexual* content is ignored. Nothing is said of masturbation, love, petting, coitus, homosexuality, premarital and extramarital sex, sexual feelings and sexual arousal, and so on. It is as if these were unimportant and should be dismissed as not being part of "wholesome" sex. These of course, are the very nub of what should constitute education in sex or, better still, education in sexuality. While contraception, pregnancy and VD are important, (and this is what most programs focus on), they are only details of sexuality. One gains the impression from these courses that they are designed solely to prevent societal problems to the exclusion of personal and interrelational problems. They seem to be saying: we know you are going to become involved in a sexual relationship, so here is what to do to prevent unpleasant surprises. One could sympathize to some extent with this elementary approach if it had some real impact, if it significantly decreased unwanted pregnancies, if it significantly decreased the incidence of venereal disease. The evidence does not support this. Even where comprehensive programs have addressed themselves to this end, the results have been disappointingly unsatisfactory.

It is not uncommon for a teacher to decide that a course in sex education would be a good thing, and with little or no preliminary preparation (in the sense of researching the characteristics of satisfactory programs) design one off the top of the head and to present this to the students, secure in the belief that what is being taught is useful. If they were to enquire, it is likely the students could set them straight.

The apparent naiveté of those responsible for sex education in the schools is incomprehensible. If teachers and administrators were to pause and review their own adolescent sexual behavior, if they were to take a close look at what their students are actually doing on a day-to-day basis, they would soon realize that much of what they are attempting to teach or convey to their students is old hat. They are talking in the abstract about things which many of the students have been practicing in a vigorous and conscientious way, in many cases, for some years.

A common failing among parents is a short memory. They appear to have little recollection of how they behaved when younger; that they practiced masturbation, that they were intensely interested in pictures of nude and seminude women, that they were necking and at least thinking of petting when they were twelve or fourteen years old, that the anatomical mysteries hidden beneath trousers and panties and bras were of some concern and topics of much speculation, that they discussed with their friends the mechanics of intercourse and its attendant feelings, and so on. All these matters seem to have been erased from their memories and they unrealistically expect their children to be, sexually, as pure as the driven snow. What father can look at his twelve- or thirteen-year-old daughter, in all her pristine innocence, and imagine that such thoughts are contained in that pretty little head? And to a lesser degree, what mother can see her adolescent son, her pride and joy, as behaving in the way her male companions (perhaps including her husband) behaved when they were her son's age? Such eventualities are seldom entertained.

Similarly with teachers. Not only have they forgotten how they themselves behaved in earlier times, they ignore the current evidence of their senses. One can only speculate on what goes through the minds of teachers when they see their junior and senior high school boys and girls walking with their arms around each other in the school, when a young couple strolls down the corridor with the boys hand in the girl's hip pocket, when they observe a young couple lying on the grass necking, when they hear from various sources what transpired at the party at Mary or John's house when the parents were absent, and so on. Surely they must recognize that their attempts at elementary sex education in this context are out of step with the times? An attempt to impress adolescents with the startling fact that babies are conceived when the father places his seed inside the mother is not likely to be crowned with success. The students are well aware of this basic fact; many of them have had a good deal of practical experience in this exercise, and some of them have been distressingly successful.

What this means in practical terms is that education in sex and sexuality should start at a fairly early age, at home and at school, before children begin to experiment in a serious way and before they acquire the kinds of misinformation and absorb the current absurdities too often associated with sex and sexual expression. To initiate this kind of education in junior or senior high school is as ridiculous as it is futile.

Inherent in sex education (and at least covertly acknowledged) is that somehow standards of sexual conduct are different for boys and for girls. This idea is so prevalent and so commonplace that it has acquired the status of an unwritten law. There can be no denying that this is operational in adolescence and in adulthood. Examples are legion. When a schoolgirl becomes pregnant she is the one shamed and ridiculed. The boy is perhaps chastized and warned to be more careful in the future. While the girl's parents often are humiliated and feel disgraced, too often the boy's mother will adopt the attitude that if the girl had not cooperated she would not now be in the fix she is in. The father may chide the boy but secretly feel proud of him—he has proven his masculinity—and anyway, if it were not his son, then it would be some other father's son.

The same is true of adults. A woman who has sex with more than one man is considered promiscuous at best and a tramp at worst. On the other hand, the number of individual "conquests" made by a man is taken as a sign that he really knows where it's at, that he has something going for him that his friends envy and would like to emulate. Extreme examples of this are where female employees are dismissed because of having sexual relations with other employees (often the boss), or where, in a coeducational training facility a cadette may be dismissed from the service for going to bed with a cadet who receives a reprimand for his part in the liaison. (The U.S. Merchant Marine Academy reinstated one such cadette after a plethora of publicity.)

In a similar fashion, Senators who hire secretaries solely to provide sex (and are caught at it) are not condemned for having sex with secretaries. Their crime in the official eye is that they used public funds for doing so. One might speculate on the reaction if the situation were reversed: if a female Senator hired a male secretary whose sole duty was to provide a sexual service.

Another aspect of the irrationality of current sexual attitudes is concerned with the fact that mixed living accommodation is becoming the norm on university campuses. However, while male and female students are allowed to share the same building, it is not expected that they will share the same bed. This expectation is not always met. This should not come as a surprise to university officials—but then they, too, are frequently not particularly realistic when it comes to dealing with sexuality. And to post regulations to the effect that sleeping together will result in expulsion from the university is as effective as proscriptions against writing on lavatory walls.

This practice becomes more unreal when, as has happened, university health services (on the instigation of boards of governors) refuse to prescribe birth control pills for students. The old argument is dragged up that if you make it possible for students to have sex, then they inevitably will. Or, among the more reactionary, if girls are going to have premarital sex, then they had better be prepared to suffer the consequences. These attitudes accomplish nothing. If girls are going to become involved in sex, they will then do so without the protection of birth control pills, or they will get them outside the confines of the university. In passing it might be mentioned that boys have little trouble purchasing condoms. They are openly displayed in virtually every drugstore.

It is no accident that these attitudes prevail. They are part and parcel of inadequate sex education. In essence, the antisexual courses offered in schools reflect the fact that what people would like to believe about sexual conduct corresponds neither to what people do nor to objective truth. A final, simple, but telling example of this is masturbation. The student gets the message that this is to be considered morally wrong. However, the effects of masturbation are useful and beneficial rather than bad, and it is fairly widely recognized to be an almost universal phenomenon.

Unfortunately there is little agreement among professionals as to the form that education in sexuality should take. This is an area where confusion abounds. The problem is further exacerbated by the fact that even if there were rational programs of sexual education, there are relatively few teachers emotionally equipped to teach them. The uncritical assumption that teaching a course in sexuality differs only in content from teaching mathematics or English is completely unwarranted. Many teachers, regardless of their motivation or enthusiasm, are simply not capable of presenting the material in ways understandable and meaningful to the students. Many do not feel comfortable enough with their own sexuality to do this convincingly, in a nonembarrassed way. They themselves recognize this and it soon becomes abundantly clear to the students. In a situation like this, it is probably not surprising that most students do not take the courses seriously or derive any great benefit from them.

Nevertheless, if future generations are not to be tormented by the same irrational fears and conditioned anxieties as their forebearers, an honest and conscientious attempt will have to be made to determine realistic and rational goals and to provide knowledgeable and qualified teachers. Furthermore, these programs will have to be assessed as to their value. Education in sexuality, like education in other areas, only has value if it has implications for future behavior. As Athanasiou (1973) points out: "The value of sex education programs lies in providing a nucleus of accurate information (beliefs) in a realistic value context which fosters the growth of healthy and functional attitudes towards human sexuality. If subsequent behavior is to be responsible and mature, the development of healthy attitudes is essential."

To this we would add: Let us be sure when we use terms like "realistic value," "functional," "responsible," and "healthy," that there is consensus as to the meaning of these. And let us be confident that what we are teaching our children does have relevance for their future behavior in ways which are adaptive and which will lead to a more mutually satisfying sexual life.

SUMMARY

There are quite pronounced differences in public attitudes towards sexual information when the source of this information is considered. The commercial exploitation of sex is readily countenanced, while attempts at rational sex education in the schools is bitterly opposed by a fairly large segment of the population. While many parents are not emotionally or intellectually equipped to provide sex education for their children, some of these resent and object to this being done in the educational system.

It seems clear that the only way in which sexual disorders can be seriously reduced will be through rational sex education. How this can be achieved—how it can be implemented and the content of sex education courses improved—is a matter of concern. There is little agreement on either of these. However, these are not insoluble problems, and their answers should be of serious concern to all parents.

References

Abel G, Barlow D, Blanchard E, Mavissakalian M (1975): Measurement of sexual arousal in male homosexuals: the effects of instructions and stimulus modality. Archives of Sexual Behavior 4:623–629

Abel G, Blanchard E, Barlow D, Mavissakalian M (1975): Identifying specific erotic cues in sexual deviations by audiotaped descriptions. Appl Behav Anal 8:247–260

Abel G, Levis D, Clancy J (1969): Effects of aversive therapy on sexual deviants. Paper presented at meeting of American Psychiatric Association, May

Annon J (1976): The Behavioral Treatment of Sexual Problems: Brief Therapy. New York, Harper & Row

Arafat IS, Cotton WL (1974): Masturbation practices of males and females. Journal of Sex Research 10: 293–307

Athanasiou R (1973): A review of public attitudes on sexual issues In Zubin J, Money J (eds.): Contemporary Sexual Behavior: Critical Issues in the 1970's. Baltimore, Johns Hopkins University Press

Athanasiou R, Shaver P, Tavris C (1970): Sex (report to Psychology Today readers.) Psychology Today 4: 37–52

Azrin NH, Naster BJ, Jones R (1973): Reciprocity Counselling—a rapid learning based procedure for marital counselling. Behav Res Ther 11 (4):365–382

Bancroft J (1971): The application of psychophysiological measures to the assessment and modification of sexual behaviour. Behav Res Ther 9: 119–130

Bancroft J, Jones H, Pullen B (1966): A simple transducer for measuring penile erection, with comments on its use in the treatment of sexual disorders. Behav Res Ther 4:239

Bandura A, Blanchard E, Ritter B (1969): Relative efficacy of desensitization and modeling approaches for inducing behavioral, affective and attitudinal changes. J Pers Soc Psychol 13: 173–199

Bandura A, Menlove F (1967): Factors determining vicarious extinction of avoidance behavior through symbolic modeling. J Pers Soc Psychol 5: 16–23

Bardwick J (1971): Psychology of Women: A Study of Bio-Cultural Conflicts. New York, Harper & Row

Barlow D (1973): Increasing heterosexual responsiveness in the treatment of sexual deviation: a review of the clinical and experimental evidence. Behav Ther 4: 655–671

Barlow D, Agras WS (1973): Fading to increase heterosexual responsiveness in homosexuals. J Appl Behav Anal 6: 355–366

Barlow D, Becker R, Leitenberg H, Agras WS (1970): A mechanical strain gauge for recording penile circumference change. J Appl Behav Anal 3: 73–76

Barr R, McConaghy N (1971): Penile volume responses to appetitive and aversive stimuli in relation to sexual orientation and conditioning performance. Br J Psychiatry 119: 377–383

Barr R, McConaghy N (1972): A general factor of conditionability: a study of galvanic skin responses and penile responses. Behav Res Ther 10: 215–227

Bentler P (1968a): Heterosexual behavior assessment. I. Males. Behav Res Ther 6: 21–25

Bentler P (1968b): Heterosexual behavior assessment. II. Females. Behav Res Ther 6: 27–30

Bergler E (1944): The problem of frigidity. Psychiatr Q 18: 374–390

Brady J, Levitt E (1965): The scalability of sexual experiences. Psychol Rec 15: 275–279

Brown IB (1866): On the Curability of Certain Forms of Insanity, Epilepsy, Catalepsy and Hysteria in Females. London, Hardwicke

Bucknill JC, Tuke DH (1874): A Manual of Psychological Medicine, 3rd ed. London, Churchill

Caird WK, Wincze JP (1974): Videotaped desensitization of frigidity. Behav Ther Exp Psychiatry 5: 175–178

Chernick AB, Chernick BA (1971): The role of ignorance in sexual dysfunction. Medical Aspects of Human Sexuality 1: 22–26

Cicero T, Bell RD, Wiest WG, Allison JH, Polakoski K, Robins E (1975): Function of male sex organs in heroin and methadone users. N Eng J Med 292: 882

Comfort A (1972): Joy of Sex. New York, Crown

Comfort A (1967): The Anxiety Makers: Some Curious Pre-occupations of the Medical Profession. London, Nelson

Commission on Obscenity and Pornography, The Report of (COP). New York, Bantam Books

Conrad S, Wincze J (1976): Orgasmic reconditioning: a controlled study of its effects upon the sexual arousal and behavior of adult male homosexuals. Behav Ther 7: 155–166

Cooke G (1966): The efficacy of two desensitization procedures: an analogue study. Behav Res Ther 4: 17–24

Cooper AJ (1969): A clinical study of coital anxiety in male potency disorders. J Psycho Res 13: 143–147

Cooper A (1969): Clinical and therapeutic studies in premature ejaculation. Compr Psychiatry 10: 285–294

Davis D (1971): Cited in Zuckerman M: Physiological measures of sexual arousal in the human. Psychol Bull 75: 347–356

Davison G (1968): Elimination of a sadistic fantasy by a client-controlled counter conditioning technique: a case study. J Abnorm Psychol 73: 84–90

Davison G (1974): *Homosexuality: The Ethical Challenge.* Chicago, Paper presented at the Annual Convention of the Association for Advancement of Behavior Therapy, November

Davison G, Neale J (1974): Abnormal Psychology: An Experimental Clinical Approach. New York, John Wiley & Sons

Dollard J, Miller N (1950): Personality and Psychotherapy. New York, McGraw–Hill

Ellis A (1962): The Art and Science of Love. New York, Lyle Stuart

Ellis A (1965): Sex and the Single Man. New York, Lyle Stuart and Dell Books

Faulk M (1971): Factors in the treatment of frigidity. Br J Psychiatry 119: 53–56

Feldman M, MacCulloch M, Mellor V, Pinschof J (1966): The application of anticipatory avoidance learning to the treatment of homosexuality. III. The sexual orientation method. Behav Res Ther 4: 289–299

Fenichel O (1945): The Psychoanalytic Theory of Neurosis. New York, WW Norton

Fisher C, Gross J, Zuch J (1965): Cycle of penile erections synchronous with dreaming (REM) sleep. Arch Gen Psychiatry 12: 29–45

Fisher S, Davis D (1971): Personal communication, cited in Zuckerman M: Physiological measures of sexual arousal in the human. Psychological Bulletin 75: 297–329

Ford CS, Beach FA (1951): Patterns of Sexual Behavior. New York, Ace Books

Fordney-Settlage D (1975): Treating sexual dysfunction: the solo female physician. In Green R (ed): Human Sexuality: A Health Practitioner's Text. Baltimore, Williams & Wilkins

Freud S (1938): Three contributions to the theory of sex. In Brill AA (ed): The Basic Writings of Sigmund Freud. New York, Random House

Freund K (1963): A laboratory method of diagnosing predominance of homo- or hetero-erotic interest in the male. Behav Res Ther 1: 83–93

Freund K (1957): Diagnostika homosexuality u muzu. Cesk Psychiat, 53: 382–394

Freund K (1960): Some problems in the treatment of homosexuality. In Eysenck HJ (ed.): Behaviour Therapy and the Neuroses. New York, Pergamon Press

Freund K, Langevin R, Barlow D (1974): Comparison of two penile measures of erotic arousal. Behav Res Ther 12: 355–359

Freund K, Langevin R, Zajac Y (1974): A note on erotic arousal value of moving and stationary human forms. Behav Res Ther 12: 117–119

Friedman D (1968): The treatment of impotence by brietal relaxation therapy. Behav Res Ther 6: 257–261

Friedman HJ (1973): An interpersonal aspect of psychogenic impotence. Am J Psychother 27: 421–429

Friedman HJ (1974): Woman's role in male impotence. Medical Aspects of Human Sexuality 8: 14–31

Friedman M (1973): Success phobia and retarded ejaculation. Am J Psychother 27: 78–84

Garfield Z, McBrearty J, Dichter M (1966): A case of impotence successfully treated with desensitization combined within vivo operant training and thought stopping. In Rubin RD, Franks CM (eds): Advances in Behavior Therapy. New York, Academic Press

Green R (1975): Human Sexuality: A Health Practitioner's Text. Baltimore, Williams & Wilkins

Greenbank RK (1961): Are medical students learning psychiatry? Pa Med J 64: 989–992

Griffith JPC, Mitchell AG (1938): The Diseases of Infants and Children, 2nd ed. Philadelphia, WB Saunders

Guttman L (1959): The basis of scalogram analysis. In Stouffer SA, Guttman L, Suchman EA, Lazarsfeld PF, Star SA, Clausen JA (eds.): Measurement and Prediction. Princeton, Princeton University Press

Hammerman S (1961): Masturbation and character. J Am Psychoanal Assoc 9: 287–311

Hare EH (1962): Masturbatory insanity: the history of an idea. J Ment Sci 108: 1–25

Herman S, Prewett M (1974): An experimental analysis of feedback to increase sexual arousal in a case of homo and heterosexual impotence: a preliminary report. J Behav Ther Exp Psychiatry 5: 271–274

Hill J, Liebert R, Mott D (1968): Vicarious extinction of avoidance behavior through films: an initial test. Psychol Rep 12: 192

Hoon E, Hoon P, Wincze J: The SAI: an inventory for the measurement of female sexual arousal. Archives of Sexual Behavior (In press)

Hoon P, Wincze J, Hoon E (1976): Physiological assessment of sexual arousal in women. Psychophysiology 13: 196–204

Hulse WC (1952): The Management of Sexual Conflicts in General Practice. JAMA 150: 846

Ince L (1973): Behavior modification and sexual disorders. Am J Psychother 27: 446–451

Jabcobson E (1938): Progressive Relaxation, 2nd ed. Chicago, University of Chicago Press

Jackson BT (1969): A case of voyeurism treated by counterconditioning. Behav Res Ther 7: 133–134

James B (1962): Case of homosexuality treated by aversion therapy. Br Med J 1: 768–770

Javanovic V (1971): The recording of physiological evidence of genital arousal in human males and females. Archives of Sexual Behavior 1: 309–320

Johnson V, Masters W (1964): A team approach to the rapid diagnosis and treatment of sexual incompatability. Pacific Medicine and Surgery 72: 371–375

Jones M (1924): A laboratory study of fear: the case of Peter. Pedagogical Seminar 31: 308–315

Jones W, Park P (1972): Treatment of single-partner sexual dysfunction by systematic desensitization. Obstet Gynecol 39: 411–417

Kaplan HS (1974): The New Sex Therapy: Brief Treatment of Sexual Dysfunctions. New York, Brunner/Mazel

Kaplan H, Kohl R (1972): Adverse reactions to the rapid treatment of sexual problems. Psychosomatics 13: 185–190

Karacen I, Goodenough D, Shapiro A, Starker S (1966): Erection cycle during sleep in relation to dream anxiety. Arch Gen Psychiatry 15: 183–189

Kerckhoff A (1974): Social class differences in sexual attitudes and behavior. Medical Aspects of Human Sexuality 8: 10–25

Kinsey A, Pomeroy W, Martin C (1948): Sexual Behavior in the Human Male. Philadelphia, WB Saunders

Kinsey A, Pomeroy W, Martin C, Gebhard P (1953): Sexual Behavior in the Human Female. Philadelphia, WB Saunders

Kohlenberg R (1974): Directed masturbation and the treatment of primary orgasmic dysfunction. Archives of Sexual Behavior 3: 349–356

Kraft T, Al–Issa I (1968): The use of methohexitone sodium in the systematic desensitization of premature ejaculation. Br J Psychiatry 114: 351–352

Lacey JI, Bateman DE, Van Lehn W (1953): Autonomic response specificity: an experimental study. Psychosom Med 15: 8–21

Lacey JI, Lacey BC (1958): Verification and extension of the principle of autonomic response stereotype. Am J Psychol 71: 50–73

Lange J (1974): Behavioral rehersal and video desensitization: an experimental investigation of their efficacy in the treatment of couples with sexual dysfunction. Unpublished MA Thesis, Dalhousie University, Halifax, Canada

Laws D, Pawlowski A (1973): The application of a multi-purpose biofeedback device to penile plethysmography. J Behav Ther Exp Psychiatry 4: 339–341

Lazarus AA (1963): The results of behavior therapy in 126 cases of severe neurosis. Behav Res Ther 1: 69–79

Lazarus AA (1963): The treatment of chronic frigidity by systematic desensitization. J Nerv Ment Dis 136: 272–278

Lazarus AA (1965): The treatment of a sexually inadequate man. In Ullmann LP, Krasner L (eds): Case Studies in Behavior Modification. New York, Holt, Rinehart & Winston, pp 243–245

Lazarus AA (1969): Modes of treatment for sexual inadequacies. Medical Aspects of Human Sexuality 3: 53–58

Lazarus AA (1971): Behavior Therapy and Beyond. New York, McGraw–Hill

Lehman RE (1974): The disinhibiting effects of visual material in treating orgasmically dysfunctional women. Behav Engineer 1: 1–3

Lobitz WC, LoPiccolo J (1972): New methods in the behavioral treatment of sexual dysfunction. J Behav Ther Exp Psychiatry, 3: 265–272

Locke EA (1971): Is behavior therapy behavioristic? (An analysis of Wolpe's psychotherapeutic methods). Psychol Bull 76:5, 318–327

Lomont JF, Edwards JE (1967): The role of relaxation in systematic desensitization. Behav Res Ther 5: 11–25

LoPiccolo J, Lobitz C (1972): The role of masturbation in the treatment of orgasmic dysfunction. Archives of Sexual Behavior 2: 163–171

LoPiccolo J, Steger J (1974): The sexual interaction inventory: a new instrument for assessment of sexual dysfunction. Archives of Sexual Behavior 3: 585–595

LoPiccolo J, Stewart R, Watkins B (1972): Treatment of erectile failure and ejaculatory incompetence of homosexual etiology. J Behav Ther Exp Psychiatry 3: 233–236

Lowrie R (1952): Frigidity in women. Western J Surg Obstet Gynecol 60: 458–462

Madsen CH Jr, Ullmann LP (1967): Innovations in the desensitization of frigidty. Behav Re Ther 5: 67–68

Malmo RB, Shagass C (1949a): Psychologic studies of reaction to stress in anxiety and early schizophrenia. Psychosom Med 11:9–24

Malmo RB, Shagass C (1949b): Physiologic studies of symptom mechanisms in psychiatric patients under stress. Psychosom Med 11: 25–29

Mann J (1970): Paper: Effects of erotic movies upon sexual behavior. Miami Beach 78th Annual Convention of The American Psychological Association

Mann J, Sidman J, Starr S (1970): Effects of erotic films on sexual behavior of married couples. Miami. Paper presented at the American Psychological Association Annual Convention, September

Marks I, Sartorius N (1968): A contribution to the measurement of sexual attitude. J Ner Ment Dis 145: 441–451

Marquis J (1970): Orgasmic reconditioning: changing sexual object choice through controlling masturbation fantasies. J Behav Ther Exp Psychiatry 1: 263–271

Masters WH, Johnson VE (1966): Human Sexual Response. Boston, Little, Brown

Masters WH, Johnson VE (1970): Human Sexual Inadequacy. Boston, Little, Brown

Mavissakalian M, Blanchard E, Abel G, Barlow D (1975): Responses to complex erotic stimuli in homosexual and heterosexual males. Br J Psychiatry 126: 252–257

McConaghy N (1974): Measurement of change in penile dimensions. Archives of Sexual Behavior 3: 381–388

McGuire RJ, Carlisle JM, Young BG (1965): Sexual deviations as conditioned behavior. Behav Res Ther 2: 185–190

Meikle S (1972): Frigidity and impotence. Medical Aspects of Human Sexuality 2: 28–33

Menninger K (1938): Man Against Himself. New York, Harcourt, Brace

Milton JL (1887): On the Pathology and Treatment of Spermatorrhoea, 12th ed. London,

Mountjoy P (1974): Some early attempts to modify penile erection in horse and human: an historical analysis. Psychol Rec 24: 291–308

Obler M (1973): Systematic desensitization in sexual disorders. J Behav Ther Exp Psychiatry 4: 93–101

O'Connor RD (1969): Modification of social withdrawal through symbolic modeling. J Appl Behav Anal 2: 15–22

Osgood C, Suci G, Tannenbaum P (1957): The Measurement of Meaning. Urbana, IL, University of Illinois Press

Patterson G, Cobb J, Ray R (1973): A social engineering technology for retraining the families of aggressive boys. In Adams HE, Unikel IP (eds.): Issues and Trends in Behavior Therapy. Springfield, IL, CC Thomas, 139–210

Paul G (1966): Insight vs. Desensitization in Psychotherapy. Stanford, Stanford University Press

Paulson M, Lin T (1970): Frigidity: a factor analytic study of a psychosomatic theory. Psychosomatics 11: 112–119

Pawlowski A, Laws D (1974): A multi-purpose, voltage controlled oscillator. Behavior Research Methods and Instruments 6: 27–28

Podell L, Perkins J (1956): A Guttman Scale for sexual experience—a methodological note. J Abnorm Soc Psychol 54: 420–422

Rachman S (1965): Aversion therapy: chemical or electrical? Behav Res Ther 2: 289–299

Rainwater L (1960): And the Poor Get Children. Chicago, Quadrangle

Ramsey RW, Barends J, Breuker J, Kruseman A (1966): Massed verses spaced desensitization of fear. Behav Res Ther 4: 205–207

Ranzani J (1972): Ejaculatory incompetence treated by deconditioning anxiety. J Behav Ther Exp Psychiatry 3: 65–67

Reith G, Caird WK, Ellis D (1974): The use of video taped induced systematic desensitization in the treatment of female sexual dysfunction. Bogota, Colombia, Paper presented at the XV Interamerican Congress of Psychology, December

Reith G, Caird WK, Ellis D (1975): Variations in the use of video induced desensitization in the treatment of female sexual dysfunction. (Unpublished manuscript)

Robinson G, Suinn RM (1969): Group desensitization of a phobia in massed sessions. Behav Res Ther 7: 319–321

Sagar C (1976): Sexual dysfunction in methadone and heroin users. Medical Tribune: Sexual Medicine Today, pp 26–27

Saghir M, Robins E, Walburn B (1969): Homosexuality I—sexual behavior of the female homosexual. Arch Gen Psychiatry 20: 192–201

Sanford D (1974): Patterns of sexual arousal in heterosexual males. Journal of Sex Research, 10: 150–155

Semans JH (1956): Premature ejaculation: a new approach. South Med J 49: 353–358

Shelton JL, Ackerman JM (1974): Homework in Counselling and Psychotherapy. Springfield, IL, CC Thomas

Shusterman LR (1973): The treatment of impotence by behavior modification techniques. Journal of Sex Research 9: 226–240

Sintchak G, Geer J (1975): A vaginal plethysmograph system. Psychophysiology 12: 113–115

Smith MJ (1975): When I Say No I Feel Guilty. New York, Dial Press

Spitz RA (1952): Authority and masturbation. Some remarks on a bibliographic investigation. Psychoanal Q 21: 490–527

Spratling EJ (1895): Masturbation in the adult. Med Rec 48: 442

Staats AW (1968): Learning Language and Cognition. New York, Holt, Rinehart, & Winston

Staats AW (1970): Social behaviorism, human motivation, and the conditioning therapies. In Maher BA (ed): Progress in Experimental Personality Research. New York, Academic Press

Steger J (1972): The assessment of sexual function and dysfunction. Portland, OR, Paper presented at the Annual Meeting of the Western Psychological Association

Suinn RM (1968): The desensitization of test anxiety by group and individual treatment. Behav Res Ther 6: 385–387

Suinn RM, Hall R (1970): Marathon desensitization groups. Behav Res Ther 8: 97–98

Szasz T (1970): The Manufacture of Madness. New York, Harper & Row

Tart CT (1971): Cited in Zuckerman M: Physiological measures of sexual arousal in the human. Psycholog Bull 75: 347–356

Thorne FC (1966): A factorial study of sexuality in adult males. J Clin Psychol 22: 378–386

Thorpe J, Schmidt E, Castell D (1964): A comparison of positive and negative (aversive) conditioning in the treatment of homosexuality. Behav Res Ther 2: 71–82

Udry JR, Morris NM (1967): A method for validation of reported sexual data. Journal of Marriage and the Family 5: 442–446

Watson J, Rayner R (1920): Conditioned emotional reactions. J Exp Psychol 3: 1–14

Williams W (1971): Desensitization: social and cognitive factors underlying the effectiveness of Wolpe's procedure. Psychol Bull 76:5, 311–317

Willoughby RR (1934): Norms for the Clark–Thurstone inventory. J Soc Psychol 5: 91–97

Wincze JP, Caird WK (1973): A comparison of systematic desensitization and video desensitization in the treatment of sexual frigidity. Miami, Paper presented at the Association for the Advancement of Behavior Therapy, December

Wincze JP, Caird WK (1976): The effects of systematic desensitization and video desensitization in the treatment of essential sexual dysfunction in women. Behav Ther 7: 335–342

Wincze J, Hoon P, Hoon E (1977): Sexual arousal in women: a comparison of cognitive and physiological responses by continuous measurement. Archives of Sexual Behavior 6:230–245

Wincze J, Hoon P, Hoon E: A comparison of the physiological responsivity of normal and sexually dysfunctional women during exposure to an erotic stimulus. Psychosom Med (In press)

Wolpe J (1958): Psychotherapy by Reciprocal Inhibition. Stanford, Stanford University Press

Wolpe J (1966): The Practice of Behavior Therapy: A Guide to the Treatment of Neuroses. Oxford, Pergamon

Wolpe J (1969): The Practice of Behavior Therapy. Oxford, Pergamon

Wolpe J, Lang P (1964): A fear survey schedule for use in behavior therapy. Behav Res Ther 2: 27–30

Wolpe J, Lazarus AA (1966): Behavior Therapy Techniques. New York, Pergamon

Woody R, Schauble P (1969a): Desensitization of fear by video tapes. J Clin Psychol 25: 102–103

Woody R, Schauble P (1969b): Videotaped vicarious desensitization. J Nerv Ment Dis 148: 281–286

Zuckerman M (1971): Physiological measures of sexual arousal in the human. Psychol Bull 75: 347–356

Appendix A
Information for Ordering

CHAPTER 3

Page 59 — Sex History Form: available at cost (for professional use) from Division of Family Study, School of Medicine, University of Pennsylvania, 4025 Chestnut Street, Philadelphia, PA 19104

Page 61 — Sexual Arousal Inventory (SAI): available at cost from John P. Wincze, Ph.D., Veterans Administration Hospital, Davis Park, Providence, RI 02908

Page 63 — Willoughby Neuroticism Scale: can be found in the appendix of Wolpe J: The Practice of Behavior Therapy, 2nd ed., New York, Pergamon Press Inc., 1973

Page 63 — Fear Survey Schedule: can be found in the appendix of Wolpe J: The Practice of Behavior Therapy, 2nd ed. New York, Pergamon Press, Inc., 1973

Page 63 — Assertive Questionnaire: a 30-item schedule for assessing assertive behavior published by Rathers S: Behavior Therapy 4:398–406, 1973

Page 64 — Sexual Behavior Record Form (Sex Inventory): available at cost from Dr. Joseph LoPiccolo, Department of Psychiatry and Behavioral Science, School of Medicine, State University of New York at Stony Brook, Stony Brook, NY 11794

CHAPTER 8

Page 148 — Film: *Squeeze Technique*. May be ordered from Multi Media Resource Center, Inc., 540 Powell Street, San Francisco, CA 94108

Page 150 — Film: *Becoming Orgasmic: A Sexual Growth Program for Women*. May be ordered from Focus International Inc., 505 West End Avenue, New York, NY 10024

Appendix B
Relaxation Training

The major points to stress prior to relaxation training are that:

1. Everyone can learn to relax. While there are individual differences in the amount of practice required and perhaps in the degree of relaxation achieved, it is something that everyone can do provided one goes about it the right way and is conscientious in practicing.
2. Training in and practicing relaxation consists of tensing and relaxing various body muscle groups and paying attention to the feeling while this is being done.
3. Learning to relax is similar to learning any other skill; the more you practice, the easier it becomes.
4. While it is easy to tell the difference between being tense and not being tense, the goal is to be able to make rather fine discriminations, to be able to detect small amounts of tension. This is a skill readily acquired.

While the client is seated in a comfortable chair, the instructions and procedures which we use are given as follows.

Straighten your leg and point your toe away from your body as hard as you can. Notice how the muscles along the top of your foot and the calf and thigh feel when you do this. With your hand feel your thigh and calf; see how tight they are. Concentrate on this tense feeling. Now gradually let the tension go; relax the muscles. Concentrate on how these muscles feel as the tension is leaving them. Now let all the tension go, let your foot rest on the floor and concentrate on how these muscles feel now that all the tension is gone. When you are doing this you should tense your muscles for about ten seconds, gradually relax them over the next ten seconds, and concentrate for about ten seconds on how they feel with all the tension gone.

All right, now do the same thing with your other leg; tense it, gradually release the tension, and concentrate on how it feels when relaxed.

This time do the opposite; point your toe towards your body as hard as you can. Notice the tension along the front part of your lower leg and thigh. Feel the muscles with your hand. Now gradually let the tension go so that your foot touches the floor. Concentrate on how the muscles feel as the tension is leaving and how they feel when it is all gone.

The same procedure is repeated with the opposite foot.

All right, now force your stomach out as hard as you can; really push. Notice how your stomach muscles feel; run your hand across your stomach, see how tight they are. Now gradually relax, release the tension. Notice how the muscles feel as the tension is leaving. Now concentrate on how they feel when they are relaxed and all the tension is gone. Now do the opposite; suck your stomach in as hard as you can. Notice the tension in your stomach and chest when you do this; concentrate on how the muscles feel. Gradually relax now and concentrate on how the muscles feel as you do this and when all the tension is gone.

This time take a deep breath and concentrate on how it feels when you are holding your breath. Hold it for about ten seconds and slowly exhale and breathe normally. Notice the feeling and the difference between holding your breath and breathing normally.

Now, clench your fist. Notice the tension in your fingers, the back of your hand and your forearm. Feel this tension with your other hand. Gradually relax; let the tension go.

Notice the feeling as the tension is leaving; now pay attention to how the muscles feel when all the tension is gone. All right, let's repeat that with the other hand.

Now your arm. Flex your arm so you can feel the tension in your biceps and shoulder. Hold it for about ten seconds and gradually release the tension. Concentrate on how your shoulder and biceps feel when they are tense, how they feel when the tension is going, and how they feel when the tension is gone. Now the same with the other arm.

This time try to force your shoulders forward as far as you can; as if you were trying to make them meet in front. Concentrate on the tension in the upper part of your arms and across your back. Now slowly relax and concentrate on how they feel, and the sensation when all the tension is gone. Now do the opposite and force your shoulders back as far as you can. Notice the tension in your back, across your chest and in your upper arms. Now let the tension go. Notice the difference as you are doing this and when all the tension is gone.

You're doing fine. What you have to remember is to concentrate on each muscle group; how it feels when it's very tense, how it feels as the tension is being released, and how it feels when all the tension is gone.

Now your neck. Try to force your chin down so that it's pressing on your chest. Notice the tension in the back of your neck. Now relax slowly and notice the change. Now the reverse; force your head back as far as you can so you can feel the tenseness in your throat. Now gradually let the tension go and bring your head upright and concentrate on how the muscles feel now.

This time squeeze your eyes closed as tightly as possible. Concentrate on the muscles around your eyes and in your forehead. Slowly release the tension and note the difference as this is happening and when all the tension is gone. Concentrate on how relaxed your eyes and forehead feel.

All right, this time force your tongue against the roof of your mouth just over your top front teeth. Really press. Notice the feeling in your mouth. Concentrate on how your tongue feels. Now, gradually relax; let the tension go and concentrate on this. Now pay attention to how your mouth and tongue feel when all the tension is gone.

Now your jaw. Clench your teeth together as hard as you can and concentrate on the muscles on each side of your jaw. Feel them with your fingers. Notice the ridge of muscles. Now, gradually relax and notice the different feeling as this is happening. Now concentrate on how your jaw muscles feel when they are relaxed.

Having demonstrated these exercises once, we explain to the client that with sufficient practice he or she will be able to become completely relaxed within a few minutes. However, the key to success is conscientious practice, and this should be done twice a day for about 15–20 minutes on each occasion. We further mention that once the skill is mastered, he or she will be able to become relaxed without actually going through the exercises—merely imagining them will be enough to induce relaxation.

SAMPLE HIERARCHIES

To illustrate the kinds of hierarchy one may encounter and to demonstrate the variability among them, the following three hierarchies from three clients are presented. Each woman found intercourse aversive and anxiety-generating.

I. Heirarchy for Mrs. A, 32 years of age. Her husband was a traveling salesman.

SUDS

1	1	Anticipating my husband coming home a week hence
3	2	Anticipating my husband coming home 3 days hence

6	3	Anticipating my husband coming home 1 day hence
10	4	My husband arriving home in the early afternoon
12	5	Being partially undressed in front of my husband—wearing skirt and bra
14	6	Being partially undressed in front of my husband—wearing panties and bra
17	7	Being partially undressed in front of my husband—wearing only panties
21	8	Husband touching my breast while I am clothed
23	9	Husband touching my breast while I am partially clothed—skirt and bra.
25	10	Seeing my husband wearing only shorts
28	11	Seeing my husband naked
32	12	Being completely naked in front of my husband
36	13	Being alone with my husband and he puts his arm around my waist
38	14	Being alone with my husband—sitting on chesterfield with his arm around me
41	15	Intercourse in the dark
44	16	In bed and my husband's hand is on my breast
47	17	Getting into my nightgown with my husband present
49	18	My husband touching my breast while I am in my nightgown
52	19	My husband touching my genitals over my clothes
55	20	In bed and my husband touching my genitals
57	21	Having intercourse after a two month interval
60	22	Having intercourse after a one week interval
62	23	Touching my husband's penis over his clothes
64	24	My husband fondling my breasts while I am naked—not in bed
67	25	Being in bed with my husband with both of us naked
71	26	My husband touching my genitals while I am naked
76	27	Getting ready for bed, knowing my husband wants intercourse
82	28	Having intercourse in the afternoon
86	29	In bed with my husband, touching his penis
89	30	Having intercourse with the lights on
94	31	Having intercourse in the morning
100	32	My husband attempting to have intercourse in the *early* morning

II. Hierarchy for Mrs. B, 27 years of age. She has never had intercourse although married for three years. Vaginismus was a major part of her problem.
SUDS

1	1	Kissing husband in the morning prior to his going to work
2	2	Sitting next to my husband on chesterfield before dinner
3	3	Seeing a sensuous type of scene in film and feeling guilty *viz a viz* husband
5	4	Having my husband display affection by kissing me—in the kitchen
7	5	Seeing other people display physical affection, kiss, etc.
10	6	Having married friends discuss starting a family
13	7	My husband putting his arm around my waist in the kitchen at 6:00 P.M.
17	8	Being with husband away from home—at parents' home, husband putting arm around me, displaying affection
22	9	Sleeping without a nightgown
27	10	Coming home after party knowing my husband wants sex—he has been drinking

29	11	Coming home after party knowing my husband wants sex—he has not been drinking
32	12	Sitting next to my husband on the chesterfield at 11:00 P.M.
35	13	Thinking about sex in advance during evening: 8–9 P.M.
39	14	When my husband suggests an attempt at intercourse with no physical lead up; talking, and he says "Let's go to bed and try."
43	15	Having my husband display affection by kissing me—in the bedroom.
48	16	My husband attempting to make love on the chesterfield
50	17	Lying down beside my husband on bed after work
52	18	Talking in bed in the morning
56	19	Kissing my husband in the evening when I have my nightgown on
61	20	Kissing my husband in the evening when I am naked
65	21	Being caressed by my husband knowing this is a prelude to intercourse
70	22	Thinking about attempting intercourse and concerned about the possibility of my vaginal muscles contracting
74	23	My husband inserting finger partially in my vagina
77	24	My husband inserting his finger completely in my vagina
80	25	My husband inserting two fingers partially in my vagina
84	26	My husband inserting two fingers completely in my vagina
88	27	Inserting my own finger in my vagina
92	28	Inserting two of my fingers in my vagina
95	29	Discussing the problem of sexual relationship with my husband; what to do about problem
98	30	Intercourse (penis partially inserted)
100	31	Intercourse (penis fully inserted)

III. Hierarchy for Mrs. C, 25 years of age. She has been married two years.
SUDS

1	1	Seeing my husband naked
3	2	Kissing my husband in front of others—at a party
4	3	Walking around naked—husband present
6	4	Touching my husband's penis over clothes
9	5	Sexual conversations with others present
11	6	Talking about having a baby
14	7	Discussing sex problems with my husband
18	8	My husband touching my breasts over my clothes
22	9	My husband touching my breasts under my clothes
27	10	Lying on the bed naked with lights on
30	11	Having intercourse in the dark with my husband using a condom
34	12	My husband touching my genitals over my clothes
37	13	My husband touching my genitals under my clothes
42	14	My husband inserting his finger in my vagina
45	15	Intercourse in dark with my husband on top
49	16	Intercourse in dark, my husband on top, no bed clothes on
54	17	Intercourse with light on, bed covers on
57	18	Being certain my husband will want intercourse in the evening
62	19	Intercourse during the day
67	20	My husband attempting intercourse in the shower
72	21	Seeing my husband with an erection
75	22	Intercourse on living room chesterfield
79	23	Intercourse on living room floor

81	24	Intercourse with the light on and bedcovers off
83	25	Intercourse with me on top in the dark
87	26	Intercourse with me on top with light on
90	27	Holding my husband's penis in bed with the lights off
95	28	Holding my husband's penis in bed with the lights on
97	29	My husband kissing and fondling my breasts while naked in bed
100	30	Intercourse in the morning with sunlight in the room

It is fairly obvious from these examples that there is a good deal of variability among women in terms of the kinds of sexual behaviors that cause anxiety. From a common sense point of view, one might expect that anxiety would be along a continuum from anticipating sex or some such innocuous situation, to actually engaging in intercourse under a variety of conditions. While this is true for some women, it is obviously not true for all. Mrs. C. is an exaggerated example of this. Many of the high anxiety items on her hierarchy were concerned with either being touched by her husband or touching her husband. This is one reason why a good deal of enquiry is required in hierarchy construction.

These examples provide only the theme of each item. In presenting these to the client the therapist would elaborate or construct a scene for each.

For week ending_____

WEEKLY SEXUAL ACTIVITY CHECK LIST*

SEXUAL ACTIVITY	Check if the activity occurred	If it occurred, check if it caused you *any* anxiety	If it occurred, check if it caused you *any* arousal
Being seen in the nude	_____	_____	_____
Orgasm (yours)	_____	_____	_____
Seeing partner nude	_____	_____	_____
Having genitals caressed	_____	_____	_____
Caressing partner's genitals	_____	_____	_____
Intercourse	_____	_____	_____
Kissing, embracing, caressing (no genital contact)	_____	_____	
Deep kissing with tongue contact	_____	_____	_____
Orgasm (partner's)	_____	_____	_____
Caressing breasts (or having breasts caressed)	_____	_____	_____

*NOTE: You should *not* include on this check list any sexual activity engaged in during the home practice sessions.

Index